CAN WE TEACH INTELLIGENCE?
A Comprehensive Evaluation
of Feuerstein's
Instrumental Enrichment
Program

CAN WE TEACH INTELLIGENCE?

A Comprehensive Evaluation of Feuerstein's Instrumental Enrichment Program

Nigel Blagg

Senior Educational Psychologist
Somerset County Council
Somerset, England

LEA LAWRENCE ERLBAUM ASSOCIATES, PUBLISHERS
1991   Hillsdale, New Jersey   Hove and London

Lawrence Erlbaum Associates, Inc., Publishers
365 Broadway
Hillsdale, New Jersey 07642

Library of Congress Cataloging-in-Publication Data

Blagg, Nigel.
    Can we teach intelligence? : a comprehensive evaluation of
Feuerstein's Instrumental Enrichment Program / Nigel Blagg.
        p.   cm.
    Includes bibliographical references (p.   ) and indexes.
    ISBN 0-8058-0793-4
    1. Mentally handicapped children—Education—Evaluation.
2. Cognition in children—Testing—Evaluation.   3. Cognitive
learning—Evaluation.   4. Feuerstein, Reuven.   I. Title.
LC4602.B48   1991
371.92′8—dc20   90-44236
                                                        CIP

Printed in the United States of America
10 9 8 7 6 5 4 3 2 1

Contents

Foreword

Robert J. Sternberg
Yale University

Consider the following problem, first posed by Sternberg and Bhana (1986): Suppose you attend a conference on modern developments in health-related research at which a pharmaceuticals salesperson discusses a new drug his/her company manufactures that he/she claims greatly improves one's general health. The salesperson is persuasive but because he/she seems to be selling a drug at a research conference, and because he/she works for the company peddling it, you decide to do a little research before buying the drug, which is quite expensive and needs to be used over a fairly long period of time.

The results of your research are disconcerting. There are few studies of the drug's effects, and most of them have been sponsored, supervised, or done "in consultation with" the manufacturer. The reports of the studies are sketchy, and many have inadequate control groups or none at all. Some amount to little more than testimonials about the drug's effects; others use outcome measures that seem to have been selected to maximize the favorability of the reports. Few of the studies have been published in refereed journals; many are reported in a company-sponsored magazine. Those studies that seem better controlled show mixed results. You are skeptical but perplexed. The drug may indeed do everything it is supposed to do, but it is hard to tell from the evidence.

Potential consumers of programs to teach thinking skills are in a similar predicament. Today, there are a number of seemingly attractive programs for teaching intellectual skills. But the gap between program development and program evaluation is truly disconcerting. My review of evaluations of intellectual-skills training programs (Sternberg & Bhana, 1986) has shown that:

1. Many of the studies were conducted or sponsored by the program developers; others involved fairly extensive consultation with them. And still

others were done by individuals with such an obvious stake in the outcome that one worries about experimenter effects.

2. Reporting was usually sketchy and often wholly inadequate. In a majority of instances, detail was insufficient for anything resembling a careful replication of what had been done.

3. Most studies involved inadequate (untrained) control groups, and some entailed none at all. Only rarely was the efficacy of one program compared with that of another program.

4. Some of the evidence offered in support of the various programs amounted to little more than user testimonials. The means of selection of such users was usually unspecified.

5. Outcome measures often overlapped program content, and thus tended to favor the program being tested. Inadequate attention was usually given both to transfer of training and to durability of training over the long term.

6. A very small proportion of the studies was published in refereed journals, or was in any way refereed at all. Such publication helps ensure independent scrutiny of methods and results.

7. Many studies were unpublished, published in media sponsored (and hence controlled) by the program developers, or were available only through the program developers. Availability through such limited channels, of course, raises questions as to just how unbiased the sampling of available studies truly is.

8. Even given these caveats on reporting, the results were generally mixed, some indicating significant gains, and others not.

Into this rather sad potpourri of program evaluations comes Nigel Blagg's evaluation of Feuerstein's Instrumental Enrichment Program, possibly the most widely used program for intellectual-skills training in the world. Blagg's evaluation is, arguably, the most thorough and carefully planned evaluation of an intellectual-skills training program that has been done, and there are few other candidates (Herrnstein, Nickerson, Sanchez, & Swets, 1986, being the main one). Blagg has evaluated the effects of Feuerstein's program not only on the students, but on the teachers as well. His evaluation is remarkable in the diversity of measures and even kinds of measures used. In order to introduce this book properly, I need first to say something about Feuerstein's program, and then about how this evaluation was done.

Feuerstein's (1980) Instrumental Enrichment (FIE) program was originally proposed for use with children showing retarded performance; it has since been recognized by Feuerstein and others to be valuable for children at all levels of the intellectual spectrum. It is based on Feuerstein's theory of intelligence, which emphasizes the executive (metacognitive) processes that control cognition, as well as the cognitive processes so controlled.

The FIE program is intended to improve cognitive functioning related to input, elaboration, and output of information. Feuerstein has compiled a long list of cognitive deficits his program is intended to correct. This list includes deficits such as: (a) unplanned, impulsive, and unsystematic exploratory behavior, (b) lack of or impaired capacity for considering two sources of information at once, (c) inadequacy in experiencing the existence of an actual problem and subsequently in defining it, (d) lack of spontaneous comparative behavior, (e) lack of or impaired strategies for hypothesis testing, and other, similar skills.

What are some of the main characteristics of the FIE program? The materials themselves are structured as a series of units, or instruments, each of which emphasizes a particular cognitive function and its relationship to various cognitive deficiencies. Feuerstein defines an instrument as something by means of which something else is effected; hence, performance on the materials is seen as a means to an end, rather than as an end in itself. Emphasis in analyzing FIE performance is on processes rather than products. A student's errors are viewed as a source of insights into how the student solves problems. FIE does not attempt to teach either specific items of information or formal, operational, abstract thinking by means of a well-defined, structured knowledge base. To the contrary, it is as content free as possible.

The FIE program consists of different types of exercises, which are repeated in cycles throughout the program. Examples of the kinds of materials in the program include: (a) orientation of dots, requiring students to identify and outline geometric figures within relatively amorphous arrays of dots, (b) comparisons, requiring students to point out how two similar-looking objects differ from each other, (c) categorization, requiring students to figure out into which of several categories pictures of common objects belong, (d) temporal relations, requiring students to indicate whether a given period of time is greater than, equal to, or less than another given period of time, and (e) numerical progressions, requiring students to generate continuations of a series of numbers.

From an armchair perspective, the program would seem to have several strengths (see Sternberg, 1984). First, it can be used for children in a wide age range, from the upper grades of elementary school to early high school and for children of a wide range of ability levels (from the retarded to the above average). Second, the program is generally well-liked by children. Third, the program is well packaged, as these programs go, and fairly easily obtainable. Fourth, the program is theory-based.

At the same time, the program seems to have some possible weaknesses. First, it requires very extensive teacher training, which must be administered by a designated training authority for the duration of the program. Second, the isolation of the program from any working knowledge or discipline base (such as social studies or reading, for example) raises questions regarding the transferability of the skills to academic and realworld intellectual tasks, especially over the long term. Feuerstein emphasizes that at least half of the time spent in the program should be devoted to "bridging," the means by which program material is related to content material. But teachers of the program may or may not do this, and in any case, they have full responsibility for doing so, a responsibility they may find overwhelming. It is easy for this or similar programs to degenerate into somewhat mindless worksheets, although I certainly would not suggest that this degeneration is common. And finally, despite Feuerstein's aversion to conventional intelligence tests, the program trains primarily those abilities that such tests tap rather than a broader spectrum of abilities that go beyond intelligence as the tests test it.

The problem with armchair analysis is that it does not tell us what really happens when a program is implemented. And this is where Blagg's comprehensive evaluation of the program comes in. The evaluation was done in Bridgwater, a small industrial town in Somerset, in the southwest of England. The evaluation was done in all four secondary schools of the town, all of which consisted of a mix of children from both urban and rural areas. The students in the program were 14 years of age and had a mean IQ of 92. They showed below-average verbal reasoning and vocabulary skills as well as depressed reading and mathematics achievement. Their work-study skills were also generally deficient. The FIE program was taught in the four schools for about 2 to 2½ hours per week for a total of up to 192 hours of training over the period of the study. Average amount of training, however, was 112 hours. The classes covered 10 of the 14 instruments, and multiple assessments of progress were taken.

The results of the program were mixed. Teachers found the materials too abstract and unfamiliar, too repetitive and poorly presented, and culturally inappropriate. Nevertheless, there were some positive outcomes for students.

On the positive side, pupils became: (a) more active contributors to class discussions, (b) more inclined to listen to other people's comments, (c) more likely to defend their opinions on the basis of logical evidence, (d) more able to describe different strategies for solving problems, (e) more likely spontaneously to read and follow instructions carefully, (f) more able to handle two or more sources of information simultaneously, and (g) more able to make spontaneous links between ideas and principles in different curriculum areas. But in terms of hard data, the study revealed no real evidence of benefits of the FIE program. Over the duration of the project, there were no significant improvements in: (a) reading skills, (b) mathematics skills, or (c) work-study skills. Nor was there evidence of (d) improved cognitive abilities as measured by the British Ability Scales, which are among the better intelligence scales available. These null findings applied to all four schools, suggesting that the failure to attain positive hard data was not situation-specific.

The study also looked at teacher outcomes. The teachers who used FIE became more assertive, confident, and self-reliant. They also became more satisfied with their jobs, more confident of their teaching abilities, more committed to their profession, and more valued in their work. Ironically, therefore, the program may have done as much or more for teachers as for students.

Blagg's study is a model for anyone who wishes to do an evaluation of an intellectual-skills training program. This is not to say that it is perfect. Far from it. For example, there were not adequate control groups in all schools, the age and ability ranges of the students were limited, and the implementation was put together in something of a hurry. But studies in the real world always have their limitations. Blagg is more honest than most in acknowledging those of his study.

It is a pleasure to read the work of someone who has put so much thought and effort into an evaluation of a training program, especially a training program that is being widely used around the world. The study reveals mixed results: Almost any well-designed study will. Before we go off teaching tens of thousands of children with any of our programs, we owe these children, as well as ourselves, the kind of comprehensive evaluation reported here.

REFERENCES

Feuerstein, R. (1980). *Instrumental enrichment: An intervention program for cognitive modifiability.* Baltimore: University Park Press.

Herrnstein, R. J., Nickerson, R. S., Sanchez, M., & Swets, J. A. (1986). Teaching thinking skills. *American Psychologist, 41,* 1279–1289.

Sternberg, R. J. (1984). How can we teach intelligence? *Educational Leadership, 42*(1), 38–50.

Sternberg, R. J., & Bhana, K. (1986). Synthesis of research on the effectiveness of intellectual skills programs: Snake-oil remedies or miracle cures? *Educational Leadership, 44*(2), 60–67.

Introduction

Certainly the "instruments" seem to have universal appeal. I have witnessed the total absorption of such disparate individuals as black adolescents in inner city Atlanta, Georgia, senior civil servants and academics perched in the corridor of a Spanish conference hotel and Autumn weary teachers "volunteered" by their LEA's [Local Education Authority]. . . . Whether it [Instrumental Enrichment] has staying power remains to be seen.
(Barry Taylor, quoted in Weller & Craft, 1983, Foreword, p. i)

Reuven Feuerstein's model for diagnosing and remedying cognitive deficiencies in poor attainers is arousing considerable interest around the world. Feuerstein claims that the Instrumental Enrichment Program can equip pupils with the basic prerequisites of thinking, thereby enabling them to become more effective learners. If this can be substantiated, the implications would be far-reaching.

Somerset Local Education Authority was introduced to Reuven Feuerstein's Instrumental Enrichment (FIE) in the early 1980s. A few schools from Somerset and four other LEA's took part in an exploratory study of the program encouraged by Barry Taylor and a number of other Chief Education Officers and organized by the Schools' Council. The study findings (Weller & Craft, 1983), which were optimistically cautious, prompted the need for a more rigorous evaluation.

In 1982, the Secretary of State for Education offered to fund pilot programs designed by LEA's specifically to help underachieving adolescents in their final 2 years of secondary school. Staff Inspector Turberfield defined the intentions of the Lower Attaining Pupil Program (LAPP) at a DES conference in May 1984:

(a) to improve the educational attainments of pupils in years 4 and 5 for whom present examinations at 16+ are not designed and who are not benefitting totally from school;

(b) to do this by shifting their education away from narrowly conceived or inappropriate teaching styles and curricular provision to approaches which are more suited to their needs, prepare them better for the satisfactions and obligations of adult life and the world of work and improve their motivation and self-respect. (Turberfield, 1984, pp. 1–2)

The LAPP objectives provided an ideal opportunity for a large scale evaluation of FIE. In September 1983, Somerset was successful in obtaining substantial LAPP funding with a large proportion of the budget allocated to investigate the application of IE to 14- to 16-year-old low-achieving adolescents in four Bridgwater secondary schools. The remainder of the funds was used to facilitate community enabling, residential experiences, and a secondment program (one teacher per school per year) to look at the problems of lower attaining pupils in different curriculum areas.

The project ran for 5 years with a formal evaluation of the effects of Instrumental Enrichment on pupils, teachers, and schools being scheduled over 3 years. During this period, approximately 1,000 pupils were exposed to Instrumental Enrichment and 30 teachers and three psychologists were trained in the program. Eight members of this group became qualified as local trainers of Instrumental Enrichment and four of these obtained further training in Israel. Over a 2-year period, 250 children and 30 teachers were closely monitored as part of a rigorous evaluation of FIE. This report will detail the findings of that extensive study.

Chapter 1 begins with a review of the literature on the teaching of cognitive skills, so that Feuerstein's work can be understood within a broad context. The chapter highlights the timeless goal of teaching intellectual skills and traces a number of important psychological influences on the school curricula that have hampered and facilitated that goal. The chapter concludes by briefly considering three cognitive intervention programs and the theories to which they relate. In each case, comparisons are drawn with Feuerstein's FIE.

Chapter 2 reviews Feuerstein's main beliefs, theories, assessment model, and intervention program (Instrumental Enrichment). The chapter opens with a discussion on Feuerstein's Learning Potential Assessment Device, picking up on issues raised in Chapter 1. It continues with an analysis of Feuerstein's mediated learning theory, the cognitive map, and the deficient functions list before going on to consider the nature of the Instrumental Enrichment Program and the current status of FIE in the research world.

Chapter 3 provides an overview of the evaluation design (used in the present study) explained in terms of Stufflebeam's Context, Input, Process, and Product Framework. It considers a whole range of issues including the background to the project, the selection of teachers and pupils, and problems associated with monitoring and assessing the mediation characteristics of the teachers and the efficacy of FIE program.

The fourth chapter focuses on the pupils and in particular their ability, attainment, and behavioral characteristics at the beginning and end of the study. Differences between control and experimental groups and differences between individual teaching groups within and across the schools are carefully analyzed before considering the evidence for pupil change. In addition to analyzing information from a comprehensive range of standardized tests, the chapter also analyzes "softer" data gathered from questionnaires, observation schedules, and formal and informal interviews with the pupils.

Chapter 5 is concerned with the teachers. It reviews their reactions to the FIE training and their reflections on FIE in the classroom. It goes on to consider evidence for personality, attitudinal, and behavioral change related to the FIE program.

The sixth chapter summarizes and critically reviews the overall findings of the study set against the constraints associated with the background context and the funding, organization, and administration of the project.

Chapter 7 reviews and discusses recurring issues identified in the study and considers their wider theoretical and practical implications in the light of general trends in the research literature and the constraints and challenges posed by the current, curriculum climate. Finally, these wider implications are considered in relation to the theoretical and design issues associated with the Somerset Thinking Skills Course (Blagg, Ballinger, & Gardner, 1988).

Acknowledgments

I am particularly indebted to the late Barry Taylor, former Chief Education Officer of Somerset (1973–1987), whose charismatic leadership and farsightedness led to the extensive trialing of Feuerstein's Instrumental Enrichment Program in Somerset. I would also like to record my appreciation to Jennifer Wisker, Chief Education Officer who quickly familiarized herself with this work and gave it her unreserved support. I am also grateful to Mr. James Clifford, Deputy Chief Education Officer; and Mr. John Cole, Chief Educational Psychologist who have endorsed this project throughout and freed me from my mainstream duties to carry out the work.

I should like to thank past and present members of the LAPP Monitoring Group who were responsible for supporting and coordinating the project work across the four Bridgwater Schools. In particular, I should like to acknowledge Mr. Don Parkinson, Principal Education Officer (Schools); Mr. Stuart Wilkinson, Education Officer (Special Education and Special Projects); Mrs. Janet Bond, Special Needs Adviser and Mr. John Rose, Area Education Officer for constant support and interest.

I am grateful to Dr. Michael Shayer, Lecturer in Science Education, Chelsea College for his interest in this project and the many hours of advice and support he gave at the planning and evaluation stages. I also appreciate the advice and help given at the beginning of this project by Dr. Bob Burden, Senior Lecturer in Psychology, Exeter University. It was Dr. Burden who suggested the adoption of Stufflebeam's CIPP analysis as a framework for this evaluation. He also assisted in the design of the Semantic Differential Scales developed to monitor teacher charge (see Tables 5.5 and 5.8) and helped with some of the initial teacher interviews. I should also like to extend my thanks to Professor Reuven Feuerstein for his observations on the issues involved in evaluating his FIE program.

In the project schools, I am especially grateful to the Head Teachers: Mr. Tom Flitton (Chilton Trinity School); Mr. Joe Fairhurst, (Blake School); Mrs. Margaret Haywood (Sydenham School) and Mr. Jack Hall (Haygrove School), for giving me open access to classrooms, teachers, and pupils, enabling a comprehensive evaluation of the effects of FIE over the 2-year project period. I am also enormously appreciative of the free time given up by the project and control group teachers (too numerous to mention) in completing diaries and observation schedules on the pupils and profiles, questionnaires, and tests exploring personal feelings about the effects of FIE on teacher attitudes and behaviors. I am, of course, deeply indebted to the pupils (too numerous to mention) for their patience and cooperation in completing lengthy assessment procedures and interviews.

With regard to testing, I should particularly like to thank the teachers in charge of FIE at the four schools who arranged and supported the group and individual assessments of the project pupils in consultation with the other staff: Dorothy Baker (Haygrove School); Marj Ballinger (Sydenham School); Mel Petty (Blake School), and Gareth Williams (Chilton Trinity School). I am also grateful to Mr. Dave Wilkinson, former Head of Science (Blake School) for his assistance with the administration of the Science Reasoning Tests and to Mrs. Jo Frew, Special Needs Support Team–Area Tutor and her team for their assistance with individual Piagetian tests. At the pre- and post-testing stages, I received much support from Mrs. Belinda Tincknell and Mr. Peter Mayhew, educational psychologists who assisted with the individual interviews with the project pupils and shared the tedious task of scoring the individual test profiles.

The business of transcribing the individual pupil profiles onto punch cards, enabling the creation of a data file, was an enormous task supervised by Mr. Graham Smith, Head of Information and Research, County Hall. Mr. Smith also assisted with a preliminary data analysis alongside Tracy Shearn, a student from Plymouth Polytechnic Psychology Department who volunteered her services. More complex analyses were supervised by Sally Barnes, Lecturer in Statistics at Bristol University and Ian Hands, Professor in Statistics, Open University. To all of these people, I record my thanks.

The data analysis, collation, and final writeup stages of this report have been completed while working on the Somerset Thinking Skills Course with my two colleagues, Marj Ballinger and Richard Gardner. I should like to thank them both for their never-ending patience and encouragement. I am also indebted to Richard for his expertise in the management of the word processor and to Marj Ballinger for the free time she gave up in helping with the data analysis and organization of the report. I should also like to thank Lynn Hearfield who was seconded from her teaching post at York to research the teaching of cognitive skills whilst on a one year fellowship to Jesus College, Oxford. Miss Hearfield saved me considerable time by sharing a number of useful articles obtained as part of her search of the American literature. Appendix 31 provides details of "The Gatehouse Observation Schedule for Teachers" together with notes on its interpretation.

This schedule was researched by Mike Lake, Senior Educational Psychologist, Buckinghamshire, and I am most grateful for his permission to include it in this book. Finally, I should like to thank Lynn Pryce for her typing and word processing skills and cheerfulness in spite of the endless reorganizations and revisions of the final report.

Chapter 1

Teaching Cognitive Skills— Issues Past and Present

You teach science; well and good; I am busy fashioning the tools for its acquisition. . . . It is not your business to teach him the various sciences, but to give him a taste for them and methods of learning them when this taste is more mature.

Rousseau (1762, pp. 90 & 134)

HISTORICAL PERSPECTIVES

The idea of teaching children to be better learners is not new. It was debated by Socrates and Plato and has been espoused by educationalists and philosophers throughout the centuries. Indeed, some teachers (especially in the humanities) have adopted Socratic methods, in which pupils are prompted to question their basic assumptions and premises in the hope that they will ultimately internalize and generalize the teacher's self-questioning model.

Of course, there have always been those who have proclaimed the wider benefits of learning particular subjects. For many, subjects like mathematics, logic, and/or Latin have provided a vehicle for "training the mind" or in current terms teaching children to "learn how to learn." Nevertheless, teaching children how to become better learners has been rarely featured as a central, coordinated, curricular aim in our schools.

At the beginning of this century, the study skills movement flirted with the idea of teaching learning techniques in a variety of books (cited in Nisbet & Shucksmith, 1986, pp. 13 & 14). Since then, numerous study skills manuals have been published. However, 60 years on, although most manuals are superior in presentation, they contain nothing new. As Nisbet and Shucksmith (1986)

1

emphasize, intuitive ideas of many years ago have become enduring truths without any theoretical or empirical basis. At a practical level, advice tends to be too general to be of use and in any case, applied too late at 16–17 years when habits and learning routines are already established. All too often, study skills amount to no more than a ragbag of tips for passing examinations or coping with specific routines in particular subjects.

More promising lines of approach are now beginning to emerge in the developmental/cognitive psychology fields, although ironically earlier notions about intelligence and learning hampered serious attempts to teach cognitive skills. For most of this century the school curriculum has been strongly influenced by Piagetian theory, psychometrics, and behaviorism. Piaget's pioneering work on the child's emerging cognitive capabilities emphasized important stages in conceptual development. During the first stage, dominated by sensory motor experiences, the baby develops an identity separate from the rest of the world. Later, the infant establishes object permanence and conservations of number, shape, volume, and so on.

Eventually, through a process of assimilation and accommodation the child begins to build up a comprehensive and predictable model of the world, which eventually enables abstract, hypothetical thinking. Piaget regarded cognitive development as a necessary prerequisite for learning rather than an outcome of educational experience. For him, the child's unfolding, reasoning abilities were largely biologically determined and the role and significance of social interaction in cognitive development was neglected. Nevertheless, he emphasized the importance of a stimulating environment with educational opportunities tailored to the child's developmental stage. In infant schools this led to "happening environments," experimental learning, and notions such as reading readiness. Unfortunately, however, it also led to a passive acceptance approach to many children who were slow to progress, encapsulated by: "They'll learn when they are ready."

Psychometrics (the business of measuring behavior and the abilities underlying it) began with Sir Francis Galton, founder of the Eugenics movement. Galton's (1869) survey of 1,000 men and their relatives demonstrated that "intellectually eminent" scientists, writers, judges, and so on tended to have similarly "eminent" close relatives and moreover, as the blood ties between relatives grew weaker, the frequency of occurrence of eminent relatives decreased. Galton concluded that intelligence was largely inherited and went on to devise simple tests of mental efficiency (e.g., reaction time and sensory discrimination tasks). Galton's work was developed in the early part of the century by Karl Pearson (a statistician) and Charles Spearman (a psychologist) who did much to promote the idea of "general intelligence" as a unitary ability underlying successful performance in many different tasks.

Of course, this notion of general intelligence as a unitary faculty has been challenged by some psychologists who have suggested that intelligent behavior relates to a number of underlying, fixed separate sources of individual differences known as factors. For instance, Thurstone (1938), held that intelligence was a function of seven primary mental abilities (verbal comprehension, verbal fluency, number, spatial visualization, reasoning, memory, and perceptual speed). Vernon (1971) regarded intelligence as hierarchical, with general intelligence (g) being underpinned by verbal-educational ability and practical mechanical ability, with performance in these two domains being influenced by numerous finer and increasingly specific skills. More recently, Gardner (1983) has proposed a theory of multiple intelligences in which individual performance is an outcome of seven different intelligences (linguistic, musical, logical, mathematical, spatial, bodily-kinesthetic, and personal).

Theoretical ideas about intelligence have fuelled the psychometric test industry, spawning the production of numerous procedures designed to provide stable indices of children's intellectual abilities. Galton's early notions of inherited intelligence have become pervasive and enduring. Moreover, the hypothetical construct "intelligence" has become inextricably intertwined with attempts to measure it. Thus, for many, IQ scores have become equated with a fixed quantity of intelligence within the child, leading to particular expectations and self-fulfilling prophecies. In spite of numerous research studies indicating the influence of educational experience on IQ's (Clarke & Clarke, 1976), outmoded notions about the invariant nature of IQ's and intelligence still persist in some educational circles.

In retrospect, it is interesting that one of the earliest constructors of mental tests (Alfred Binet, 1857–1911) was not so much interested in measuring the intellectual potential of pupils, as concerned to identify slow learners in need of remediation. He rejected the idea of intelligence as a unitary faculty and regarded it as being made up of numerous smaller modifiable functions such as observation, memory, judgment, attention, and so on. He strongly protested against the pessimism associated with fixed notions of intelligence and set out to demonstrate that intelligent behavior could be trained with his program of "mental orthopaedics."

Nevertheless, it is the notion of assessing rather than teaching cognitive abilities that has captivated the educational and psychological world for the majority of this century. Many would argue that psychometrics have been useful for predictive purposes or the analysis of individual strengths and weaknesses, but nowadays even these functions are being called into question. The overgeneralization of IQ tests to population groups for whom they were not devised or standardized has caused a backlash in some parts of the world. For instance, in certain USA states traditional IQs have been outlawed on grounds of their cultural bias. The need to find more effective, appropriate, and fairer ways of assessing individuals of varying abilities from many different cultures has led to an increased emphasis on nonverbal tests that are allegedly based on culture-fair or culture-free items. In spite of this, however, problems remain with many of the procedures because of inappropriate assumptions about the nature of intelligence and assessment.

The dangers of psychometrics led many educationalists to embrace behaviorism. Early behaviorists avoiding examining internal, hypothetical processes that defied measurement and concentrated instead on immediately observable interactions between the individual and the environment. Behaviorism has been responsible for programmed learning, task and curriculum analysis, precision teaching, behavioral objectives approaches, and a shift from normative assessment procedures to criterion referenced approaches. However, although behaviorism has made significant contributions to the teaching of basic skill hierarchies and the management of certain kinds of behavioral difficulties, it has not been able to tackle more complex behavior. In contrast to the Piagetian approach, the behavioral focus on task and curriculum analysis has deflected attention away from the need to examine cognitive competencies within the child. However, in common with the Piagetian approach, it has overlooked the critical role of social interaction in learning and development. For instance, Skinner's operate conditioning paradigm reduces people to mere dispensers of reinforcement while ignoring the subtle complexities of human interaction.

RECENT DEVELOPMENTS

Of course, there have been many overlapping and interacting developments in the fields of cognitive psychology, psychometrics, and behaviorism. For instance, behaviorism has broadened its scope with the various techniques developed in the 1960s now being seen as a set of resources to be deployed as part of a sensitive and comprehensive problem solving approach (Blagg, 1987). Moreover, with the emergence of the cognitive behavior therapy movement in particular, it is beginning to be acceptable to consider and analyze feelings and internal processes.

Meichenbaum (1985) illustrated how "a set of strange bedfellows" were brought together to give rise to a particular cognitive-behavioral training approach. He mentions the influence of social learning theory and in particular, the finding that children's cognitive strategies help them to delay gratification and control their behavior. He cites related research in the early 1970s, demonstrating that impulsive children were not so much *intrinsically* impulsive but rather, lacked certain self-mediating cognitive strategies that caused them to stop and think. This connected with the work of the Soviet psychologists, Luria (1961) and Vygotsky (1962). Luria (1959) proposed three stages of development in which children gradually learned to control their motor behavior. It was hypothesized that in the first stage, very young children were controlled by the speech of others (mainly adults). In the second stage, their own overt speech began to regulate and mediate their behavior until finally, in the third stage, "inner" speech took on a self-regulatory function.

It was on the basis of this model that Meichenbaum and Goodman (1971) developed their cognitive-behavior modification (CMB) training approach, which has led to a range of related procedures sharing a number of common features:

- The child is very actively involved in the learning process.
- Some form of "self talk" is typically encouraged, including positive self-affirmations, questioning tactics and prompts to promote caution where necessary.
- The teacher models the kinds of behaviors needed by the learner.
- In the course of training, the teacher's explicit verbalizations are overtly—and subsequently, covertly—copied and practiced until the learner begins to regulate his or her own behavior without external prompts.

This kind of self-instructional training has proved useful with impulsive children (Meichenbaum & Goodman, 1971) although benefits have tended to be restricted to specific training contexts (i.e., transfer and generalization have been elusive). Perhaps this is not surprising as training procedures have been closely tied to particular tasks and notions of the transitions from external speech to inner thought have been rather simplistic. Meichenbaum (1977) acknowledged these problems and suggested a number of ways in which transfer might be enhanced. Many CMB manuals have now been published which include promising suggestions in need of further study and elaboration.

In the psychometric field, the Illinois Test of Psycholinguistic Abilities (ITPA) caused a wave of excitement in the early 1960s by providing a model for assessing and teaching deficiencies in skills regarded as essential for learning. Unfortunately, the early promise of the ITPA movement turned out to be an illusion. The ITPA training programs (Kirk, McCarthey, & Kirk, 1968) did not lead to general improvements in attainments or learning abilities. Moreover, fundamental weaknesses in the assumptions underlying the ability training model were detailed by Ysseldyke and Salvia (1974); Hammill and Larsen (1974); Newcomer, Larsen, and Hammill (1975). As Bradley (1983) pointed out:

> disillusion and disappointment were widespread. More tragic than that disappointment was the fact that children were the victims of an iatrogenic educational programme, one that deprived them of potentially effective instruction while they were being subjected to interventions that excited the educators but that were of unproven effectiveness . . .   (p. 81)

These convincing critical appraisals led to the widespread abandonment of ability training procedures based on the ITPA. On a wider scale, the psychometric model has not been useful in suggesting ways of training intelligent behavior. Factors such as verbal comprehension or reasoning, simply do not tell us what it is that should be trained (Sternberg, 1985).

For these and other reasons, there is now a growing interest in dynamic approaches to intellectual assessment and a useful review of the state of the art can be found in Lidz (1987). More than 50 years ago Vygotsky (1935/1978a) talked about the need to identify the child's "zone of proximal development," which he defined as "the distance between the actual (mental) developmental level as determined by independent problem solving and the level of potential (mental) development as determined through problem solving under adult guidance or in collaboration with more capable peers" (Vygotsky 1935/1978a, pp. 85–86).

Quite independently in the 1950s and 1960s, Feuerstein and his colleagues were talking in similar terms about the need to assess a child's potential for learning by carefully analyzing the amount and nature of mediation required to help a child acquire a new concept, idea or skill. Over a number of years, the Feuerstein team have been experimenting with alternative ways of assessing an individual's potential for learning. Their approaches have evolved into an experimental package of materials known as the Learning Potential Assessment Device (LPAD) the basis of which is explicated in the *Dynamic Assessment of Retarded Performers* (Feuerstein, Rand, & Hoffman, 1979). Task types are rather similar to IQ and aptitude tests but, the traditional, formal approach to assessment in which the examiner is constrained by standardized instructions has been transformed into an interactional approach in which the examiner plays a crucial mediational role.

In summary, a much more optimistic view of human development currently prevails. The Vygotskyan premise that intellectual development is an outcome of educational experience now overrides the more pessimistic, biologically based Piagetian view. Thus, active learning approaches that consciously attempt to change an individual's cognitive skills are now gaining favor over a passive acceptance approach to individuals with learning problems. The role of social interaction as a crucial developmental force is now being recognized alongside the self-regulatory functions of language.

THINKING ABOUT THINKING

Since Flavell (1977) coined the term *metacognition* (referring to an individual's conscious awareness of his own thought processes) there has been an explosive growth in research on "thinking about thinking." It has been demonstrated that young children and low achievers are less able than adults or high achievers to talk about techniques and methods of learning and problem solving employed in specific tasks (Campione, Brown, & Ferrara, 1982). The implication is that if learners can become more aware of their own thought processes and learning strategies, they could not only widen their repertoire of such strategies, but also gain conscious control over them (i.e., by knowing when to select and apply them). This could provide the key to transfer and generalization. Indeed, Annett and Sparrow (1985) proposed an information processing theory of transfer in which a skill is regarded as a complex pattern of behavior controlled by a plan or schema that specifies and controls the actions appropriate in particular situations. Thus, as Annett (1989) suggested:

> When detailed skills are not readily transferred from one situation to another, this is an indication that they are not under the control of the plan which is currently in operation. . . . This theory of transfer leads, then, to a different prescription of what to do to encourage transfer and that is to identify the higher level skills which should be controlling behavior in a given problem area and to teach these in such a way that they incorporate a set of appropriate, and if necessary, varied specific skill components. (p. 12)

Annett (1989) aligned transfer skills with metacognitive skills. However, here we enter a hugely complex and confusing area. What exactly are these higher level metacognitive skills? How are they distinguished from specific skill components? Can they be defined with sufficient clarity that they can be taught? Does giving a name to an important process necessarily tell you what that process involves? For instance, one of Feuerstein's (Feuerstein, Rand, Hoffman, & Miller, 1980) essential cognitive functions refers to the need for the learner to be able to distinguish relevant from irrelevant. This is an important consideration but begs the question of how to go about it.

Developmental and cognitive psychologists, curriculum experts, teachers, and trainers have suggested a multitude of candidate metacognitive skills and processes. As yet, there is no accepted taxonomy nor even a commonly accepted list of these skills. However, although the fine detail of metacognition has yet to be teased out and clarified, there does seem to be broad agreement in the literature over the main domains that need attention. Nisbet and Shucksmith's (1987) review illustrates the lack of a common language for discussing metacognitive processes, but at the same time highlights the overlapping views of many researchers.

For example, lower order processes are referred to as mediational skills (Resnick & Beck, 1976), control processes (Belmont & Butterfield, 1977), and microstrategies (Kirby, 1984). These same authors refer to higher order processes as general strategies (Resnick & Beck, 1976), executive functions (Belmont & Butterfield, 1977), and macro-strategies (Kirby, 1984).

In essence, high-level control processes are regarded as being responsible for the selection, coordination, and sequencing of many lower order skills, in order to create purposeful, cognitive strategies. The distinction between control strategies and skills has been helpfully clarified by Nisbet and Shucksmith (1986) who made a simple analogy with a football team and its trainer. Individual players need to practice many skills, including heading, dribbling, ball control, and so on. Prior to a particular match or at half time, groups of players may plan certain tactics or strategies which involve a careful selection, sequencing, and coordination of skills for a particular purpose. Nisbet and Shucksmith took the analogy further by querying what happens when the strategy does not work. A poor team might continue with the same tactics, irrespective of the outcome. A good team would be able to monitor and assess the situation and flexibly adapt the strategy to achieve the desired goals. It does not matter how proficient the individual players are at particular skills like tackling and sprinting if they cannot coordinate them into useful strategies. Furthermore, the analogy demonstrates that there are different levels of strategic thinking, with monitoring, checking, and revising procedures requiring higher-level processes than generating and planning tactics.

Sternberg's information processing model of cognition puts some flesh on Nisbet and Shucksmith's analogy. Sternberg (1985) analyzed intelligent performance into a number of component processes. In keeping with the other researchers, his analysis refers to two levels of cognitive process:

1. **metacomponents** or **executive skills,** which are higher-level processes used for decision making, planning, monitoring, evaluating, and so on;

2. **lower order components,** which are sub-divided into:

    (a) **performance components** or **non-executive skills,** which carry out the steps and procedures selected by the metacomponents. These processes might include coding elements of a problem or combining elements into a working strategy or comparing one solution against another option and so on.

    (b) **acquisition components,** which are involved in learning new information.

    (c) **retention components,** which are involved in the retrieval of information.

    (d) **transfer components,** which are involved in carrying information from one context to another.

Sternberg's model does not provide comprehensive guidance on how to go about teaching the component processes involved in all intelligent behavior, but it does provide a structure for the experimental analysis and teaching of many different aspects of intelligent behavior.

PROGRAMS THAT TEACH COGNITIVE SKILLS

In the USA there are now numerous cognitive skills programs that claim to provide the materials to teach various component processes involved in intellectual tasks. Many of these programs, including Feuerstein's FIE (Feuerstein et al., 1980), are comprehensively reviewed, discussed, and compared in Chipman, Segal, and Glaser (1985a & 1985b). Although the style, content, and intention of the different programs overlap, their theoretical underpinnings are varied and each tends to emphasize different higher- and lower-order metacognitive processes. Feuerstein's FIE (1980) is, perhaps, one of the most comprehensive programs and it is linked to a series of clinically eclectic, over-lapping theoretical frameworks, which I will consider in the next chapter. However, at this point I will briefly consider three other programs that contrast with FIE:

- de Bono's CoRT System
- Lipman's Philosophy for Children
- Sternberg's Componential Training Program

thereby illustrating some of the recurring theoretical, content and teaching issues associated with cognitive skills courses.

de Bono's CoRT System

Some course designers have been more concerned with pragmatic than theoretical issues, being content to link their programs to loose metaphors for the mind while concentrating on the practicalities of teaching particular skills and strategies. The well known CoRT system (de Bono, 1976, 1979, 1981) falls into this category. It comprises a 2-year course involving a number of student instruction packs with accompanying teacher notes. Each pack is graded into six levels with each level covering one aspect of thinking (breadth, organization, interaction, creativity, information, and feeling and action). These areas are developed and elaborated through a series of ten lessons. The CoRT program has been used with a variety of age and ability levels and has been especially popular in the industrial world.

De Bono has been responsible for a technique that he calls "lateral thinking" which concerns ". . . rearranging available information so that it is snapped out of the established pattern and forms a new and better pattern. This rearrangement has the same effect as insight" (de Bono, 1969, p. 237). He believes that lateral as opposed to "vertical" or "logical" thinking is especially valuable in problem solving and practical decision making, considering that it generates numerous, unconstrained innovative alternatives.

CoRT lessons are tightly controlled and structured with the emphasis being placed on pupils becoming efficient in particular strategies and techniques explained in the materials. For example, the first lesson in CoRT 1—concerned with breadth of thinking—involves pupils in learning and practicing PMI (deliberately considering good, bad, or interesting points about an idea rather than immediately accepting or rejecting it). In contrast to Feuerstein et al. (1980), de Bono avoids the use of abstract, contextually bare tasks and instead draws upon everyday practical problems (e.g., "What are the consequences of quarrelling with your parents?" "If you were running a school, what rules would you insist upon?") Also, unlike FIE the pupil activities rely on an entirely verbal mode. Nevertheless, the specific thinking skills that are highlighted and taught have much in common with many of the metacognitive, self-monitoring strategies referred to by Feuerstein et al. (1980) and other authors. Like FIE the CoRT program is separate to mainstream curricula and has to be taught as a "bolt on" course.

Although the role of group work and discussion is recognized, the teaching approach seems to be more consistent with rote learning of techniques than the exploration of ideas with the teacher acting more as an instructor than a sensitive mediator. As such, there seems to be little room within the program for pupils to learn to take on responsibility for their own learning and problem solving. Indeed, an extensive, independent evaluation of the CoRT materials used with primary school children produced no hard evidence of any generalizable cognitive benefits arising from the course (Hunter-Grundin, 1985).

Although the program seems to have a practical appeal, the skills and procedures covered by the course do not seem to fit into a coherent theoretical framework. De Bono makes an artificial distinction between thinking and intelligence:

> Innate intelligence or IQ can be compared to the intrinsic power of the car. The skill with which this power is used is the skill of thinking. Thinking is the operating skill through which innate intelligence is put into action. A high intelligence may be allied to a high degree of thinking skill, but this is not necessarily so. Conversely a more modest intelligence may be accompanied by a high degree of thinking skill.
>
> (de Bono, 1976, p. 45)

The analogy does seem confusing. Apart from the muddled implication that innate intelligence equates with IQ, it is difficult to see how thinking can be separated from intelligence as both concepts are inextricably linked. Nevertheless, de Bono's basic premise appears to be that, although intelligence is fixed, his thinking skills lessons can enable us to use what intelligence we have in the most effective way. Thus, as Wolfe Mays (1985) has observed, in de Bono's view a "750cc intelligence" could be trained to function more effectively than an untutored "3 litre intelligence"!

Lipman's Philosophy for Children

The Philosophy for Children Program (Lipman, Sharp, & Oscanyan, 1980) is very different to both the CoRT and FIE programs and yet seeks to promote the development of many similar intellectual skills. The program is not based on psychological theory as such but rather has its roots in the nature of philosophical thinking. Although it is very difficult to define philosophical thinking in any precise terms, Lipman et al. (1980) argued that it not only involves thinking and reasoning but also thinking about thinking. Socrates emphasized that there were criteria that could be used to evaluate thinking such as the *internal consistency of arguments and the nature of the assumptions underlying arguments*. Thus, as Bransford, Arbitman-Smith, Stein, and Vye (1985) concluded in their analysis of Lipman's program, philosophical thinking is about:

> . . . a concern for coherence (internal consistency), for the correspondence between ideas and available data, and for the assumptions that underlie one's arguments. Philosophical thinking is also imaginative; for example, one must search for alternative sets of assumptions.   (p. 156)

Lipman and his colleagues have extended Socrates' idea that thinking things through in a logical and philosophical way can improve people's well-being. They suggest that it can not only benefit adults but also children, pointing out that the child's natural wonderment about the world leads them to spontaneously question similar issues that exercised the minds of early philosophers.

Accordingly, Lipman and his colleagues have analyzed the teachings of traditional philosophy, stripped away complex terminology and exposed a wealth of ideas that can be debated and discussed with reference to the discipline of logic. The resulting philosophical framework has been presented in the context of children's novels in which the characters spend much of their time reflecting on ways in which better thinking can be distinguished from poorer thinking.

The novels, associated activities, and exercises are explained in the accompanying teachers' manuals. Each lesson involves pupils in reading the texts and discussing the stories in relation to the follow-up exercises. The stories are stimulating and exciting to the point that pupils identify with and rehearse the characters' thinking processes and moral dilemmas.

Each novel provides opportunities to explore different reasoning processes, leading to the formulation of general principles that could apply to everyday life. Within the novels, each chapter includes a number of leading ideas that the pupils reflect on in the accompanying exercises and relate them to everyday concrete situations. For instance, under the heading of "Discovery and Invention," pupils are given a series of items such as television, light bulbs, and Pacific Ocean and asked to classify them as either "discovery" or "invention," justifying their answers.

Many of these activities seem to make assumptions about pupils possessing the lower-level prerequisite skills that FIE seeks to develop. In other words, it appears to be targeted at children who already have reasonable cognitive abilities. Lipman identifies 30 thinking skills that the teaching program intends to foster and many of these overlap with some of the higher-level metacognitive skills promoted in FIE including: constructing hypotheses, generalizing, drawing inferences from hypothetical syllogisms, classifying, and categorizing.

Unlike FIE, the very essence of the program is discussion and very little emphasis is placed on recording answers. In addition, while the need to read is greatly restricted in FIE, it is extensively used in Philosophy for Children. In contrast to both the CoRT and FIE programs, Lipman's course attempts to integrate with school curricula. The key novel (*Harry Stottlemeier's Discovery*) concerns itself with basic reasoning and inquiry skills but the contexts of the novel include ethics and science. A brief quote will give a flavor:

> Maria looked thoughtful, "But people are always jumping to conclusions. If people meet one Polish person or one Italian person or one Jewish person or one black person, right away they jump to the conclusion that this is the way all Polish people are or all black people, or all Italians or all Jews."
> "That's right," said Harry, "The only exercise some people get is jumping to conclusions."   (Lipman, 1974, p. 22)

The other novels apply the procedures of philosophical enquiry to familiar, concrete situations involving science, social studies, ethics, and the arts.

The program has been field tested and evaluated with encouraging findings although the quality and objectivity of the evaluation studies has been seriously questioned by Sternberg and Bhana (1986) who highlighted major flaws in the 20 studies that they reviewed. Nevertheless, at a face-validity level the program seems to have a lot to offer for pupils who already possess the minimal cognitive resources to cope with the course.

Sternberg's Componential Training Program

In contrast to programs associated with loose metaphors for the mind or philosophic inquiry, some programs, such as Sternberg's (1985) and Feuerstein's (1979) are more closely linked to psychological theory. However, although both programs relate to theories with an information processing orientation, the manner in which this orientation is expressed differs greatly in the two approaches.

In a sense, the two theories and their related intervention programs complement each other in that they analyze and train different aspects of intellectual performance but in a slightly different way. For instance, Feuerstein's *deficient cognitive functions list* (detailed in chap. 2) addresses similar issues to Sternberg's listing of the various kinds of information processing components. Both Sternberg and Feuerstein take a very optimistic view about the potential to modify intellectual development but each author dwells on different aspects of this dynamic process. Whereas Feuerstein emphasizes mediated learning experience (described in chap. 2), Sternberg concerns himself with the mechanisms by which the various components of intelligent behavior interact. Acquisition, retention, and transfer components provide the mechanisms for a steadily developing knowledge base. Increments in knowledge enable more sophisticated forms of acquisition, retention, and transfer and possibly improvements in performance components. Higher-order, self-monitoring metacomponents enable individuals to learn from their own mistakes. Finally, indirect feedback from lower-order components to one another, alongside direct feedback to the metacomponents, should result in improved efficiency in performance.

Feuerstein tends more toward clinical ecclesticism in his theoretical frameworks in an attempt to be both pragmatic and holistic. As such, his theoretical formulations and FIE program are difficult to test. In contrast, Sternberg's componential theory, referred to earlier, is less inclusive but more rigorous and experimentally biased. As Sternberg (1985) admits, his componential theory probably cannot be disproved. For example, it would be difficult to find a way of deciding whether the distinction between acquisition and transfer components was justified. However, he argues that particular examples of each of the five main components of his theory can, and have been, empirically tested.

Sternberg argues that intellectual development can be enhanced by improvements in any of the lower- or higher-order information processing components. Thus, his componential program aims to train individuals in metacomponential skills, performance componential skills as well as those skills that involve components of knowledge acquisition, retention, and transfer. Each section of Sternberg's training program includes material that:

- relates the instruction to his overall theory of intelligence;
- provides training in the particular processes of interest;
- uses "real world" and researched examples of the component skills being developed;
- illustrates model examples of applications of the component skills;
- provides multiple exercises that enable independent practice in the use of the component skills.

For example, metacomponential training is broken down into seven areas:

1) recognizing and defining problems,
2) selecting lower order components for solution of problems,
3) selecting a strategy for combining components,
4) selecting a representation upon which components and strategy act,
5) allocating processing resources,
6) monitoring progress and solution of problems,
7) utilizing feedback from problem-solving.   (Sternberg, 1985, p. 234)

The modular activities dealing with the first metacomponent (recognizing and defining problems) begin with real life examples of individuals faced with various difficulties. In each case, the difficulties can be overcome by a reframing of the problem (e.g., a professor misses a plane because he fails to catch a limousine). In fact, he could have caught the plane if he had used alternative transportation. He made the mistake of perceiving the problem as one of catching the limousine rather than the plane and therefore did not seek other ways of reaching the airport in time.

These examples from real life are followed up by researched-based training examples; for instance, ones which illustrate the kinds of mistakes that young children make when solving analogies because of their failure to recognize and define the problem. After these tasks students are given direct advice on ways of improving their ability to recognize and define problems such as rereading or reconsidering the question. Finally, further abstract and naturalistic tasks are used to "stretch" pupil ability to apply recognizing and defining skills. Similar procedures are used for each of the remaining metacomponential skills. Training in the performance, acquisition, retention, and transfer components is also broken down into several levels, with each level focusing on aspects of each component.

In summary, Sternberg's (1977) theory of intelligence provides a useful framework within which to analyze and investigate various aspects of intelligent behavior. His models overlap with, and are complementary to, Feuerstein's (Feuerstein et al., 1979, 1980) theories. Sternberg's componential training program is only partially completed and undergoing further development, elaboration, and testing. Nevertheless, it appears to offer a promising way of training intellectual skills. Sternberg's emphasis on the need to develop models and training programs that can be experimentally tested is to be welcomed.

SUMMARY

This first chapter has reviewed a number of theoretical, empirical, and practical issues associated with the idea of teaching cognitive skills in order to provide the reader with a broad background to Feuerstein's Instrumental Enrichment. The chapter began by highlighting the timeless goal of teaching intelligence, referring to the intentions and aspirations of the early philosophers. It went on to trace the development of a number of important psychological influences on the school curricula that have hampered progress toward any serious attempts to develop cognitive skills.

The chapter continued with a review of more recent overlapping and interacting developments in the fields of behaviorism, psychometrics, cognitive, social, and developmental psychology, which all point toward promising possibilities for teaching cognitive skills. The concluding section of the chapter briefly considered three cognitive intervention programs and their associated theories. Some comparisons were drawn with Feuerstein's FIE as a way of sensitizing the reader to some of the many issues that will be raised in this book.

Chapter 2

Feuerstein's Beliefs, Theories, Assessment Model, and Intervention Program

Feuerstein, a clinical psychologist and former pupil of Piaget, developed his ideas and beliefs about intelligence and learning while working for the Youth Aliyah Movement during the 1950s where he was dealing with the assessment and education of orphaned, traumatized immigrants coming to Israel after the Holocaust. Over many years of clinical work, Feuerstein came to believe in the enormous plasticity and modifiability of the human intellect and the crucial role played by significant adults in mediating the child's cognitive development.

> Except in the most severe instances of genetic and organic impairment the human organism is open to modifiability at all ages and stages of development.
>
> (Feuerstein et al., 1980, p. 9)

LEARNING POTENTIAL ASSESSMENT DEVICE

In assessing many holocaust survivors from Asia, Africa, and Europe, Feuerstein became disillusioned with the use of standardized intelligence tests for planning educational programs or predicting likely success rates. Traditional IQ tests merely indicated what a child had been able to learn to date, rather than potential for learning in the future. Accordingly, Feuerstein began to select and adapt conventional testing materials so they lent themselves to a dynamic rather than static assessment procedure. Gradually, over a number of years, the Israeli team brought together a collection of materials and approaches that are now collectively called *The Learning Potential Assessment Device* (LPAD).

Feuerstein, Rand, Jensen, Kaniel, and Tzuriel (1987) describe the basic elements of the LPAD model and emphasize the benefits of their particular dynamic

15

approach. They reject attempts to produce "culture free" intelligence tests or culture specific norms to allow for fairer interpretations of intelligence test results. They also criticize "functional" dynamic assessments (typified by the work of Budoff & Friedman, 1964, or Brown & Ferrara, 1985) based on a teach-test-teach paradigm where the aim is to produce quantitative measures as well as qualitative observations on the child's ability to learn efficiently.

This functional dynamic assessment approach basically involves assessing the child on a set of problem-solving tasks in a traditional way without assistance. This is followed by a training period in which the adult attempts to teach important processes involved in the tasks. The child can then be reassessed on a range of graded materials (from closely related through to quite distanced tasks) to check for the acquisition, retention, and generalization of the processes that have been taught. Naturally, the assessor monitors the nature and extent of the kinds of prompts necessary for the child to effect transfer.

Feuerstein et al. (1987) refer to their LPAD approach as "structural" dynamic assessment. The goal in LPAD goes beyond exploring changes in the child's immediate levels of functioning on tests in search of fundamental changes in basic cognitive processes that underpin many areas of mental activity. Feuerstein and his colleagues believe that the establishment of baseline measures (in a kind of formal test situation) might undermine the development of a positive relationship between the child and the examiner, put the child's confidence at risk, and constrain the examiner's flexibility to assist the child to perform at the highest possible level. It is the child's peaks of performance and the conditions of their appearance that become objects of analysis and scrutiny in the LPAD. Every effort is made to facilitate the recurrence and generalization of these peaks of performance.

Naturally, the lack of any baseline data on the child's performance makes it difficult to quantify observations and changes that occur during the assessment. In other words, the LPAD sacrifices the chance of quantitative measures of learning potential in favor of obtaining richer qualitative data. Using a range of selected, abstract, "IQ-like" tasks the examiner sensitively interacts with the child, mediating where necessary to bring about changes in the child's "deficient cognitive functions." The use of progressively dissimilar problem-solving materials involving more complexity (bits of information), changes in mode (verbal, pictorial, numerical, etc.), and tasks involving different mental operations in theory provides the opportunity to assess flexibility and generalizability of the cognitive skills exposed and/or developed during the assessment procedure.

Feuerstein et al. (1987) claim that the LPAD materials have been carefully chosen because they:

1. involve the use of "higher mental processes";

2. have an "optimal rather than minimal level of complexity in order to reflect

the molar nature of the real life situation, and, by this, offer the necessary prerequisites to further learning" (Feuerstein et al., 1987, p. 45);

3. offer opportunities for detecting very small changes in pupils' problem-solving behavior following limited mediation; and

4. are intrinsically motivating to children, adolescents, and adults.

There are theoretical and empirical problems associated with these claims. In an ideal world, it would be extremely useful to assess an individual's ability to acquire skills and processes that have universal application to commonly agreed examples of intelligent behavior. If this were possible, we might be able to assess an individual's learning potential in relation to the acquisition of skills relevant to many important, real-life contexts. However, there is no universal agreement on what constitutes intelligent behavior and no accepted taxonomy of cognitive abilities that offers guidance on the relative importance of these functions. What is meant by "higher mental functions" and what constitutes an "optimal level of complexity"?

The link with real-life is also questionable, as the tasks Feuerstein uses are similar in style and content to intelligence and aptitude tests. The problem arises that the LPAD may just be assessing an individual's ability to learn psychological test items. In other words, any observed improvements in cognitive functions may be specific to the rather artificial LPAD items. Such learning, even if it can be clearly demonstrated, may not transfer and generalize to more naturalistic contexts. Thus, it is not entirely clear whether potential for learning assessed by the LPAD equates with potential for learning in other contexts.

In any case, the examiner's interpretations of the child's responses to the LPAD depend on an intimate understanding of the deficient functions list and the elements in the cognitive map. However, both of these clinical "tools" include items that are fuzzy and difficult to operationalize. Moreover, the materials are quite complex and the child-examiner interaction paradigms provided in the manual are lengthy and involved. Undoubtedly, the materials would require many hours of use with many different client groups before enough clinical experience could be built up to make interpretation meaningful.

Perhaps even more fundamental than this, the whole procedure rests on the examiner's ability to mediate effectively and to organize, control, and record the nature and extent of the mediation. There may be individuals who do not appear to learn in the context of the LPAD. Such individuals could be regarded as being of "low modifiability" in contrast to others who gain much from the experience and are designated "highly modifiable." There is already evidence in the dynamic testing literature to indicate that low modifiability may be just as much related to the nature and quality of the mediation as to any enduring characteristics of the individual being assessed.

In spite of these reservations, the LPAD may be invaluable in assessing more profoundly handicapped children for whom traditional forms of assessment would be entirely inappropriate. Moreover, dynamic assessments offer another vantage point from which to gather important cognitive and affective information complementing the more traditional diagnostic process. Nevertheless, just as conventional IQ tests can be abused by assuming that a low IQ is synonymous with low ability and consequent low expectations, likewise the LPAD can be very dangerous if it is assumed that low modifiability is necessarily synonymous with a low potential to become a more effective learner.

In Israel, the LPAD is being used in some schools as a group procedure. This would appear to undermine its potential strength as a clinical tool by reducing the opportunity for the mediator to adapt and monitor the teaching interventions to suit the needs of the individual. Furthermore, the degree of modifiability as assessed by the group LPAD is being used as a means of deciding which individuals are most likely to respond to teaching and should therefore qualify for the most intensive help. This seems a highly suspect procedure quite at variance with the philosophy and belief systems on which Professor Feuerstein's work is built. As individual administration of a range of LPAD materials is quite time consuming—normally a minimum of 4 to 6 hours—it is not surprising that Feuerstein and his colleagues are experimenting with group LPAD procedures. However, it would be unfortunate if this led to the approach being abused and discredited.

DIRECT EXPOSURE LEARNING AND MEDIATED LEARNING

Feuerstein's work is underpinned by a powerful belief system. He views the human intellect as being highly malleable and modifiable at all ages and stages of development. While accepting that this belief can be easily eroded by realities such as the severity of an individual's condition, Feuerstein argues that a person's age or the nature of the problem cannot be used as a basis for predicting change. To account for the causes of differential cognitive development he proposes that humans learn through two modalities. In addition to direct exposure experiences emphasized by the stimulus-organism-response (S-O-R) model advocated by Piaget he argues that cognitive development is more crucially effected by mediated learning experiences (MLE). This is a subtle process in which adults emphasize, interpret, extend, and embellish the environment so that the child builds up an internal model of the world in which disparate aspects of experience are meaningfully related. Whereas direct stimuli impact on the child in a haphazard random fashion, mediated stimuli cannot escape the child's attention and recognition. Salient features of the environment are amplified, transformed, and rescheduled while others are blocked out so that the child is helped to systematize, select, and appreciate what to ignore and what to notice. Thus, Feuerstein emphasizes the role of the parent, teacher, and significant adult (H) in coming between the child and the world of stimuli or the world of responses changing Piaget's S-O-R model into S-H-O-H-R.

He distinguishes between many aspects of mediation, some of which he regards as being culturally determined and others universal. The three universal criteria for MLE are:

1. Intentionality/Reciprocity
2. Meaning
3. Transcendence.

As Chapter 3 will demonstrate, these criteria are difficult to operationalize. However, in general terms they can be explained as follows:

1. **Intentionality** is the imposition of the mediator on the mediatee. The adult must find ways of creating a state of vigilance in the child and a way of orienting the child to particular stimuli and experiences. Reciprocity refers to feedback from the child that the adult's intentions are understood. This may take several sessions to establish.

2. **Meaning** concerns the way in which the mediator endows the learning experience with a purpose, relevance and excitement, whether this means simply "do this for me" or "do this because it will help you . . . ."

3. **Transcendence** refers to the need to embellish the learning experience with a purpose and significance that goes beyond the particular needs of the task. For instance, the act of feeding a baby becomes a mediated transcendent interaction if it goes beyond satisfying the child's biological needs. In most cases, feeding is associated with temporal/spatial correlations (e.g., "we eat now, not later," "we eat here, not there," "wash your hands before eating" etc.).

Feuerstein believes that low attainment is caused primarily by a lack of mediation. This may be associated with many factors. For various reasons a child may not be offered sufficient mediation. Alternatively, there may be issues that reduce the child's accessibility to mediation (e.g., sensory difficulties or emotional problems). Nevertheless, in Feuerstein's view, such handicaps need not necessarily lead to impaired cognitive development provided the adult can ensure that the child receives enough mediation.

COGNITIVE MAP

In attempting to understand the notion of intellectual modifiability, Feuerstein proposes the use of a "cognitive map." This is meant to be a model of the mental act that covers seven dimensions, each of which is open to change. The dimensions are as follows.

Content

This refers to the subject matter of a particular task. Some pupils may experience problems with an activity because they are not sufficiently familiar with the subject matter. They may not have the basic knowledge prerequisites required by the task or they may simply fail to understand the technical vocabulary involved.

Mode

The mode refers to the main communication medium adopted in the pupils' learning. Modalities could include verbal, pictorial, numerical, diagrammatic, tabular, and so on. Undoubtedly many pupils perform better in some modes than others. For instance, there are many pupils in the low-attaining groups who experience great problems with the verbal mode while coping very well with pictorial or diagrammatic modes.

Operation

Feuerstein uses the term *operation* to refer to the mental structure through which information is processed, ranging from the business of simple recognition through to the use of analogies. In this aspect of Feuerstein's work, there is considerable overlap with Piaget's formulations. Feuerstein accepts Piaget's description of mental operations but adds a number of others. He implies that high-level operational thinking is based on a series of lower level fundamental processes, which are open to change with the right kind of mediated experiences. Mental operations are of course hypothetical constructs that are difficult to define in behavioral terms.

Phase

This is a somewhat artificial way of breaking down a mental act into three broad areas: input, elaboration, and output. Undoubtedly, there are children in the low-attaining groups who experience major problems with one particular aspect of phase. For instance, there are pupils who perform poorly on intellectual tasks because they simply fail to gather the prerequisite information at the input stage.

Complexity

The mental act increases in complexity according to the amount of information involved. In reality it is difficult to quantify the number of "bits" of information that any one task involves. However, it is well known that many pupils fail to cope with certain tasks because of their complexity rather than their content, mode, or the operations involved.

Level of Abstraction

As the mental act moves further away from the concrete events on which it operates, the more abstract it becomes. Ultimately, abstract thinking would involve purely hypothetical propositions. Once again, it is difficult to quantify and measure the relative levels of abstraction across different task types.

Level of Efficiency

This concerns the speed and precision of the mental act at the *input, elaboration,* and *output* stages. To some extent, it is probably a function of some of the other dimensions of the cognitive map, but it is also influenced by factors like anxiety and motivation.

THE INSTRUMENTAL ENRICHMENT PROGRAM

Feuerstein (1987) regards the Instrumental Enrichment Program as a "crystalized form of MLE." The program consists of 15 modules, or as Feuerstein calls them "Instruments" each made up of a series of paper-and-pencil tasks. Each task provides the basis for a 1-hour teaching session, with the intention being that pupils receive three to five sessions a week over a 2- to 3-year period. The program is accompanied by a highly detailed teacher's manual. The course involves:

1. Organization of Dots
2. Orientation in Space I
3. Comparisons
4. Analytic Perception
5. Categorization
6. Family Relations
7. Temporal Relations
8. Numerical Progressions
9. Instructions
10. Syllogisms
11. Transitive Relations
12. Orientation in Space II
13. Orientation in Space III
14. Representational Stencil Design
15. Cartoons (Illustrations).

Each instrument is meant to provide the teacher with activities to help the child overcome specific problems in gathering, thinking through, and responding to information. Feuerstein claims to have identified a number of regularly recurring problems at this phase level undermining the child's ability to think and learn. He itemizes these difficulties in his "deficient cognitive functions" list (Feuerstein et al., 1980, p. 73). This clinically based, non-exhaustive list covers a broad range of issues. For example, it includes loose descriptors of aspects of the child's functioning related to: cognitive style, knowledge base and concepts, motivation and processing capacity.

Thus, at the phase level concerned with gathering and organizing information, Feuerstein et al. (1980, p. 73) highlight such issues as: "blurred and sweeping perception [and] unplanned, impulsive and unsystematic exploratory behavior." At this input level, they also refer to deficiencies in the childs': "receptive verbal tools," "spatial orientation," "temporal concepts," "conservation of constancies," and "need for precision and accuracy in data gathering." Moreover, they point out that some children show a "lack of capacity for considering two or more sources of information at once."

At the elaboration or thinking through stage, Feuerstein et al. (1980, p. 73) identify a further range of issues including an: "inability to select relevant vs. non-relevant cues in defining a problem," "narrowness of mental field," "episodic grasp of reality," as well as deficiencies in knowledge of or need for "planning," "hypothesis testing" and "inferential thinking."

Similarly, at the response level, Feuerstein and his co-workers emphasize various issues such as:

> trial and error responses; lack of, or impaired receptive verbal tools for communicating adequately elaborated responses; lack of, or impaired need for precision and accuracy in communicating responses; deficiencies in visual responses; impulsive acting out behavior.   (Feuerstein et al., 1980, p. 73)

In selecting the teaching materials to overcome these and other problems, Feuerstein drew on the "tools of his trade" (i.e., different kinds of aptitude and ability tests, many of which were no longer in general use at the time). The test items were extended, elaborated, and compiled into modules, which he referred to as instruments. The term *instruments* emphasized the notion that it was not so much the content of the activities that was so important but rather the way in which they were used by the teachers.

Within each instrument, the content and mode of presentation of each task is very similar although the activities gradually increase in complexity. At critical stages in each instrument, a mastery page is introduced summarizing and assessing the child's growing competence. I will briefly review the contents of each of the instruments that were used in the study reported in this book.

Organization of Dots was derived from an aptitude test developed by André Rey. It consists of 26 similar but increasingly difficult tasks in which the pupil is required to locate and draw model figures hidden in amorphous clouds of dots. The use of overlapping shapes, non-universal shapes, and, later, 3D shapes adds to the complexity.

Orientation in Space I concentrates on developing the pupil's sense of spatial awareness. The first part deals with the relationship between four stable objects and a boy who changes position in relation to the objects, thereby increasing awareness of personal orientation in space. A higher level of abstraction is reached in the second part of the instrument as symbols are introduced, intended to encourage pupil ability to perceive other points of view.

Analytic Perception uses task types often associated with perceptual training programs. Once again, the layout and style of each page is similar throughout the module with the pupils exploring and explaining various part/whole relationships using different geometric configurations.

Comparisons is the fourth instrument in the first year program of study. This instrument analyzes the nature of comparison, distinguishing it from description with the intention of enhancing pupil ability to make appropriate and spontaneous comparisons to suit the needs of particular problems. The tasks require the pupil to isolate relevant attributes when making comparisons and to understand and describe the relationship between objects, events, and ideas in terms of their similarities and differences.

The instruments covered in the second year of the program are Categorization, Instructions, Numerical Progressions, Temporal Relations, and Family Relations. The instrument Cartoons (Illustrations) is recommended for use at any appropriate time throughout the program.

Categorization consists of 31 pages and is a development of Comparisons. The modes of presentation are more varied with the tasks focusing on the procedures and processes involved in elaborating and organizing different forms of data into superordinate categories. Pupils are meant to learn the difference between sorting and categorizing and between a relationship based on association and one based on grouping according to a principle selected to suit a particular need.

Instructions consists of 41 pages and uses verbal and figural presentation modes. It focuses on the need for precision in both giving and receiving instructions. At various points the tasks involve describing a given drawing so precisely that it can be replicated from the description; also correcting a given drawing so that it corresponds to the written instructions and vice versa.

Numerical Progressions is presented in numerical and diagrammatic modes. This 35-page instrument does not aim to teach arithmetical skills; numbers have been used because relationships based on the intervals between numbers are relatively easy to see. The basis of the instrument is rhythmic patterning of events and recurring cycles. The instrument aims to develop pupil ability to identify and apply rules either in the continuation of given progressions or in the construction of new ones, thereby encouraging pupil potential to make predictions.

Temporal Relations consists of 35 pages divided into six units, each of which introduces, explores, and develops a different aspect of time. They focus on the relationship between time, distance, and speed; measurable intervals of time; interrelationship between past, present, and future; the relativity of time through the pupils own subjective viewpoint; the precision of temporal concepts; and causal relationships.

Family Relations comprises 36 pages and uses verbal, graphic, and symbolic modes of presentations. It requires more reading skills than the other instruments. The instrument focuses on a system of conceptually defined relationships by which to link separate entities or categories.

Cartoons (Illustrations) is presented in pictorial mode. It is not intended to be taught sequentially, but as separate pages interspersed among those of other instruments. The tasks present a series of problem-solving situations, randomly ordered, intended to promote pupil ability to apply thinking skills learned so far in the program.

As the FIE program has drawn largely from the world of psychometrics, it is based on a rather limited range of task types and presentation modes. Feuerstein argues that the relatively context-free nature of the materials are necessary for this kind of work, as they allow important principles to be exposed without the child being distracted by "contextual clutter." At the same time, he emphasizes that the precise content of each instrument is not important, merely serving as a means of highlighting the need for particular kinds of thinking processes.

The business of transferring and generalizing the cognitive processes used in the lesson to everyday life is attempted via "bridging." In theory, throughout each lesson, the teacher should relate cognitive processes involved in the FIE tasks to real-life applications. It is hoped that eventually pupils will spontaneously bridge (i.e., make their own connections between the lessons and real life without prompting or assistance). Unless bridging can be successfully engineered, transfer and generalization will not occur and the whole point of the FIE program will be lost.

EXISTING RESEARCH EVIDENCE FOR AND AGAINST FIE

On the face of it, FIE sounds like the miracle cure we have all been waiting for. What evidence is there to support the claims for the program?

Feuerstein's work on changing cognitive abilities began in the early 1950s. His Instrumental Enrichment Program was developed in the 1960s and was disseminated widely by Curriculum Development Associates of the USA in the late 1970s. Empirical support for the program came later when Feuerstein, Rand, Hoffman, and Miller (1979a) published a paper in the *American Journal of Mental Deficiency,* reporting the effects of FIE on retarded adolescents. This paper was followed by two substantial books (Feuerstein et al., 1979b, 1980).

Since then, there have been a number of well-designed studies of FIE reported by Feuerstein's co-workers at Vanderbilt University in the USA (Arbitman-Smith, 1982; Arbitman-Smith & Haywood, 1980; Arbitman-Smith, Haywood, & Bransford, 1985; and Haywood & Arbitman-Smith, 1981). There have also been many small-scale studies in the form of Master's and Doctoral Theses. For instance, in the UK, Beasley (1984) undertook a small-scale study on the effectiveness of FIE with respect to adolescents with moderate learning difficulties attending a special school. Finally, there have been numerous low-key, anecdotal exploratory studies of FIE that have been generally poorly designed and executed using assessment measures of unknown characteristics.

The Feuerstein message has spread beyond the technical, academic, and educational research journals into a wide range of professional journals, magazines, and lay literature. In the UK, articles have appeared in the national press (The *Times Educational Supplement,* The *Sunday Times,* The *Telegraph*), as well as *Special Children* and *New Society.* Recently, a journalist (Sharron, 1987) wrote a eulogy to Feuerstein that strongly criticized the British education system's commitment to outmoded notions of intelligence and learning and proposed Feuerstein's theories, ideas, and program as the way ahead. The book provided an easy to read account of Feuerstein's ideas but made largely unsubstantiated claims about the effectiveness of FIE linked to a very episodic, flimsy, and distorted account of the research literature.

Unfortunately, in spite of the burgeoning mass of studies since the late 1970s, there is to date relatively little convincing research evidence to substantiate the claims made for FIE. A detailed, penetrating, and critical review of the status of Feuerstein's ideas is reported in Bradley (1983, p. 83):

> The most crucial question when the claim is made that an intervention improves cognitive functioning is "Do the experimental procedures improve intellectual performance?" The response from the proponents of the program is generally on the order of . . . "The results while modest, are promising. . . ." I would suggest a more appropriate description of the results: "At present they are very modest, perhaps promising but, more likely, at best clouded."

The current situation remains much as Bradley reported it. The literature generally suggests that Instrumental Enrichment leads to statistically significant gains on certain measures of intellectual ability, inconsistent gains on various measures of subject achievement, and positive effects on attitudes, classroom behavior, and motivation. However, close scrutiny of the research reveals many inadequacies, methodological flaws, and over-optimistic interpretations.

Feuerstein's work is permeated by an eclectic web of overlapping theoretical models that are clinically and heuristically useful but imprecise and difficult to evaluate. Quite apart from the inherent research problems that this poses, Bradley (1983) points to many other technical shortcomings in the published research, which cast doubt on the findings. In particular, he argues that many of the measures chosen to assess the effectiveness of FIE have been either unreliable or inappropriate. Furthermore, he cites the failure of most studies to use multivariate research designs and statistical analyses to overcome experimental error rates and allow for the simultaneous investigation of changes in various dependent variables. He quite rightly points out that an effective cognitive intervention program is likely to produce changes in various aspects of the child's behavior and development and that studies must be able to monitor and distinguish these various effects over and above chance fluctuations in the data.

Shayer and Beasley (1987) carried out a substantial review of the American and Israeli FIE research subjecting the data to a meta-analysis. Their interpretation is more optimistic than Bradley's but still it only points to moderately interesting gains on intelligence test items closely related to the FIE program and very limited and modest gains on certain achievement measures. In the same paper, Shayer and Beasley report on their own FIE study using special school adolescents (10 experimental and 10 control subjects). They report interesting and substantial effects on pupil ability to process fresh information but, once again, there is little evidence of this translating into improved achievement in school. The authors argue that their evidence is sufficient to warrant the time and effort involved in the FIE program. However, given the very small numbers involved and the optimal conditions under which the study was mounted and supported, it would be unwise to over-generalize these findings.

In his review article, Burden (1987) argues that the FIE research carried out so far has paid relatively little attention to the conditions (training, support, choice of groups, opportunities for bridging, etc.) under which the intervention has been delivered. Instead, most studies have focused almost exclusively on changes in various dependent variables. Moreover, Burden agrees with Bradley (1983), that outcome measures utilized have often been inadequate as a means of assessing FIE's main goals. Perhaps more controversially, Burden (1987) suggests that the main obstacle to understanding the effects of FIE is not so much a lack of appropriate assessment techniques but the "inadequacy of traditional, laboratory-based experimental design methodology when applied to complex, real-world interventions" (p. 14). He intimates that Bradley's (1983) suggestions for dealing with the research complexities are impracticable, as multivariate designs would require very large samples and the use of many different measures. Given the need for 2- and 3-year follow-up studies, it is doubtful that many researchers would have the time and energy to implement Bradley's ideas. Burden (1987) calls for an entirely different style of evaluation. He commends the "illuminative" approach advocated by Hamilton (1976) and suggests that the context/input/

process/product (CIPP) model proposed by Stufflebeam (1971) is perhaps the most promising framework for examining the complexities of implementing and evaluating Instrumental Enrichment and mediated learning experiences.

Some researchers would argue that a purely illuminative approach would fall short of being able to provide definitive evidence of a cognitive development program's efficacy. They would argue that such an approach would be far more open to experimenter bias. Nevertheless, the traditional experimental design methodology does not seem incompatible with the looser illuminative approach. Indeed, both approaches can be comfortably accommodated within Stufflebeam's CIPP analysis. Accordingly, the Somerset evaluation of FIE utilized Stufflebeam's CIPP model; but within this framework, a range of input and output measures were considered within a multivariate design.

Chapter 3

Instrumental Enrichment
Evaluation Design

CIPP
context / input /
process / product

Any school-based action research study is fraught with problems. There are so many factors that can affect pupil behavior and learning. Every school is unique with a different catchment area, organization, and curriculum. The charisma or otherwise of particular teachers can have dramatic, positive or negative influences. Issues like these make it very difficult to distinguish the individual and special contribution of one particular intervention. Beyond this, proponents of FIE argue that there is "no quick fix in cognitive modifiability" (Link, 1977). In other words, the program takes time to work, and to monitor its effects a longitudinal study of at least 2 years is required. However, longitudinal studies pose problems. Apart from the time involved, there are difficulties in maintaining and monitoring coherent pupil groups over long periods. Furthermore, the longer the study, the greater the chance of other home and school related factors influencing pupil change.

Stufflebeam's (1971) CIPP model provided a useful framework within which to monitor and observe the effects of Instrumental Enrichment on pupils, teachers, and the curriculum. As Fig. 3.1 shows, the model involves attention to: (a) the Context in which the innovation took place; (b) the Input to the teachers and pupils in terms of who was selected and what was received; and (c) the Process of what happened and the Product of the intervention in terms of the achievement of previously stated aims and objectives.

In order to cover the range of possible effects involved in the Instrumental Enrichment Program, the evaluation needed to be both formulative and summative, with attention to the assessment of cognitive and affective changes in both pupils and their teachers. Quantitative assessments needed to make use of normative and criterion-referenced testing procedures and where possible control

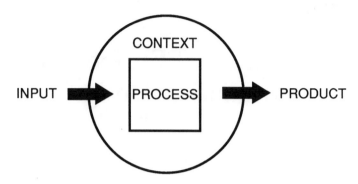

FIG. 3.1.   Stufflebeam's (1971) CIPP Model

groups were established. Sensitive and detailed qualitative data was gathered throughout the period of study.

This chapter will present a broad overview of the study and consider some of the technical problems associated with evaluating and monitoring the potential effects of FIE. More specific details relating to the selection and characteristics of the pupils and teachers and outcome effects on pupils and teachers will be reserved for Chapters 4 and 5.

THE CONTEXT

Background Issues

Bridgwater is a small industrial town situated in Somerset, in the southwest of England. Somerset is a rural county that earns its revenues from agriculture. Bridgwater is unusual in that its economy depends heavily on Hinckley Point Nuclear Power Station and a range of light industries such as British Cellophane and Clark's Shoes.

The town has a secondary school population of approximately 3,000 pupils who attend one of four schools (referred to in the report as Schools A, B, C, and D). Each school takes children from both urban and outlying rural primary schools. However, two of the schools (A and B) are regarded as having a slightly poorer social intake as they draw more heavily from two large council estates (subsidized housing owned and maintained by the county council).

It is important to note that the application for LAPP funding was centrally organized by the then Chief Education Officer, Barry Taylor. The location for the project, the four Bridgwater secondary schools, was also centrally determined. Thus, the project did not arise out of local enthusiasm for FIE. Final funding details did not materialize until the term before the intervention program was due to begin. Implementation plans were therefore hastily arranged.

The need to impose FIE on timetables that had already been drawn up created considerable disruption during the first year of the project. Both staff and pupils, in some schools, were hostile and cynical about being withdrawn from chosen options to participate in an unknown course. Although these timetabling problems were overcome during the formal experimental period (i.e., the second and third years of the project) the unfortunate initial implementation period left a legacy of discontent in some schools.

On the positive side, the LAPP schools received enhanced staffing and resources with extra teachers being given positions of responsibility, linked with improvements in salary. Improved pupil/teacher ratios were also possible for the FIE lessons with class sizes varying from 12 to 18.

The attitude of senior management toward Instrumental Enrichment, at the outset of the project in each of the four schools would be best described as neutral and relatively uninformed. Two terms before the project was to be implemented, FIE teachers were recruited from within each of the schools by inviting volunteers to attend a one-week FIE training course. There was also a responsibility allowance available to one teacher in each school to take overall responsibility for the FIE program. In general, teachers were confused about the nature of FIE and uncertain about what would be involved in teaching the program. As the cartoon on this page illustrates, even the senior management were unable to offer any relevant information to potential FIE teachers.

Unfortunately, funds for training courses did not extend to whole staff awareness days or to teachers other than those to be directly involved in teaching the program. Brief discussions and a cursory glance at the FIE materials did little to stimulate a positive and optimistic attitude toward the program amongst the senior management. Indeed, in at least one school there was some cynicism toward the

FIG. 3.2.

notion of trying to artificially improve children's intelligence and learning ability. Moreover, one deputy head teacher commented that almost any teacher given extra resources and smaller classes could bring about significant improvement in children's performance, irrespective of the nature of the intervention.

The four schools operated different timetable arrangements. The two schools A and B, with slightly poorer social intakes, favored banding and streaming. In each case, whole-year groups were divided into upper- and lower-ability bands, with individual's classes within each band further differentiated according to ability. In these schools, ability largely equated with reading and mathematics quotients supplied by feeder primary schools. Subsequent movement between classes was determined by performance in school examinations. Schools C and D favored more flexible setting arrangements which enabled pupils to be in higher- or lower-ability groupings for different activities according to their achievements in particular subjects. In all schools, fourth and fifth year pupils followed a set of core (compulsory) subjects as well as options (other subjects selected by the pupils and parents). In the lower-achieving groups, options were strongly guided (i.e., teachers helped pupils and parents to choose subjects that would be appropriate and manageable).

Establishing the Broad Aims and Objectives

Discussions were held with senior members of the Local Education Authority administration as well as the headteachers, deputy headteachers, and other staff in each of the four project schools. It was quite clear that the central administration and senior management in the schools were looking for powerful evidence to support the case that Instrumental Enrichment improves pupil motivation, attitudes, and, perhaps most important of all, does indeed remediate specific cognitive deficiencies leading to improved learning ability in situations beyond the training tasks involved in Instrumental Enrichment. Undoubtedly, Instrumental Enrichment challenged traditional teaching styles and methods. Barry Taylor, the then Chief Education Officer, was particularly interested in the effect that this may have on teachers.

Thus it was at the input stage that the selection and formal pre-testing of both pupils and teachers took place and the problems associated with the design and selection of assessment procedures were considered. A comprehensive range of pre-assessment procedures was eventually implemented with FIE and control pupils. In a separate but related project, a larger group of FIE teachers were compared over time with a group of control teachers in order to assess the wider impact of FIE on teacher attitudes and behavior.

In considering the potential effects of FIE on the pupils, the main goals and sub-goals of FIE were analyzed and translated into testable hypotheses. Feuerstein et al. (1980) describe the major goal of FIE:

—to increase the capacity of the human organism to become modified through direct exposure to stimuli and experiences provided by the encounters with real life events and with formal and informal learning opportunities. (p. 115)

This major goal is elaborated by six sub-goals:

1. The correction of the deficient functions that characterize the cognitive structure of the culturally deprived individual.
2. The acquisition of basic concepts, labels, vocabulary, operations, and relationships necessary for FIE.
3. The production of intrinsic motivation through habit formation.
4. The production of reflective, insightful processes in the student as result of his confrontation with both his failing and succeeding behaviors in the FIE tasks.
5. The creation of task-intrinsic motivation.
6. To arouse the learner from his role of passive recipient and reproducer of information and turn him into an active generator of new information.

(Feuerstein et al., 1980, pp. 115–117)

Unfortunately, it was difficult to devise appropriate, accurate, and reliable procedures that would test the aforementioned hypotheses. These issues will be returned to in later sections.

THE INPUT (PUPILS)

Selecting the Pupils

As the introduction of this book makes clear, the project was the result of a government-based initiative, designed to explore ways and means of improving the educational opportunities for 14- to 16-year-old, low-achieving adolescents. Thus, within the four project schools, the program was targeted at this age range with pupils receiving the program from the beginning of their fourth year until they left school at the end of their fifth year. The project schools were mainstream not special schools and the term "low-achieving" meant low-achieving in relation to the public examination system (GCE) in operation at the time.

Low-achieving is a very inclusive and loose descriptor, covering a wide range of pupils showing many different kinds of attitudinal, emotional, behavioral, and learning difficulties ranging in severity. The final choice of pupils from the many possible candidates for the project was left to individual schools. Although each school adopted slightly different selection procedures, the attitudinal, ability, and attainment characteristics of the teaching groups at the start of the study were remarkably similar across and within the schools, according to a number of test indices reported in Chapter 4.

School A

Fourth and fifth year pupils were organized into upper- and lower-ability bands. All pupils in the lower-ability band followed the FIE program as a core subject eliminating the possibility of establishing control groups in this school. There were four fourth year FIE groups (15, 16, 17, 18) with approximately 18 pupils in each. The study assessed and monitored change in all four of these groups over the 2-year period. It was planned to place special emphasis on video work in this school.

School B

Fourth and fifth year pupils were organized into upper- and lower-ability bands. Staff were asked to nominate pupils from the lower-ability band who might benefit from FIE. Three groups, (4, 5, and 6), with approximately 15 pupils in each were selected on the same basis and regarded as equivalent in ability terms. It was initially intended that each group would receive FIE but unfortunately, one of the newly trained FIE teachers refused to teach the program (group 5) and an experienced FIE teacher (group 6) was promoted during the first term of the program. This meant that groups 5 and 6 acted as controls, with both groups receiving extra mathematics instead of FIE. The remaining group (4) received the FIE program.

School C

Prior to the project, a group of fourth and fifth year pupils in this unstreamed school were identified as not coping with the full range of school subjects. This group was designated a limited range group and FIE was offered to all pupils in this group as a guided option choice. There were enough pupils to form three equivalent FIE groups (11, 12, 13) with approximately 15 pupils in each.

There were no possibilities for establishing formal control groups. Under the circumstances, assessment and monitoring were mainly confined to the three fourth year Instrumental Enrichment groups. However, FIE pupils did not remain together as a coherent group for all lessons. Indeed, beyond FIE lessons, these students were mixed with other low-attaining pupils who did not receive the FIE program. This provided an opportunity to compare progress over time of FIE versus non-FIE, low-attaining pupils across a range of different subjects. For instance, in Applied Science, FIE pupils were grouped with other non-FIE children who happened to be very weak at science. Thus, it was possible to ask the applied science teacher to rate the whole class in terms of various behavior indices at various points during the experimental program allowing a comparison of behavioral changes between those receiving FIE and those not.

School D

Fourth and fifth year pupils were normally taught in mixed ability groups with the exception of a few subjects, including mathematics and English. FIE was offered as a guided option to those pupils who did not study a foreign language. Two FIE groups (7 and 8) were selected with approximately 15 pupils in each. However, within this school it was possible to identify a third group (9) of fourth year children (who had similar difficulties and ability levels). These children did not receive FIE but were assessed and monitored carefully as a control group. As in school C, it was also possible to carry out a series of small-scale controlled comparisons of FIE and non-FIE lower-attaining pupils.

The control groups in schools B and D acted as quasi controls for schools A and C.

Project Pupil Characteristics

In general terms, some of the project pupils were disenchanted with school life and poorly motivated toward studying, with their dissatisfaction being demonstrated in a variety of ways; including disruptive behavior, truancy, or a failure to participate in lessons in anything other than a token way.

Some of the project pupils were reasonably positive about school but showed pervasive and inappropriate learning styles that handicapped their performance. For instance, the project sample contained many impulsive pupils typified by those who rush into tasks without knowing what the problem is or spend insufficient time thinking through, planning, and checking their work.

At the other end of the impulsive/reflective continuum, some of the project pupils seemed to be so highly anxious about making mistakes that they were constantly rehearsing approaches and answers in private but rarely committing themselves in public. Many of these children were reluctant to take part in discussions and when obliged to put something on paper, often produced highly neat, tidy, and constrained examples of work. These children rarely managed to finish any of the activities that their teachers set them.

Quite apart from learning-style problems, many of the project pupils gave the impression of having a limited repertoire of relatively inflexible cognitive strategies. It seemed as though they had learned particular skills and routines that they automatically used, irrespective of whether they were appropriate or not. Often, these pupils did not seem to question their approach to tasks, being more concerned to appear occupied and busy than to consider whether their tactics were correct.

In some instances, limited and inflexible strategies seemed to relate in part to low self-esteem, a fear of taking risks, and a consequent willingness to adopt the role of a less able pupil rather than experience failure. Amongst some of the pupils, low self-esteem, inappropriate learning styles, and a limited strategic repertoire interractted with specific gaps in cognitive resources and knowledge (e.g., poor language and communication skills, reading difficulties) so that achievement was poor across many different areas.

There were some problems associated with selecting appropriate test procedures that would be sufficiently sensitive to the kinds of attitudinal, behavioral, and learning process issues that needed to be studied in the evaluation. These issues are fully discussed later in this chapter. More precise psychometric characteristics of the project pupils at the start of the study are defined in Chapter 4 in Tables 4.1, 4.2, and 4.3. However, at this stage, it may be helpful to the reader to summarize the main features of the attainment and ability profiles of the pupils.

The total sample of project pupils showed:

- a mean IQ = 91.7 based on a sample of verbal and non-verbal tests from the British Ability Scales.
- a normal distribution of ability on certain spatial reasoning and visual memory tasks. Indeed, there were some so called low-attaining pupils with quite remarkable abilities in these areas.
- generally below average verbal reasoning and vocabulary skills
- consistently depressed reading and mathematics attainments
- consistently poor work study skills.

Timetable Arrangements

In the four project schools, FIE was established as a kind of quasi department. It was timetabled as a separate subject and given a specific time allowance in each school.

It was important to distinguish the amount of FIE teaching that each pupil received as this would be likely to effect pupil outcomes. The project was scheduled to run for 2 years, but in practice, pupils only received five terms teaching as most were Easter leavers. Timetable arrangements varied from school to school as follows:

School A—Two double periods, amounting to two 1-hour-and–10-minute sessions each week.

School B—Two double periods, amounting to two 1-hour sessions each week.

School C—Two double periods, amounting to two 1-hour-and–10-minute sessions each week.

School D—Four single periods, amounting to four 45-minute sessions each week. In addition, FIE pupils were kept together for mathematics and English and attempts were made within these lessons to apply the cognitive skills exposed and practiced in the FIE tasks.

However, the timetable allocation could not be literally interpreted as the input to each pupil. Natural interruptions to timetabling like staff absenteeism, Inservice Training for Teachers (INSET), sports days, speech days, and so on can vary both within and across schools as can pupil attendance. Accordingly, in order to calculate the precise number of hours of FIE teaching that each pupil received it was necessary for each teacher to keep a detailed record of:

- the number and duration of each FIE lesson taught by the FIE teacher.
- the attendance of each pupil at the above lessons.

On the basis of this information, each pupil was given an attendance figure. Within the total sample of FIE pupils there was a very wide variation in attendance, with pupils receiving from only 30 hours up to 192 hours FIE teaching over the study period. The mean FIE teaching time received by the total project sample was 112 hours.

Teaching Materials

Within each school the FIE classes covered 10 of the 14 FIE instruments available at the time:

Organization of Dots
Orientation in Space 1
Comparisons
Analytic Perception
Categorization
Family Relations
Temporal Relations
Numerical Progressions
Instructions
Cartoons.

Issues in Assessment

The Use of Ability Tests

FIE is derived from extended aptitude and ability tests. As such, it contains abstract materials, modes of presentation, and styles of task commonly found in existing assessment procedures purported to measure intelligence or learning ability. Improved scores on closely related test materials would not amount to convincing evidence of the effectiveness of FIE.

One way around this might involve assessing the degree of overlap between test materials and the FIE program. In this way, some tests could be regarded as potential indicators of "close" transfer and others "distanced" transfer. However, this raises the further problem of how one quantifies the degree of overlap. Inevitably, subjectivity comes into this with the result that what is judged as evidence of close transfer by some researchers would be regarded as evidence of distanced transfer by others.

FIE seeks to transform pupils' cognitive process skills; however, most existing standardized ability tests assess the products of learning rather than the processes by which learning takes place. In an ideal world it would be desirable to construct a range of cognitive assessment procedures specifically designed to test the efficacy of FIE. Unfortunately, designing, piloting, and standardizing tests so that the scores are reliable and valid is a long-term process. As a result, researchers are posed with the dilemma of using inappropriate, standardized procedures with known characteristics or newly designed procedures, inadequately researched and therefore of unknown reliability and validity (see Newland, 1980).

The Limitations of Standardized Attainment Tests

FIE does not claim to teach mathematics, reading, and the like directly, but rather claims to prepare pupils to be more effective learners. In theory, FIE should boost pupil self-esteem; promote positive attitudes about being able to learn to learn and bring about the kinds of cognitive improvements that will make this possible.

Previous studies have suggested that self-esteem changes can occur quite early in the FIE program and many research studies unrelated to FIE have demonstrated a positive relationship between achievement and self-esteem enhancement. Accordingly, some improvement in basic educational attainments might be indirectly expected as a result of FIE in association with improvements in self-esteem. However, cognitively linked, dramatic improvements in attainment areas would not be predicted from FIE in the short term, as fundamental cognitive improvements are said to take time to achieve. If, as the proponents claim, it takes a minimum of 2 years to bring about significant improvements in the ability to learn it will only be after that period that improvements in the acquisition of knowledge in basic attainment areas would begin to show.

The Availability of Suitable Attitudinal, Behavioral Change Measures

Perhaps the most fundamental issue on which FIE should be judged is the extent to which FIE pupils show evidence of improved functioning in other areas of the school curriculum and their personal lives. One way of exploring this involves monitoring changes in attitude, motivation, and behavior in different school and social contexts. However, once again, researchers are faced with the problems of having a limited range of standardized assessment tools suitable for the job.

Assessing the Pupils

In view of the issues just raised, the final choice of pupil assessment procedures was a compromise, resulting in the use of the following ability, attainment, attitudinal, and behavioral measures.

Ability Measures

Six individually administered tests from the British Ability Scales were used to assess pupil change in specific cognitive areas.

In view of the general linguistic and communication skill demands of the FIE program (e.g., the need to explain and justify ideas and points of view and the general emphasis on vocabulary development) it was predicted that FIE pupils should show evidence of improved scores on:

- **Word Definitions (BAS WD),** a test requiring an oral response, assessing changes in vocabulary development.
- **Similarities (BAS SIM),** a test assessing changes in verbal reasoning ability. It should be noted that the test essentially involves comparing groups of items and explaining why they belong together (i.e., supplying an appropriate category name). There are numerous very similar reasoning activities contained in the third FIE instrument (Comparisons). The test is entirely oral beginning with items low in abstraction (e.g., milk, lemonade, coffee) and ultimately finishing with high-level abstraction (democracy, justice, equality).

Given the FIE emphasis on reducing impulsivity, promoting planning behavior and generally developing pupil cognitive functions (e.g., the ability to attend to detail, analyze, label and describe accurately, notice cues and clues, visualize, and mentally orientate and transport images) it was predicted that FIE pupils should show significant improvements on IQ test items where these functions were required. This should apply on both verbal and visual tasks. However, evidence of improvement in cognitive functioning should be more noticeable on certain visual reasoning tasks because of their close relationship to the original FIE program. Accordingly, it was predicted that there would be particularly significant improvements amongst the FIE pupils on the following tests:

- **Block Design—Level (BAS BD),** a spatial reasoning test requiring pupils to make up three-dimensional geometric patterns to match two-dimensional drawings.

- **Block Design—Power (BAS BDP).** This is identical to 3, but it assesses pupils efficiency by scoring for speed as well as accuracy.
- **Matrices—(BAS MAT),** an abstract visual reasoning test involving pupils in seeing patterns and relationships between shapes and visual symbols. The test requires a written response.
- **Recall of Designs—(BAS RD),** a short-term visual memory test requiring pupils to observe, memorize, and recall a series of diagrams using shapes and symbols. The pupils are given a short time to look at each diagram and then they have to accurately draw the shapes and symbols in their correct relationship to one another.

The results of these tests were considered separately but were also used to compute an intelligence quotient for each child. It was predicted that FIE pupils should show improvements in IQ as a reflection of better functioning on the individual tests.

In addition to these BAS ability measures the CSMS Science Reasoning tasks were also used in an attempt to note any changes in cognitive operations as assessed by typical Piagetian reasoning tasks:

- spatial relationships
- volume and heaviness
- the pendulum and equilibrium in the balance.

The CSMS tasks were extended downwards to include measures of "early concrete operations," where necessary, by an:

- individually administered Piagetian Test Battery. The items chosen were originally developed for primary-aged children by the Pakistan National Institute of Psychology (1977–1981) with Shayer, Lovell, and Opper acting as consultants. This was rewritten by Blagg and Tincknell (1984), under Shayer's supervision for the present study.

It was anticipated that if the FIE pupils showed significant improvements in terms of Feuerstein's cognitive functions list, this should translate into measurable improvements in cognitive operations. For example, FIE pupils at a concrete operational level at the beginning of the study should show evidence of shifting toward concrete generalization or early-to-late formal operational reasoning. In view of the foregoing it was predicted that FIE pupils would show significant improvements on the CSMS tasks and Piagetian test battery. Such improvements had already been demonstrated with a small group of special school adolescents (N = 10) receiving FIE under optimal conditions (Shayer & Beasley, 1987).

Attainment Measures

Information on reading ability was already being gathered at the input stage of the project independent on the FIE evaluation as the Edinburgh Reading Test was normally given to all fourth year pupils as part of the county screening procedure. Accordingly, this test was also used as a posttest measure at the end of the study as a means of monitoring changes in pupils' reading ability. It was predicted that FIE pupils should show positive improvements in Edinburgh Reading Test quotients associated with gains in self-esteem.

In addition, five other group procedures were selected from the Richmond Attainment Test Battery as shown below:

- Richmond Work study skills RW–1—Map reading
- Richmond Work study skills RW–2—Reading graphs and tables
- Richmond Work study skills RW–3—Knowledge and use of reference materials
- Richmond Mathematics skills RM–1—Concepts
- Mathematics skills RM–2—Problem solving.

Although the work study skills tests do involve some knowledge about conventions in representation and so on, most of the tasks involve the interpretations of given rather than assumed information. If FIE does result in reduced impulsivity, improved planning behavior, and generally improved cognitive functions, this should translate into improved abilities to gather, organize, and interpret information. Thus, it was hypothesized that FIE pupils would show significant improvements in scores on the Richmond Work Study Skills Tests. Performance on the Richmond Tests of Mathematics Skills is more reliant on assumed knowledge outside the scope of the FIE program. In view of this, it was predicted that FIE pupils would not show any significant improvements in the mathematics skills tests.

Attitudinal/Behavioral Measures

Feuerstein's reference to FIE producing intrinsic motivation through habit formation and transforming passive recipients of information into active generators of new information suggests that FIE pupils should show evidence of:

- Positive behavioral change in the classroom on a range of critical incidents.
- Developing more positive attitudes toward school and school work.
- Developing more positive views of themselves as learners and problem solvers.

The first of these hypotheses was explored by a specially formulated observation schedule in which teachers could rate pupil behavior in class at the beginning and end of the study on a range of critical incidents (see chap. 4, Table 4.4). The schedule was not factor analyzed and in view of this, each item was treated separately.

The second hypothesis was explored by using an individually administered rating scale, recording pupils' attitudes toward FIE and their core school subjects with respect to:

- personal enjoyment
- personal relevance
- personal participation
- lesson format
- class cooperation

as detailed in Chapter 4. The information gained here was extended with a small sample of the pupils using the Semi-Structured Interview Schedule shown in Appendix 1.

The third hypothesis was investigated using the Coopersmith Self Esteem Questionnaire (group administered) anglicized by Dr. Peter Gurney, Exeter University. It was predicted that FIE pupils would show significant gains in self-esteem.

THE INPUT (TEACHERS)

Selecting the Teachers

Details of the project were posted in each of the four project schools and staff were invited to participate in the program and apply for the available scale posts. During the first year, eight teachers were trained together with the Senior Educational Psychologist who was monitoring the program. During the second year the project was widened to involve seven more teachers. Teachers applied from all subject disciplines, and probationers through to heads of department took part in the program. Out of the four schools involved, only one member of the senior management was trained and taught the program. In general, those that wished to participate were encouraged to do so. Only one cohort of pupils was studied and followed up over 2 years. Table 3.1 provides details of the FIE teachers (trained in years 1 and 2 of the project) who taught those pupils.

TABLE 3.1
The Status, Subject Specialisms, FIE Training and
FIE Teaching Experience of the Teachers Who Taught Pupils
Involved in the Evaluation

School	Teaching Group	Project Year	FIE Teaching Experience	Status	Subject Specialism	No. of FIE Training Courses
A	15	1st	3	Asst. teacher	History/ Careers	4
A	15	2nd	1	Head of Dept.	PE	2
A	16	1st & 2nd	3	Asst. teacher	Woodwork	4
A	17	1st & 2nd	2	Asst. teacher	English	2
A	18	1st & 2nd	2	Asst. teacher	Biology	2
B	4	1st & 2nd	3	Asst. teacher	Art & Design	4
C	11	1st	3*	Scale 2	PE & RE	4
C	11	2nd	3	Scale 2	Geog/Careers	3
C	12	1st & 2nd	3	Dep. Head	Science	2
C	13	1st	1	Head of Dept.	English	2
C	13	2nd	3*	Scale 2*	PE & RE*	4*
D	7	1st & 2nd	3	Asst. teacher	English	3
D	8	1st & 2nd	2	Asst. teacher	English	2

NB: * Refers to the same teacher.

Training the Teachers

The teachers who were involved in the program from its inception were more extensively trained than those who joined later. They received a 1-week residential course in conjunction with a larger group of teachers from Oxford prior to the project and three further 1-week residential training courses in the second and third years of the project. The members of this original group maintained their interest and cohesion with formal and informal contacts both in Somerset and between the two counties.

Teachers who joined the program in the second year of the project were trained as part of a much larger national residential week. Unfortunately, timetabling constraints meant that these less experienced FIE teachers were teaching at the same time as the more experienced, thereby preventing any opportunity for interchange and support in the classroom. Moreover, the newly trained FIE staff were unable to attend in service training days with the Oxford staff because of a combination of industrial action and supply cover limitations. In summary, of the 12 teachers who taught the evaluated pupils, 5 were extensively prepared and supported during the intervention (teaching groups: 4, 7, 11, 13, 15, and 16 shown in Table 3.1) while the remaining teachers were adequately trained but insufficiently supported during the program.

A further 14 teachers attended a new training course toward the end of the second year in preparation for year 3 of the project. Some of these teachers were needed to replace those who left the project, whereas others were trained in an attempt to extend knowledge about FIE to other curriculum areas.

Assessing the Teachers

Instrumental Enrichment calls for an interactive teaching style in which the teacher becomes a facilitator/mediator rather than a transmitter of a set body of knowledge. In order for a teacher to be effective in FIE, the theory predicts that he or she must first learn to operate comfortably within this framework. For some teachers this may involve a radical change in classroom behavior, with associated changes in attitude and possibly even personality. On the other hand, it may be the case that the most effective Instrumental Enrichment teachers are those who start off with certain personality traits and attitudes toward themselves and their work as teachers. In any event it was as important to assess changes in teachers involved in Instrumental Enrichment as it was to assess changes in pupils.

This particular aspect of the study was broadened to include all teachers who taught FIE at some stage in the project and not just those who taught the project pupils. In this way it was possible to obtain a larger and more representative sample of trained FIE teachers. Of course, it could be argued that any positive changes in Instrumental Teachers over a 2-year period might be the natural outcome of the experience of teaching in a particular comprehensive rather than the specific outcome of any contact with Instrumental Enrichment. This could especially apply to young teachers or those new to their secondary school. In order to control for this, an equivalent number of non-Instrumental Enrichment teachers (matched for sex, age, and experience) from each of the four comprehensive were also studied.

The mere business of taking part in a Department of Education and Science (DES)-funded project involves the participants in many novel experiences, not least being the frequent exposure to observation and questions by Local Education Authority (LEA) officials, university representatives, Her Majesty's Inspectorate, and other interested parties. It would be unreasonable to think that these experiences should have no effect on teachers. In view of this, an equivalent number of teachers in a nearby comprehensive school, involved in a quite different DES funded project (Technical and Vocational Educational Initiative: TVEI), were also interviewed and monitored over the same period.

There were many possible research hypotheses that could have been explored relating to teacher change. Many of the points already raised within the pupil section on Issues in Assessment, have parallel implications for the assessment of teachers. For instance, there are no existing standardized instruments for assessing attitudinal and behavioral change in teachers. For the purposes of this study, all FIE teachers and their controls were given a pre-post testing assessment package involving the following:

1. Completion of Cattell's 16 Personality Factor Questionnaire (an individually administered, standardized personality questionnaire) to check teacher change across a range of personality dimensions.
2. Three Semantic-Differential Scales designed for the study to assess attitudinal change over time in a number of areas relevant to the FIE program:
   - Myself as a Teacher (Table 5.5)
   - The Characteristics of Less Academic Pupils (Table 5.8)
   - Attitudes Towards Instrumental Enrichment (Table 5.1).

These scales are discussed in detail in Chapter 5. However, at this stage it should be noted that these scales were not factor analyzed or checked for reliability and validity. In view of this, each item on each scale, was treated independently at the analyses of results stage.

This pre-post assessment package was supplemented by semi-structured interviews with each teacher.

THE PROCESS

In order to understand the practical implications and applications of Instrumental Enrichment, accurate and detailed records of significant events were kept within the process of the intervention. A summative diary was designed, as shown in Appendix 2, which was completed by each teacher on a termly basis. In addition, each class was visited regularly by the evaluator with a view to making observations about pupil developments and also to provide teachers with feedback on the extent to which lessons kept to the Feuerstein model.

A fundamental component in Feuerstein's theoretical frameworks is his notion of the role of the adult as a mediator. As noted previously, Feuerstein argues that the main cause of low attainment is a lack of effective mediation. Instrumental Enrichment is meant to provide the teacher with a means to make up for that lack of mediation. The success of the program, therefore, depends on the teacher being an effective mediator.

Thus it might be predicted that the extent to which a child's cognitive and affective development will be modified will depend heavily on the amount of exposure to FIE and the quality and nature of the child's mediated learning experiences. This means that any study exploring the effects of Instrumental

Enrichment needs to observe and monitor the teachers as much as the pupils. Unfortunately, however, the meaning of mediation has not been adequately translated into a set of behavioral descriptors. It is only in the last few years that Feuerstein has begun to address this area, long after the original publication of FIE. Consequently, there are no reliable schedules for recording and measuring "effective mediation in teachers." In view of these issues, it was felt important to develop some means of regularly monitoring teacher behavior in the classroom with a view to exploring the relationship between this and pupil outcomes.

At the very beginning of the project, an FIE Lesson Observation Form developed in Nashville was used. However, this was quickly replaced by a more comprehensive schedule, as shown in Table 3.2, designed to record teacher behavior in the following areas:

- Classroom organization
     preparation and planning
     lesson beginning
     transitions
     lesson ending

- General teaching style

- Lesson process
     introduction
     independent work
     discussion
     summary.

The items in this schedule were based on ideas drawn from the original Nashville Lesson Observation Form, The Preventative Approaches to Disruption Package (Chisholm et al., 1986) and aspects of teacher behavior that seemed important in relation to Feuerstein's early writings on Mediated Learning Experiences.

This checklist was used as a structured way of recording observations on FIE teachers and also as a self-appraisal instrument for the teachers to review their own classroom teaching. There was consistent and close agreement between my own ratings and the teachers' self ratings. Inter-rater reliability was also investigated with the assistance of a team of post-graduate students from Exeter University who visited FIE classes in pairs, independently recording their observations and then comparing their ratings. Once again there was very high correspondence between the independent observer ratings on each item.

At the end of the study, the items in this checklist were recorded and regrouped

TABLE 3.2
FIE Lesson Observation Form

INSTRUMENTAL ENRICHMENT
LESSON OBSERVATION FORM (BLAGG, 1983)

Teacher _____ Date _____

School _____ Class _____

Module and Page _____

Number of students present _____

Duration of lesson from _____ to _____ total length _____

Please rate each item according to the following criteria:
1 = never applies   2 = rarely applies   3 = sometimes applies   4 = often
applies   5 = always applies

A. CLASSROOM ORGANIZATION:

  1. PREPARATION AND PLANNING:

   (a) Creation of a pleasant classroom environment (attention
       to decor, good display work by both pupil and teacher;
       homely touches).   1 2 3 4 5

   (b) Chairs/desks arranged to provide good eye contact
       between pupil-pupil and teacher-pupil.   1 2 3 4 5

   (c) Materials well organized and easily accessible.   1 2 3 4 5

   (d) Preparation of visual aids and support materials that
       interest, excite, and broaden the meaning of the lesson. 1 2 3 4 5

  2. LESSON BEGINNINGS:

   (a) Pupils entering the classroom in an orderly fashion.   1 2 3 4 5

   (b) Lesson is started in lively stimulating fashion.   1 2 3 4 5

   (c) The aims and objectives of the lesson are clearly outlined
       to the pupils.   1 2 3 4 5

  3. TRANSITIONS :

   (a) Transitions from class discussion work to independent
       work are organized efficiently and smoothly.   1 2 3 4 5

   (b) Transitions from independent work to class discussion
       work are organized efficiently and smoothly.   1 2 3 4 5

   (c) Pupils are given clear instructions of what to do when an
       activity has been completed.   1 2 3 4 5

(Continued)

TABLE 3.2
(continued)

(d) Any deterioration in pupils behavior at transition times is dealt with effectively through refocusing. 1 2 3 4 5

4. LESSON ENDINGS:

(a) Pupils pack-up their equipment and materials when told to do so by the teacher. 1 2 3 4 5

(b) Packing-up time is organized in such a way that there is just enough time to put away equipment and materials in an orderly fashion before the bell goes. 1 2 3 4 5

(c) Adequate time is allowed for a summary of the lesson topic and activities with both pupils and teachers giving feedback on the lesson. 1 2 3 4 5

(d) Teacher organizes an orderly quiet exit of pupils from the classroom. 1 2 3 4 5

B. GENERAL TEACHING STYLE:

(a) Teacher makes good use of pupil feedback to avoid over-stressing points that have already been grasped. 1 2 3 4 5

(b) A well-balanced use of class, group, and independent work to maintain momentum and pupil interaction and involvement. 1 2 3 4 5

(c) Pupils are encouraged to be the main contributors in class discussions. 1 2 3 4 5

(d) Pupil ideas and contributions are carefully considered, even if they do not appear to be entirely relevant. 1 2 3 4 5

(e) Teacher quickly refocuses pupils attention in the event of distraction from main topic. 1 2 3 4 5

(f) Pupils are allowed to assume the role of expert at certain points in the lesson. 1 2 3 4 5

(g) Pupils are encouraged to use visual aids (blackboard/overhead projector) in explaining their problem-solving approaches or difficulties. 1 2 3 4 5

(h) Teacher moves about the classroom a great deal throughout the lesson. 1 2 3 4 5

(i) Teacher activity encourages and values individual pupil contributions. 1 2 3 4 5

(j) The pupils are attentive and responsive during the lesson. 1 2 3 4 5

(k) Rate, fluency, and emotional tone of speech are appropriate to the message. 1 2 3 4 5

C. LESSON PROCESS AND CONTENT:

Instrument and Pages _____

_____ _____

Generalization Topics _____

_____

1. INTRODUCTION—from _____ to _____ total length _____

   (a) Teacher gains pupil attention and involvement by using
       appropriate stimulus material.   1 2 3 4 5

   (b) Teacher is clearly enthusiastic about the topic.   1 2 3 4 5

   (c) Teacher clearly defines aims and objectives.   1 2 3 4 5

   (d) Teacher develops clear exploration of vocabulary relevant
       to the lesson content with appropriate use of diaries,
       dictionaries, and pupil discussion.   1 2 3 4 5

   (e) FIE tasks for the lesson are effectively related to other
       school and/or real-life situations.   1 2 3 4 5

   (f) Teacher uses probe questioning to check and extend pupil
       understanding of FIE tasks.   1 2 3 4 5

   (g) Teacher uses open-ended and relational questioning to
       facilitate pupil discussion, involvement and understanding. 1 2 3 4 5

   (h) Teacher actively discourages impulsivity through the
       development of planning skills.   1 2 3 4 5

   (i) Pupils are encouraged to anticipate possible difficulties on
       FIE tasks.   1 2 3 4 5

   (j) Important cues and possible problem-solving strategies
       are elicited from the pupils.   1 2 3 4 5

   (k) Teacher elicits concepts, principles, and processes that go
       beyond the immediate needs of the task.   1 2 3 4 5

   (l) Teacher helps pupils to relate the present subject matter
       to the previous and/or future activities.   1 2 3 4 5

2. INDEPENDENT WORK—from _____ to _____ total time _____

   (a) The majority of the pupils work on task most of the time.   1 2 3 4 5

   (b) Teacher encourages explicit awareness of cognitive skills
       required for the FIE tasks.   1 2 3 4 5

   (c) Pupils in difficulty are helped to notice relevant cues and
       develop appropriate problem-solving strategies.   1 2 3 4 5

(Continued)

49

TABLE 3.2
(continued)

(d) The majority of pupils have their work checked. 1 2 3 4 5

(e) Pupils who finish early pursue appropriate activities set. 1 2 3 4 5

3. DISCUSSION—from _____ to _____ total time _____

(a) Problem-solving procedures are elicited from pupils. 1 2 3 4 5

(b) Pupils are helped to analyze their errors. 1 2 3 4 5

(c) Pupils are encouraged to evaluate the most efficient problem-solving approaches. 1 2 3 4 5

(d) Self-checking strategies are elicited from and evaluated by the pupils. 1 2 3 4 5

(e) Pupils outline cognitive skills required in solving problems. 1 2 3 4 5

(f) Overall principles are clearly summarized by the teacher with students contributing. 1 2 3 4 5

(g) Teacher makes use of prepared generalization (related to: school work, personal relationships, other FIE modules, and domestic and vocational issues). 1 2 3 4 5

(h) Pupils are able to provide spontaneous applications of processes involved in the lesson. 1 2 3 4 5

(i) The majority of the pupils actively participate in the discussions. 1 2 3 4 5

(j) Discussion work provokes significant numbers of pupils to higher levels of thinking. 1 2 3 4 5

(k) Discussion work is balanced by constructive pupil/pupil interaction and pupil/teacher interaction. 1 2 3 4 5

(l) Pupils are encouraged to infer from the specific instances to the general rule or principle involved. 1 2 3 4 5

4. SUMMARY—from _____ to _____ total time _____

(a) Teacher rounds off the lesson by relating activities covered to the aims and objectives outlined at the beginning of the lesson. 1 2 3 4 5

(b) Overall ideas and principles are restated and applied and related to other modules and contexts outside the course. 1 2 3 4 5

(c) Pupils remain alert and contribute to summary discussion. 1 2 3 4 5

(d) Teacher gives feedback to the pupils on their progress. 1 2 3 4 5

(e) Pupils are encouraged to express their feelings about the lesson.   1 2 3 4 5

Comments:

D. SUMMARY   MEDIATION RATINGS FOR:

Mediation of—

1. **Intentionality/Reciprocity.** (Teacher demonstrates commitment, enthusiasm, and persistence in communication and received appropriate feedback from the children.)   1 2 3 4 5

2. **Meaning.** (Teacher communicates the relevance and purpose of the activities.)   1 2 3 4 5

3. **Transcendence.** (Teacher takes every opportunity to broaden the context of specific learning opportunities arising during the lesson).   1 2 3 4 5

4. **Feeling of competence.** (Teacher makes minimal use of criticism. Pupils comments are valued and shaped to fit appropriately to the discussion in hand).   1 2 3 4 5

5. **Regulation and control of behavior.** (Teacher inhibits impulsivity while encouraging speed and accuracy.)   1 2 3 4 5

6. **Challenge and search for novelty.** (Teacher moves pupils beyond the stage of exposing existing skills through to truly challenging situations beyond expected pupil capabilities.)   1 2 3 4 5

7. **Sharing behavior.** (Pupils are encouraged to take turns and listen while others are talking in discussions, etc.)   1 2 3 4 5

8. **Individuation/differentiation.** (Pupils are given every opportunity to develop their own ideas and viewpoints.)   1 2 3 4 5

9. **Goal-seeking, goal-setting, planning, and goal-achieving behavior.** (Teacher illustrates, develops, and elicits the sequence of processes involved in efficient problem-solving behavior.)   1 2 3 4 5

according to the nine most important mediated learning experience (MLE) parameters proposed by Feuerstein:

*—intentionality/reciprocity

*—meaning

*—transcendence

—competence

—regulation and control of behavior

—sharing behavior

—individuation and psychological differentiation

—goal seeking, goal setting, planning, and goal achieving behavior

—challenge/search for novelty and complexity.

The recording process was far more difficult than initially anticipated, for two reasons:

- **The lack of explicit behavioral descriptors to characterize each MLE parameter.** For instance, item C2(c): "pupils in difficulties are helped to notice relevant cues and develop appropriate problem-solving strategies," certainly refers to: mediating for competence, regulation, and control of behavior and goal seeking, goal setting, planning, and goal achieving behavior. However, depending on the meaning of the word "help" it could also encompass mediating for intentionality/reciprocity, meaning, individuation, and psychological differentiation.

- **The fact that some teacher behaviors address only one aspect of MLE, whereas others address many.** For example, item A4(a): "pupils pack up their materials and equipment when told to do so by the teacher," might conceivably refer to one aspect of the regulation and control of behavior whereas, item C1(g), "teacher uses open ended and relational questioning to facilitate pupil discussion, involvement and understanding," could be interpreted as addressing many MLE parameters including: intentionality/ reciprocity, meaning, transcendence, sharing behavior, individuation, and psychological differentiation as well as goal setting, goal seeking, planning, and goal achieving behavior.

In this respect it seems likely that certain teacher behaviors are more important than others in terms of mediated learning experience theory. Thus, the original teacher behavior items in Table 3.2 appear one or more times in the recoded MLE schedule (Appendix 3) depending on their relationship with each of the MLE parameters. Using this revised record form it was possible to rate each teacher's implementation of the FIE program in terms of the nine MLE parameters. However, given the large number of items and their degree of overlap it was felt important to explore a means of simplifying the teacher rating procedure. Accordingly, teachers were first considered according to their ratings on all of the items and then re-rated according to the first three starred(*) universal, essential MLE parameters.

In fact, the rank order distribution of the teacher ratings was very similar whether the nine MLE or the three universal MLE scores were used (Spearman's Rank Order correlation coefficient = +0.98; N = 10; P>0.001). Accordingly ratings based on the first three items only were utilized to divide the FIE teachers into two groups (high-MLE and low-MLE). It was hypothesized that high-MLE teachers would be more likely to produce cognitive, affective, and behavioral changes in the pupils than their low-MLE colleagues. The final list of behavioral

TABLE 3.3
**The behavioral descriptors used for rating teachers in terms
of the three universal MLE criteria (Intentionality/reciprocity [I],
Meaning [M], Transcendence [T])**

	I	M	T
A. CLASSROOM ORGANIZATION:			
Creation of a pleasant classroom environment (attention to decor, good display work by both pupils and teacher, homely touches.).	*	*	
Chairs/desks arranged to provide good eye contact between pupil-pupil and teacher-pupil.	*		
Materials well organized and easily accessible.	*		
Preparation of visual aids and support materials that interest, excite, and broaden the meaning of the lesson	*	*	
Lesson is started in lively stimulating fashion.	*	*	
The aims and objectives of the lesson are clearly outlined to the pupils.	*	*	
Pupils are given clear instructions of what to do when an activity has been completed.	*		
Adequate time is allowed for a summary of the lesson topic and activities with both pupils and teachers giving feedback on the lesson.		*	
B. GENERAL TEACHING STYLE:			
Teacher makes good use of pupil feedback to avoid over-stressing points that have already been grasped.	*		
A well-balanced use of class, group, and independent work to maintain momentum and pupil interaction and involvement.	*	*	
Pupils are encouraged to be the main contributors in class discussions.	*	*	
Pupil ideas are carefully considered and explored even if they do not appear to be entirely relevant.	*	*	
Teacher quickly refocuses pupils attention in the event of distraction from main topic.		*	
Pupils are allowed to assume the role of expert at certain points in the lesson.	*	*	
Pupils are encouraged to use visual aids (blackboard/overhead projector) in explaining their problem-solving approaches or difficulties.	*	*	
Teacher moves amongst the pupils during the lesson.	*		
Teacher actively encourages and values individual pupil contributions.	*		

(Continued)

TABLE 3.3
(continued)

	I	M	T
The pupils are attentive and responsive during the lesson.	*		
Rate, fluency, and emotional tone of speech are appropriate to the message.	*	*	

C. LESSON PROCESS:

1. INTRODUCTION

	I	M	T
Teacher gains pupil attention and involvement by using appropriate stimulus material.	*		
Teacher is clearly enthusiastic about the topic.	*		
Teacher clearly defines aims and objectives.	*	*	
Teacher develops clear exploration of vocabulary relevant to the lesson content with appropriate use of diaries, dictionaries, and pupil discussion.		*	*
FIE tasks for the lesson are effectively related to other school and/or real-life situations.		*	*
Teacher uses probe questioning to check and extend pupil understanding of FIE tasks.	*	*	*
Teacher uses open-ended and relational questioning to facilitate pupil discussion, involvement, and understanding.	*	*	*
Teacher actively discourages impulsivity through the development of planning skills.	*	*	*
Pupils are encouraged to anticipate possible difficulties on FIE tasks.	*	*	
Important cues and possible problem-solving strategies are elicited from the pupils.	*	*	*
Teacher elicits concepts, principles, and processes that go beyond the immediate needs of the task.	*	*	*
Teacher helps pupils to relate the present subject matter to the previous and/or future activities.	*	*	*

2. INDEPENDENT WORK

	I	M	T
The majority of the pupils work on tasks most of the time.	*		
Teacher encourages explicit awareness of cognitive skills required for the FIE tasks.		*	*
Pupils in difficulty are helped to notice relevant cues and develop appropriate problem-solving strategies.	*	*	
The majority of pupils have their work checked.	*	*	

3. DISCUSSION

	I	M	T
Problem-solving procedures are elicited from pupils.	*	*	*
Pupils are helped to analyze their errors.	*	*	

	I	M	T
Pupils are encouraged to evaluate the most efficient problem-solving approaches.		*	*
Self-checking strategies are elicited from and evaluated by the pupils.	*	*	*
Pupils outline cognitive skills required in solving problems.	*	*	*
Overall principles are clearly summarized by the teacher with students contributing.	*	*	*
Teacher makes use of prepared generalization (related to: school work, personal relationships, other FIE modules, and domestic and vocational issues).		*	*
Pupils are able to provide spontaneous applications of processes involved in the lesson.	*	*	*
The majority of the pupils actively participate in the discussions.	*		
Discussion work provokes significant numbers of pupils to higher levels of thinking.			*
Discussion work is balanced by constructive pupil/pupil interaction and pupil/teacher interaction.	*		
Pupils are encouraged to infer from the specific instances to the general rule or principle involved.	*	*	*

4. SUMMARY

	I	M	T
Teacher rounds off the lesson by relating activities covered to the aims and objectives outlined at the beginning of the lesson.	*	*	
Overall ideas and principles are restated and applied and related to other modules and contexts outside the course.	*	*	*
Pupils remain alert and contribute to summary discussion.	*		
Teacher gives feedback to the pupils on their progress.	*	*	
Pupils are encouraged to express their feelings about the lesson.			

descriptors used for rating teachers in terms of their MLE characteristics is given in Table 3.3.

In the early stages of the project, it was planned to videotape a series of lessons in the life of a particular Instrumental Enrichment group, over the 2-year period, as a means of observing change. Unfortunately, technical difficulties and lack of time made this impractical.

THE PRODUCT

At the product stage, detailed post-testing was carried out related to the previously agreed aims and to the pre-testing program undertaken at the Input stage. Full details are given in Chapters 4 and 5.

The overall findings of the project are reviewed in Chapter 6 and wider implications are considered in Chapter 7.

The Pupils

The notion of "Lower-Attaining" pupils carries with it the need to identify and select pupils for the intervention. The means of doing this varied from school to school. In schools A and B, the project children were timetabled together for most subjects and as such were seen to have a definite "lower-attaining identity." As the pupils' comments later in this chapter show, some pupils in schools A and B were adversely affected by being so clearly labelled as less able. This was less of a problem in schools C and D where more flexible timetabling arrangements pertained and the lower-attaining pupils (LAP) were less identifiable as a particular group. During the life of the project, a new cohort of fourth year pupils was introduced to FIE each year. The formal evaluation began during the second year of the LAP Project. All FIE pupils in this year (teaching groups 4, 7, 8, 11, 12, 13, 15, 16, 17, and 18) were formally evaluated.

Within the overall design, it was felt important to establish matched groups of lower-attaining pupils in each project school to act as controls. It was envisaged that these pupils would not receive FIE but might well participate in other aspects of the LAPP program (i.e., residentials and work experience). These pupils would be assessed and observed on the same range of procedures as the FIE pupils. There were, however, some difficulties in achieving this including:

- The time available to assess and monitor additional groups of children other than those involved in Instrumental Enrichment.
- The difficulties in finding matched groups of lower attaining children who were not already selected to receive FIE in each of the four project schools.

Involving too many pupils would have made the assessment procedures unwieldy. Nevertheless, selecting, monitoring, and assessing too few would have made any generalizations difficult. Furthermore, it was decided not to introduce a comparison group from another school as this would have introduced numerous contaminating curriculum and school variables defeating the object of a control group. In view of these considerations control groups were established in only two of the project schools (B and D).

One of the critical tests of Instrumental Enrichment concerned the extent to which skills and attitudes developed in the FIE lessons transferred to other situations. During the course of the intervention program, it was hoped, where possible, to involve non-Instrumental Enrichment teachers in qualitative assessments of pupil change amongst FIE and non-FIE lower-attaining pupils. In this connection, it was fortunate that FIE pupils did not remain in the same teaching groups in some schools for all subjects. Thus, in many instances there were similar numbers of FIE and non-FIE children in particular classes, making within-class comparisons between the two groups possible.

ABILITY AND ATTAINMENT CHARACTERISTICS OF THE PUPILS AT THE BEGINNING OF THE STUDY

Differences Between Groups

At the beginning of the study, each pupil was screened on the full range of assessment procedures detailed in Chapter 3. The data were then subjected to a number of analyses of variance to check for differences between:

- Schools
- Experimental and control groups
- High-MLE, low-MLE, and control groups
- Teaching groups within schools.

I will deal with each of these analyses in turn.

Differences Between Schools

In spite of the differing catchment areas of the four project schools and the different procedures for selecting the low-attaining pupils, there were relatively few school differences between the project pupils on the various standardized attainment and ability measures. There were no significant differences on any of the British Ability Scale Measures. Similarly, the project pupils in each school were well matched in terms of reading ability (Edinburgh Reading Test); map reading (Richmond W–1), and mathematics problem solving (Richmond M–2). Nevertheless, as Table 4.1 shows slight differences did emerge at the 0.05 level

TABLE 4.1
Differences Amongst the Lower Attaining Pupil Samples (From the Four Project Schools) on a Range of Standardized Attainment Measures at the Pre-Test Stage (Using Analysis of Variance).

Variable	School A		School B		School C		School D		F Ratio	P
	Mean	N	Mean	N	Mean	N	Mean	N		
ERT quotient	82.62	60	84.27	33	82.12	41	84.89	38	1.39	NS
RW1 quotient	83.18	60	87.12	41	86.95	39	88.37	35	2.47	NS
RW2 quotient	82.47	60	80.46	41	85.23	39	87.23	35	3.73	<0.05
RW3 quotient	81.20	60	83.95	441	78.46	39	83.51	35	2.78	<0.05
RM1 quotient	80.85	60	82.17	42	87.97	39	87.17	35	6.19	<0.0005
RM2 quotient	87.92	60	85.50	42	88.93	40	90.26	35	1.74	NS

N = Number of Subjects.
F RATIO = From ANOVA tables.
P = Probability Levels.

of probability on pupil ability to read graphs and tables (Richmond W–2) and understand and use reference materials (Richmond W–3). However, such slight differences could have occurred by chance given the many tests and comparisons to which the data were subjected. Nevertheless, lower-attaining pupils in schools A and B were significantly poorer than their counterparts in schools C and D with respect to knowledge of mathematical concepts (Richmond M–2; $P<0.0005$).

Differences Between Experimental and Control Pupils

Control and experimental pupils (Schools B and D) were extremely well matched with no statistically significant differences emerging on any of the pretest measures.

Differences Between Control, High-MLE, and Low-MLE Pupils

Further analyses were conducted to check whether there were differences, at the beginning of the study, between those pupils being taught by teachers who showed more evidence of being comfortable with the teaching style advocated by FIE (high-MLE teachers) in comparison to those pupils who were being taught by the low-MLE teachers. There were no differences between the pupils from the low- and high-MLE teaching groups. However, the control pupils were found to be marginally better than either the low- or high-MLE experimental groups on the

Edinburgh Reading Test at the 5% level. Apart from this, there were no other statistically significant differences between the groups at the start of the study on any of the psychometric attainment or ability measures (see Appendix 4).

Differences Between Teaching Groups

Finally, the data was analyzed to check for differences between the individual teaching groups (both control and experimental) across the four schools. Marginal differences were noted between teaching groups at the 0.05 level of probability on Richmond W–2 and Richmond M–1. Apart from this, there were no significant differences on the other psychometric measures at the start of the study (see Appendix 5).

As this table illustrates, the majority of LAPP pupils at the start of the study showed: (a) a poorly developed vocabulary (BAS Word Definitions Scale); (b) poorly developed verbal reasoning skills (BAS Similarities Scale); and (c) impulsivity (as shown by rapid trial-and-error responses on the BAS matrices test leading to below average scores). In contrast, these same pupils showed: (a) a normal distribution of scores on a timed spatial reasoning test (BAS Block Design Power) and (b) a normal distribution of scores on a visual memory test (BAS Recall of Designs).

The Attainment Characteristics

Although slight differences occurred between project pupils within and across the schools, all pupils showed a consistent pattern of well below average reading and mathematical ability, and poorly developed work study skills as shown in Table 4.3

TABLE 4.2
The Mean Centile Ranks, Mean 'T' Scores, and Standard Deviations
of the Low-Attaining Project Pupils at the Beginning of the Study
on a Range of Tests From the British Ability Scales.

British Ability Scales	Centile Ranks	Mean 'T' scores	Standard Deviations
Word Definitions	24th	41.9	5.76
Similarities	32nd	44.5	7.26
Matrices	35th	45.3	7.51
Block Design	39th	45.67	9.45
Block Design (Power)	50th	50.3	8.54
Recall of Designs	46th	48.7	9.90

N = 177; BAS Mean IQ = 91.7 (S.D. 12.7)
N.B. average 'T' Score = 50 (range 23–73)
average centile = 50th (range 1–99)

TABLE 4.3
The Mean Quotients and Standard Deviations of the
Low-Attaining Project Pupils at the Beginning of the Study
on a Range of Attainment Tests.

Test	N	Mean Quotient	Standard Deviation
Richmond Work-Study Skills			
W-1: Map Reading	175	86.0	10.25
W-2: Reading Graphs and Tables	175	83.6	9.88
W-3: Knowledge and use of Reference Materials	175	81.7	9.60
Richmond Mathematics Skills			
M-1: Mathematics Concepts	176	84.0	9.99
M-2: Mathematics Problem Solving	177	88.0	9.60
Edinburgh Reading Test	172	83.3	7.18

NB: An average quotient = 100 (range 75–125)

Summary

These results illustrate that the lower-attaining pupils in the four project schools showed a normal distribution of ability on certain spatial reasoning and visual memory tasks. Indeed there were lower-attaining pupils with quite exceptional abilities in these areas. In contrast, the majority of lower-attaining pupils showed below average language skills, below average mathematics and reading attainments, and poor work study skills. It seems highly likely that many pupils who end up in lower-attaining groups do so because of poorly developed language skills and/or inadequate progress with reading rather than globally limited intellectual ability. It seems likely that, inadequate reading attainments restrict access to the curriculum, leading to generally depressed attainments, impoverished linguistic opportunities, and consequent poor verbal reasoning and vocabulary scores on intelligence test items.

CHANGES IN PUPIL ABILITIES AND ATTAINMENTS

Introduction

At the end of the 2-year study, all FIE and control pupils were followed up on the full range of attainment and ability measures outlined in Chapter 3 with a view to checking whether there were any significant changes in the FIE pupils with respect to: (a) cognitive abilities, (b) study skills, or (c) reading and mathematics attainments.

If there were any positive and significant changes, could they be attributable to the effects of the Instrumental Enrichment program? Moreover, if there were significant FIE effects, were these related to teacher effectiveness (rated in terms of their MLE characteristics as defined in Chapter 3, Table 3.3) or the number of hours of FIE tuition that each pupil received?

Treatment of Results

Change over time can be studied in a number of ways. However, with two time points (one for pre- and one for post-test) the most straightforward way involves calculating an explicit change score for each pupil on each of the performance measures. In this way, differences between the pupils at the beginning of the study (minimal though they were) are irrelevant as change becomes the object of the analysis.

The basic analytic technique adopted for these data was analysis of variance of change scores. This statistical technique explores whether or not different groups of subjects have different mean scores. This is achieved by comparing the obtained differences between the means in the FIE sample with the size of the difference one might reasonably expect to get by chance alone. If the difference is larger than one would expect by chance or, if such a size difference in the sample would only occur very rarely by chance, then the difference is said to be statistically significant.

This aspect of the study introduces a number of complications beyond this simple pattern. There were many competing variables that might have explained differences between FIE and control pupils. The following factors were taken into account:

- Treatment (the effects of the FIE program)
- Sex (Differential effects between boys and girls)
- School (Differential effects between the four schools)
- Teacher effectiveness (rated in terms of mediation characteristics)
- Attendance (referring to the number of hours of FIE tuition that each pupil actually received).

Initially, the first three explanatory factors were considered with the cross-classification of these factors producing multiple groups (e.g., experimental subjects who are male in school A, control subjects who are female in school B, and so on). By analyzing each group, it was possible to partition the differences between the sample mean change scores (for each test) so that the components of the difference could be attributed to each of the explanatory factors. In this way, it was possible to say to what extent any observed changes in the pupils could be explained in terms of treatment, sex, and school.

Unfortunately, the analysis was complicated because the groups defined by the cross-classification had different numbers in each. This meant that differences could not be uniquely attributed to the experimental factors unless certain additional restrictions were imposed. In order to remove any possible source of criticism, the treatment, sex, and school effects were estimated in turn, eliminating each of the others. In other words, the differences between means that could be attributed to the differential treatment of the control and experimental pupils was calculated over and above any effect that might have arisen due to sex and school.

A second complication arose because control groups did not exist in all schools. Therefore, some of the groups defined by the cross-classification of the first three explanatory factors did not have any subjects. In view of this, only main effects of the three factors are reported (i.e., possible interaction effects are ignored).

Differences between groups were analyzed according to treatment, sex, and school effects, considered in terms of the following response variables:

- Edinburgh reading test change
- Richmond work-study skills
  RW–1 change (Map Reading)
  RW–2 change (Reading graphs and Tables)
  RW–3 change (Knowledge and use of Reference Materials)
- Richmond Mathematics skills
  RM–1 change (Mathematics Concepts)
  RM–2 change (Mathematics Problem Solving)
- British Ability Scales
  BAS IQ change (Intelligence Quotient)
  BAS WD change (Word Definitions)
  BAS RD change (Recall of Designs)
  BAS SIM change (Similarities)
  BAS BD change (Block Design—Level)
  BAS BDP change (Block Design—Power)
  BAS MAT change (Matrices)
- CSMS Science Reasoning Tasks (supplemented by an individually administered Piagetian Test Battery).

Finally, the contribution of teacher effectiveness and the number of hours of FIE teaching time that each pupil received was considered in relation to the above response (dependent) variables using an analysis of covariance.

The analysis of covariance is an extension of the analysis of variance that tests for equality of means *after* allowance is made for *concomitant* variables or *covariates*, which may differ between groups and which may affect the dependent variable of interest. The assumption is made that the covariates are linearly related to the dependent variable with the regression coefficient being the same in each group. The analysis of variance now tests the equality of group means on the dependent variable after adjusting the covariates to have equal means in the group. The analysis of variance F tests now answer the question, "Given that the groups have the same means on the covariates, do the means on the dependent variable differ?"

Results (Analysis of Variance)

Bearing in mind the comprehensive battery of group and individual psychometric test procedures used at the beginning and end of this evaluation, it was surprising to find relatively few significant changes over time amongst any of the teaching groups. Considering treatment, school, and sex factors on all 12 response variables, analysis of variance revealed only three significant results (and even then, significance was only at the 5% level). Two treatment effects were observed (one negative and one positive) and one school effect was noted, favoring school A. There were no differential pupil outcomes with respect to sex. The detailed outcomes will be considered in relation to each of the groups of psychometric response variables (attainments, work study skills, and reasoning abilities) discussed in detail in Chapter 3. Full statistical details on those effects that were significant will be included in the body of the text. The remaining analyses will be itemized in the Appendices 6 through 16.

Attainments

There were no differential sex, school, or treatment effects among the project pupils with respect to their: (a) reading skills (Edinburgh Reading Test) as shown in Appendix 6 or (b) mathematical problem solving abilities (Richmond Mathematics Skills RM2) as shown in Appendix 9. There was, however, a significant school effect favoring school A with respect to pupil understanding of mathematical concepts (Richmond Mathematics Skills RM1). The school effect was marginal and only significant at the 5% level. By referring to tables 4.4, 4.5, and 4.7, it can be seen that school A has shown a significant improvement over time on the RM1 test of mathematical concepts, whereas schools B and C deteriorated over time and school D has shown a very slight improvement. It is probably significant that at the beginning of the study, school A was significantly poorer than the other schools on the RM1 test. Starting from this lower base line lower-attaining pupils in school A had a greater margin within which to improve.

The finding that FIE pupils did not significantly improve in relation to the control pupils over the period of the project in relation to their reading and/or mathematical skills was broadly in line with expectations. Both the mathematics and reading tests rely on assumed knowledge outside the scope of the FIE program. In other words, improvements in these attainment areas would have

TABLE 4.4
The Effects of Treatment (the Impact of the FIE Program),
Sex (Differential Outcome Between Boys and Girls), and
School (Differential Outcomes for Schools A, B, C, and D)
on Richmond Mathematics Test (RM1) (Change Scores
Using Analysis of Variance (Anova).

Source	S of Squares	Degrees of Freedom	Mean sq.	F (ratio)	P (variance)
Treatment	312.554	1	312.554	3.175	.079
Sex	29.037	1	29.037	.295	.589
School	1085.52	3	361.834	3.676	.016
Explained	1155.279	5	231.056	2.347	.049
Residual	7579.684	77	98.437		

depended on a distanced transfer effect. Nevertheless, previous studies have demonstrated a consistent relationship between enhanced self-esteem and reading gains (Lawrence, 1988). Accordingly, reading gains might have been expected as an incidental spin-off had the pupils shown significant gains in self-esteem as a result of the FIE program. As the findings later in this chapter will demonstrate, no consistent long-term benefits in self-esteem were noted among the FIE pupils in comparison with the controls.

Work Study Skills

There were no differential sex, school, or treatment effects observed in the project pupils regarding their: (a) ability to read graphs and tables (Richmond Work Study Skills RW2) as shown in Appendix 7 or (b) ability to interpret and use various kinds of reference materials (Richmond Work Study Skills RW3) as

TABLE 4.5
The Mean Cell Values for Each of the Sub Groups Generated
by the Anova Shown in Table 4.4. The Numbers of Boys and Girls
From the Experimental and Control Groups in Schools A, B, C, and D
are Shown in Parentheses.

Treat	School A Sex		School B Sex		School C Sex		School D Sex	
	Boy	Girl	Boy	Girl	Boy	Girl	Boy	Girl
Exp.	4.75	6.43	−6.33	−8.00	.62	−1.44	−2.50	−4.60
	(16)	(14)	(3)	(3)	(13)	(9)	(6)	(5)
Cont.	—	—	−4.33	6.00	—	—	8.00	−2.67
			(3)	(3)			(5)	(3)

Exp. = FIE pupils
Cont. = Control pupils
Treat = Treatment

TABLE 4.6

A Multiple Classification Analysis of the Richmond Mathematics Concepts (RM1) Change Scores Which Elaborates the Anova Results in Tables 4.4 and 4.5. It Illustrates the Estimated Effect Sizes Expressed as Deviations From the Grand Mean for Each of the Treatment, Sex, and School Groups (Adjusted for the Other Factors).

Factor	Group	N	Estimated effect sizes (deviation from the grand means)*	Average change scores*
Treatment	Exp.	70	0.06	0.58
	Cont.	20	−0.20	0.32
Sex	Boy	51	−1.23	−0.71
	Girl	39	1.61	2.13
School	A	24	4.49	5.01
	B	19	−3.00	−2.48
	C	27	−1.86	−1.34
	D	20	−0.03	0.49

Grand Mean = 0.52
* Adjusted for each of the other factors

shown in Appendix 8. However, a negative treatment effect was observed in relation to map reading skills (Richmond Work Study Skills RW1) as shown in Table 4.7, 4.8 and 4.9.

Table 4.7 shows the analysis of variance (Anova) of the RW1 change scores with respect to treatment, sex, and school. Table 4.8 illustrates the mean cell values for each of the groups generated by the Anova. These results are explained further in the form of the multiple classification analysis shown in Table 4.9. This latter table shows the effect sizes for each group (listed in Table 4.8) adjusted for the other factors and expressed as deviations from the grand means. The final column, which illustrates average change scores for each group (adjusted for the

TABLE 4.7

The Effects of Treatment (the Impact of the FIE Program), Sex (Differential Outcome Between Boys and Girls), and School (Differential Outcomes for Schools A, B, C, and D) on Richmond Work Study Skills (RW1) Change Scores Using Analysis of Variance (Anova).

Source	S of Squares	Degrees of Freedom	Mean sq.	F (ratio)	P (variance)
Treatment	484.266	1	484.266	4.540	.036
Sex	4.930	1	4.930	.046	.830
School	702.234	3	234.078	2.195	.095
Explained	834.638	5	166.928	1.565	.180
Residual	8213.049	77	106.663		

TABLE 4.8
The Mean Cell Values for Each of the Sub Groups Generated
by the Anova Shown in Table 4.7. The Numbers of Boys and Girls
From the Experimental and Control Groups in Schools A, B, C, and D
are Shown in Parentheses.

Treat	School A Sex		School B Sex		School C Sex		School D Sex	
	Boy	Girl	Boy	Girl	Boy	Girl	Boy	Girl
Exp.	2.19	6.17	−3.00	−9.33	4.92	2.33	2.17	−0.60
	(16)	(14)	(3)	(3)	(13)	(9)	(6)	(5)
Cont.	—	—	−2.67	8.33	—	—	14.20	−1.67
			(3)	(3)			(5)	(3)

Exp. = FIE pupils
Cont. = Control pupils
Treat = Treatment

other factors), has been calculated by adding the grand mean to each group effect score.

Thus, as the RW1 change score is calculated by subtracting the pre-study score from the post-study score, it can be noted that both the FIE and control groups improved over time in map reading. However, the increase in the RW1 score over the period of the study is significantly less for the experimental groups than for the control groups (+ 1.31 for the FIE groups and 9.47 for the control groups).

These findings were contrary to expectations as the work study skills tests

TABLE 4.9
A Multiple Classification Analysis of the Richmond Work Study
(Map Reading) Skills (RW1) Change Scores Which Elaborates the
Anova Results in Tables 4.7 and 4.8. It Illustrates the Estimated Effect
Sizes Expressed as Deviations From the Grand Mean for Each of the
Treatment, Sex, and School Groups (Adjusted for the Other Factors).

Factor	Group	N	Estimated effect sizes (deviation from the grand means)*	Average change scores*
Treatment	Exp.	70	−1.81	1.31
	Cont.	20	6.35	9.47
Sex	Boy	51	−0.13	2.99
	Girl	39	0.17	3.49
School	A	24	2.87	5.99
	B	19	−4.12	−1.00
	C	27	1.77	4.89
	D	20	−1.91	1.21

Grand Mean = 3.12
* Adjusted for each of the other factors

largely involve the interpretation of given rather than assumed information. It had been predicted that if the FIE program made significant improvements to pupil cognitive functions at the phase level of the cognitive map (see chap. 2) this should translate into improved abilities to gather, organize, and interpret information. Moreover, the style and layout of the Richmond Work Study Skill Tests (using diagrams, pictures, charts, and so on) suggest that they represent a set of relatively close transfer tasks (in relation to FIE). In spite of this, there was no evidence of transfer effects from the FIE program to the study skills tasks.

Ability Measures

Finally, dealing with the individually administered British Ability Scale (BAS) Tests and the CSMS Science Reasoning Test, there were no differential sex, school, or treatment effects observed in the project pupils over the period of the study with respect to changes in their:

- BAS IQ Scores
- BAS Word Definitions Scores
- BAS Recall of Designs Scores
- BAS Similarities Scores
- BAS Block Design (Level) Scores
- BAS Matrices Scores
- CSMS Science Reasoning Scores.

Full details of the Anovas are given in Appendices 11 to 16. The only significant effect noted in the British Ability Scales Test Battery was a positive treatment effect on the BAS Block Design (Power) Change Score as shown in Tables 4.10, 4.11, and 4.12.

Table 4.10 shows the analysis of variance (Anova) of the BAS Block Design (Power) change scores with respect to treatment, sex, and school. Table 4.11 illustrates the mean cell values for each of the groups generated by the Anova. These results are explained further in the form of the multiple classification analysis shown in Table 4.12. By analyzing the various group effect sizes (adjusted for other factors) in Table 4.11, it can be seen that there was considerable variation in pupil outcomes on the Block Design Power Test in the four schools. Pupil's scores in schools A and C appeared to stay relatively stable over time, whereas pupils scores in schools B and C improved over time. These variations however, were not statistically significant.

Over and above any variations in the data relating to sex and school, there was a significant treatment effect on the Block Design (Power) change scores. This treatment effect related to an improved performance among the FIE pupils

TABLE 4.10
The Effects of Treatment (The Impact of the FIE Program), Sex
(Differential Outcome Between Boys and Girls), and School
(Differential Outcomes for Schools A, B, C, and D) on British Ability
Scales Block Design Power Test Change Scores Using Analysis
of Variance (Anova).

Source	S of Squares	Degrees of Freedom	Mean sq.	F (ratio)	P (variance)
Treatment	3507.253	1	3507.253	4.818	.032
Sex	43.508	1	43.508	.060	.808
School	4809.581	3	1603.194	2.202	.098
Explained	5519.694	5	1103.939	1.516	.199
Residual	41495.734	57	727.995		

and a relative deterioration in performance among the controls. Interestingly, there was no significant difference between the FIE and control groups on the untimed version of the Block Design Test (Level). This may have been because of a ceiling effect, with most pupils (both FIE and controls) managing to reach the limits of the test. The difference between the FIE and controls on the block Design Power Test, however, suggests that relative to the controls the FIE pupils had become more efficient at spatial reasoning tasks, that is, they were able to complete test items accurately more rapidly than the controls.

The findings on the BAS Block Design (Power) Test were in line with expectations in that the FIE program gives pupils plenty of practice in working with visual materials. More particularly, the program emphasizes issues such as the importance of: precision and accuracy in description and labelling; the use of various analytic and visual search procedures; visualizing, transporting, and

TABLE 4.11
The Mean Cell Values for Each of the Sub-Groups Generated
by the Anova Shown in Table 4.10. The Numbers of Boys and Girls
From the Experimental and Control Groups in Schools A, B, C, and D
are Shown in Parentheses.

Treat	School A Sex		School B Sex		School C Sex		School D Sex	
	Boy	Girl	Boy	Girl	Boy	Girl	Boy	Girl
Exp.	4.60	−3.40	37.75	11.25	−5.29	−2.00	14.00	13.20
	(5)	(10)	(4)	(4)	(7)	(5)	(4)	(5)
Cont.	—	—	−2.75	−.75	—	—	−7.57	11.00
			(4)	(4)			(7)	(4)

Exp. = FIE pupils
Cont. = Control pupils
Treat = Treatment

TABLE 4.12
A Multiple Classification Analysis of the British Ability Scales Block
Design Power Test Change Scores Which Elaborates the Anova Results
in Tables 4.10 and 4.11. It Illustrates the Estimated Effect Sizes
Expressed as Deviations From the Grand Mean for Each of the
Treatment, Sex, and School Groups (Adjusted for the Other Factors).

Factor	Group	N	Estimated effect sizes (deviation from the grand means)*	Average change scores*
Treatment	Exp.	70	4.94	11.5
	Cont.	20	−17.29	−10.73
Sex	Boy	51	2.85	9.41
	Girl	39	−3.73	2.83
School	A	24	−8.37	−1.81
	B	19	13.21	19.77
	C	27	−9.73	−3.17
	D	20	10.63	17.19

Grand Mean = 6.56
* Adjusted for each of the other factors

mentally orienting images. As such, there is considerable overlap between the kinds of cognitive functions required by the Block Design Task and those required in the FIE program. Furthermore, the presentation of at least part of the Block Design Task (where the pupil is required to analyze the 2-dimensional drawings) is very similar to some of the FIE tasks. In these circumstances, it is surprising that the FIE pupils did not improve over time far more on the Block Design (Power) Test.

The BAS Matrices Scale involves pupils in noticing patterns and abstracting relationships between shapes and visual symbols so that they can draw in the missing parts of a matrix. As such, it represents an even closer context within which to check for transfer effects of the FIE program. Nevertheless, as Appendix 16 demonstrates, no significant differences emerged between the FIE pupils and the controls on the BAS Matrices change scores.

The BAS Recall of Designs Test provides another set of tasks, closely related in content and format to the FIE program. The tasks require pupils to observe, memorize, and draw a series of diagrams (involving abstract shapes and symbols). Once again, as Appendix 13 shows, there was no evidence to suggest that the FIE program had helped the FIE pupils to perform consistently better than the controls on this task.

In view of the positive anecdotal comments regarding the linguistic benefits of the FIE program (referred to later in this chapter), it was surprising that no differences emerged between the FIE and control pupils change scores on the BAS Word Definitions Scale (see Appendix 12). Additionally, in view of the close overlap between the items on the BAS Similarities (Verbal Reasoning) Scale and the third FIE instrument (Comparisons), it was even more surprising to find no differential treatment effects favoring the FIE pupils (see Appendix 14).

Finally, as Appendix 10 shows, there was no evidence to suggest differential cognitive development favoring the FIE pupils as assessed by the CSMS Science Reasoning Tests (supplemented where necessary by the individually administered Piagetian Test Battery) referred to in Chapter 3. The tasks involved here were assessing a number of Piagetian cognitive operations from concrete through to formal operational reasoning levels. These results contradict the findings in Shayer and Beasley's (1987) small-scale study, referred to in Chapter 2.

Results (Analysis of Covariance)

Some pupils received relatively little FIE teaching time because of poor attendance and so on. In addition, some of the FIE classes were taught by less experienced FIE teachers, a few of whom did not feel comfortable with the sensitive mediator role. Thus, it could be argued that the disappointing results recorded so far were due largely to the combined effects of the two additional variables:

- attendance (used here to refer to the number of hours of teaching time each pupil actually received).
- MLEU (referring to teacher effectiveness rated in terms of their ability to mediate for intentionality/reciprocity, meaning and transcendence).

The importance of these variables is discussed in Chapter 2 and the means of assessing them is detailed in Chapter 3. The essential question considered here is: Did those pupils who received the most FIE teaching time and/or were taught by the most effective mediators, show any evidence of significant gains on the various dependent variables in comparison to those pupils who received less of the FIE program or were taught by the least effective mediators?

This question was answered by re-analyzing all of the change scores on all 12 dependent variables, using an analysis of covariance. The results are detailed in Appendices 17 to 30. Also given in these appendices are the adjusted means for the various schools. The results show only one additional significant effect beyond those already noted and that was a school effect at the 5% significance level when the dependent variable was the Richmond Mathematics Concepts (RM1) change scores.

The two covariates, Attendance and MLEU, made no significant differences to pupil outcomes within the FIE groups. Contrary to expectations, these two variables appear largely unrelated to any of the psychometric change scores.

Summary and Conclusions

To summarize, the analyses of variance on all 14 response variables showed:

1. No evidence of FIE having any negative or positive effect on pupils' reading and mathematics attainments over the period of the study. A positive effect would have represented some evidence of distanced transfer.

2. No evidence of FIE having any positive effect on pupils' work study skills with respect to map reading, interpreting graphs and tables, or using reference materials. Indeed, there was a slight suggestion of a negative transfer effect with the FIE pupils' performance on the RW1 test (map reading) appearing to deteriorate over time (significant at the 5% level). These results were not predicted as the Richmond Work Study Skills Tests were judged to represent a set of reasonably close transfer tasks.

3. Relatively little evidence of FIE having any positive effect on pupils' cognitive abilities. Only one significant treatment effect was noted—an improvement in the FIE pupils relative to the controls over the project period on a timed spatial reasoning task (BAS Block Design Power). This treatment effect (which was only significant at the 5% level) was unfortunately due, in part, to a major deterioration in the performance of the control group over time. In view of FIE's heavy concentration on abstract visual tasks using geometric shapes, this finding represented only modest evidence of a close transfer effect. Positive treatment findings favoring the FIE pupils were predicted but not found on two other tests (BAS Matrices and BAS Recall of Designs) which involve tasks similar in format and content to activities in the FIE program. In addition, anecdotal evidence reported later regarding the possible positive effects of FIE on pupils' linguistic skills was not supported by the Anova findings on the BAS Word Definitions and Similarities Scale change scores. Finally, no evidence was amassed to suggest enhanced cognitive development among the FIE pupils relative to the controls as assessed by changes in their pre- and post-CSMS Test Profiles, which investigated pupil competence on a range of Piagetian reasoning tasks.

It might have been suggested that potential treatment effects were diluted by some pupils receiving relatively little of the FIE program and/or by some of the FIE teachers being less experienced, inadequately supported during the study, and uncomfortable with the interactive teaching style. The analysis of covariance explored this by introducing the additional explanatory factors of pupil attendance and teacher effectiveness. There was no evidence to suggest that either factor made any significant difference to pupil outcome.

BEHAVIORAL CHARACTERISTICS OF THE PUPILS AT THE BEGINNING OF THE STUDY

At the beginning of the study, the classroom behavior of a sample of the FIE pupils was assessed using a specially devised Teacher Observation Schedule (TOS) as shown in Table 4.13. Observations were largely restricted to FIE pupils in FIE classes but, in one school it was also possible to obtain observations of FIE pupils in other lessons by non-FIE teachers.

The Teacher Observation Schedule was not factor analyzed and in view of this each item was treated separately. Mean teacher ratings of the FIE pupils at the beginning of the study on each of the 25 Teacher Observation Schedule items is given in Table 4.14. The results suggest that on almost all items, the non-FIE teachers were more negative about pupil behavior than were the FIE teachers. However, these findings need to be treated cautiously as many non-FIE teachers found the schedule difficult to complete because their lessons did not provide opportunities to notice the behaviors under scrutiny. In particular, non-FIE teachers found it hard to comment on items 13 (pupil use of logical evidence), 14 (ability to describe different problem-solving strategies), 15 (use of precise problem-solving vocabulary), 21 (ability to handle two or more sources of information simultaneously), 24 (ability to make spontaneous links across different curricular areas), and 25 (spontaneous use of a dictionary).

Many of the mean scores fell within the range 2.5–3.5, suggesting no marked preference for either of the extreme statements on these particular items. Nevertheless, on some items mean scores did suggest a preference for one or other of the statements. For example, somewhat surprisingly, both FIE and non-FIE teachers reported the majority of low attaining pupils as being:

- punctual for lessons (item 16)
- arriving with appropriate equipment (item 17).

In contrast, both FIE and non-FIE teachers reported problems with pupils:

- use of precise problem-solving vocabulary (item 15)
- ability to make links across different curricular areas (item 24)
- spontaneous use of a dictionary (item 25).

TABLE 4.13
The Teacher Observation Schedule Developed for the FIE Study
to Note Changes in Pupil Behavior on a Range of Critical Incidents

TEACHER OBSERVATION SCHEDULE (BLAGG, 1983)

School _____ Pupil's Name _____

Name of Teacher _____ Year Group _____

Subject _____

Date _____

Please tick the appropriate number on the 1 to 5 scale for each of the
dimensions listed below. The lower the score the more positive the pupil's
behavior; the higher the score the more negative the pupil's behavior.

TYPICALLY THIS PUPIL:

1. Is self-disciplined in class.   1 2 3 4 5   Is disruptive in class.

2. Settles down to work quickly.   1 2 3 4 5   Takes a long time to settle
                                                     down to work.

3. Concentrates right up to the   1 2 3 4 5   Tends to become unsettled
    end of the lesson.   toward the end of the lesson.

4. Is highly responsive to direct   1 2 3 4 5   Is unresponsive to direct
    questioning.   questioning (i.e., remains
                                                     silent and sullen).

5. Actively contributes to class   1 2 3 4 5   Switches off during class
    discussion work.   discussion.

6. Is self-motivated toward   1 2 3 4 5   Is unmotivated toward
    classwork.   classwork.

7. Asks for help when in   1 2 3 4 5   Never asks for help when in
    difficulty.   difficulty.

8. Produces neat carefully   1 2 3 4 5   Produces untidy slapdash
    organized work.   work.

9. Strives toward precision and   1 2 3 4 5   Does not appreciate the
    accuracy.   relevance of precision and
                                                     accuracy.

10. Usually gives relevant and   1 2 3 4 5   Frequently supplies irrelevant
    complete answers to   or incomplete replies to
    questions.   questions.

11. Willingly helps other pupils in 1 2 3 4 5   Shows no evidence of
    the class.   concern for other pupils.

12. Listens to other pupils   1 2 3 4 5   Never listens to other pupils
    comments during discussion.   comments during discussions.

13. Will defend own opinions on the basis of logical evidence.   1 2 3 4 5   Fails to supply logical evidence to support opinions.

14. Can describe to others a number of different strategies for solving a problem.   1 2 3 4 5   Is unable to describe more than one way of solving a particular problem.

15. Shows evidence of using precise problem-solving vocabulary.   1 2 3 4 5   Shows no evidence of using precise problem-solving vocabulary.

16. Arrives at lesson on time.   1 2 3 4 5   Is frequently late for lessons.

17. Arrives with appropriate equipment.   1 2 3 4 5   Never arrives with appropriate equipment.

18. Produces work with relatively few errors.   1 2 3 4 5   Produces work showing frequent errors and erasures.

19. Takes responsibility for catching-up on work missed.   1 2 3 4 5   Never spontaneously bothers to make-up for work missed.

20. Spontaneously reads and follows instructions carefully before starting on a task.   1 2 3 4 5   Is constantly making mistakes because of failing to consider all of the instructions carefully beforehand.

21. Shows evidence of being able to handle two or more sources of information at one time when solving problems.   1 2 3 4 5   Approaches problems using a random trial and error strategy or only one source of information/dimension at one time.

22. Readily completes homework assignments on time.   1 2 3 4 5   Rarely manages to complete homework.

23. Approaches new tasks and work with confidence.   1 2 3 4 5   Tends to be apprehensive about unfamiliar tasks and new work.

24. Spontaneously makes links across different curricular areas.   1 2 3 4 5   Has difficulty in making links between different curricular areas.

*25. Uses a dictionary spontaneously.   1 2 3 4 5   Actively avoids dictionary work.

(* Please complete only if pupil has a dictionary available in class).

COMMENTS:

_____

_____

_____

TABLE 4.14

Mean Ratings Given by FIE and Non-FIE Teachers for a Sample of the FIE Pupils on the Teacher Observation Schedule (Table 4.13) at the Beginning of the Study. NB: For Each Item in Table 4.13 Scores of 1–2 Favor the Left Statement; Scores of 4–5 Favor the Right Statement; a Score of 3 Shows no Particular Preference for Either Statement.

Teacher Observation Schedule Item	Concerning	FIE Teachers Mean ratings N = 126	Non-FIE Teachers Mean ratings N = 38
1	Self discipline	2.6	2.6
2	Approach to work	2.6	3.1
3	Concentration in lesson	3.1	3.5
4	Response to questioning	2.9	3.6
5	Contribution to discussion	3.0	3.7
6	Self motivation	2.7	3.3
7	Requests help	2.7	3.1
8	Neatness in work	2.8	3.5
9	Precision in work	2.8	3.6
10	Relevance in answers	3.1	3.7
11	Willingness to help	3.2	3.6
12	Listening skills	2.9	3.1
13	Use of logical evidence	3.3	3.8
14	Flexibility in strategy use	3.4	4.2
15	Use of problem-solving vocab.	3.5	4.3
16	Punctuality	1.9	2.1
17	Appropriate equipment	2.2	2.3
18	Errors in work	2.8	3.5
19	Responsibility for work	2.9	3.6
20	Instruction following	3.0	3.6
21	Managing complexity	3.1	4.0
22	Homework completion	2.6	3.2
23	Confidence with new tasks	3.0	3.6
24	Ability to generalize	3.6	4.2
25	Use of dictionary	3.5	3.7

Non-FIE teachers reported concerns on many more of the Teacher Observation Schedule items. Thus, in non-FIE lessons in one school, FIE pupils were regarded as:

- tending to be unresponsive to direct questioning (item 4)
- inclined to switch off during class discussions (item 5)
- failing to appreciate the relevance of precision and accuracy (item 9)
- often supplying irrelevant or incomplete answers to questions (item 10)
- often showing no evidence or concern for other pupils (item 11)
- often failing to supply logical evidence to support opinions (item 13)

- tending to be unable to describe more than one way of solving a problem (item 14)
- showing little evidence of being able to use precise problem-solving vocabulary (item 15)
- failing to spontaneously make up for work missed (item 19)
- often failing to consider instructions carefully (item 20)
- tending to adopt a random trial-and-error strategy (item 21)
- tending to be apprehensive with unfamiliar tasks (item 23)
- finding difficulty in making links between different curriculum areas (item 24)
- being inclined to avoid dictionary work (item 25).

CHANGES IN PUPIL BEHAVIOR

The previous section confirmed that at the beginning of the study, low-attaining pupils exhibited a range of behavioral problems likely to prevent them from becoming effective learners. Indeed, the problem areas highlighted are the very behaviors that a program like Instrumental Enrichment ought to be able to tackle. The FIE program has produced very disappointing findings with respect to changes in pupils' cognitive abilities, work study skills, and reading and maths attainments. Is there any evidence to suggest that there were important behavioral changes in the FIE pupils during the period of the study that might have led to ability and attainment improvements in the longer term? Moreover, if there were any significant behavioral changes were these confined purely to FIE classes or did the improvements generalize to other lessons? This section will now explore these questions using FIE and non-FIE teacher observations of FIE and control pupils on the Teacher Observation Schedule (Table 4.13).

Behavioral Changes within FIE Classes

Unfortunately, it was not possible to obtain follow-up data on all FIE pupils rated at the beginning of the study. Nevertheless, pre and post observations were obtained from FIE teachers on 72 FIE pupils. Treating each item independently, the data was subjected to the Wilcoxon Matched-Pairs Signed-Ranks test and a number of positive trends reached statistically significant levels suggesting the following tentative conclusions about pupil change.

FIE teachers felt that within the FIE classes, over the period of the study, FIE pupils became:

- more active contributors to class discussion work (Item 5, N = 72, Z = −2.56, p = 0.01)

This was the only item significant at the 1% probability level. There were, however, a number of other significant findings at the 5% probability level. Thus, FIE pupils were also regarded as becoming:

- more self-disciplined in class (Item 1, N = 72, Z = −2.19 p<0.05)
- more inclined to listen to other pupils comments in class discussions (Item 12, N = 72, Z = −2.30, p<0.05)
- more inclined to defend their own opinions on the basis of logical evidence (Item 13, N = 72, Z eq −2.43, p<0.05)
- more able to describe to other pupils a number of different strategies for solving problems (Item 14, N = 71, Z = −2.18, p<0.05)
- more likely to spontaneously read and follow instructions carefully before starting on a task (Item 20, N = 71, Z = −2.24, p<0.05)
- more able to handle two or more sources of information at one time when solving problems (Item 21, N = 71, Z = −2.00, p<0.05)
- more able to make spontaneous relationships between ideas and principles in different curricular areas (Item 24, N = 70, Z = −2.28, p<0.05).

Given the large number of items being investigated, it is likely that some effects at the 5% probability level will have occurred by chance. Nevertheless, the many positive trends in the data and the absence of any statistically significant negative effects on the TOS does add weight to the findings. To summarize, within the FIE classes FIE teachers reported significant improvements in pupil behavior, learning style, discussion skills, and conceptual thinking.

Changes in Behavior Beyond FIE Classes

Were the positive behavioral changes noted by the FIE teachers amongst the FIE pupils also noticed by other teachers? Did non-FIE teachers also report similar behavioral improvements over time among the FIE pupils in their other subject areas? Moreover, were any behavioral improvements over time confined to FIE pupils only? How did the control pupils (those low attainers not receiving the FIE program) fare over the same period? In other words, was there any evidence of positive behavioral transfer effects from FIE to non-FIE classes?

In the two schools where control groups were established (see details in chap. 3) it was possible to obtain observations of pupil behavior (both control and experimental pupils) by non-FIE teachers both at the beginning and end of the study. This data was used to compute a change score for each pupil and the data was then analyzed to explore changes over time within the control and FIE groups.

Using the Wilcoxon Signed Rank test, no significant positive changes over time were recorded by the non-FIE teachers for the FIE pupils attending their lessons. In fact the FIE pupils were perceived as becoming significantly more troublesome over the 2-year period with respect to items 1, 17, and 22. At the same time non-FIE teachers perceived the control pupils as becoming even worse, with significant negative trends occurring on items 5, 6, 7, 12, and 17.

Given the apparent lack of positive behavioral transfer from the FIE classes to the non-FIE classes, the data was analyzed further to distinguish between those pupils who received more effective teaching in terms of Feuerstein's Mediated Learning Experience parameters (see chap. 3, Table 3.2 and 3.3, and Appendix 3). Each of the FIE teachers involved with the project pupils was rated in terms of their mediation characteristics using the schedule shown in Table 3.2. Only those items concerned with the mediation of intentionality/reciprocity, meaning, and transcendence were used to obtain a mediation score according to the proforma detailed in Appendix 3. An average mediation rating for the total sample was computed and on the basis of this, pupils taught by FIE teachers below the median were allocated to a low-MLE group and those taught by FIE teachers above the median to a high-MLE group.

Analyzing the changes over time on the Teacher Observation Schedule noted by the non-FIE teachers within the three groups (Control, low-MLE, and high-MLE) the following effects were noted. Among the pupils who in theory received less effective (low-MLE) teaching, the majority of the trends in the data were negative. However, among these trends only one item showed a statistically significant negative effect. According to the non-FIE teachers, the low-MLE group children became:

- less likely to give complete and relevant answers to questions (TOS Item 10, $N = 12$, $Z = -2.00$, $p<0.05$).

The results among the pupils who in theory received more effective (high-MLE) teaching were even more disappointing. Once again, the trends in the data were entirely negative with three of these trends reaching statistically significant levels. According to the non-FIE teachers, the high-MLE pupils became:

- less likely to manage to complete homework set (TOS Item 22, $N = 20$, $Z = -3.29$, $p<0.001$)
- less disciplined in the class (TOS Item 1, $N = 20$, $Z = -2.22$, $p<0.05$)
- less likely to bring the appropriate equipment to the lesson (TOS Item 17, $N = 20$, $Z = -2.05$, $p<0.05$).

A similar but if anything more negative picture emerged among the control pupils. The majority of trends in the data were negative. In fact there were only 6 out of 25 possible positive trends and none of these reached levels of statistical significance. A number of the negative trends were statistically significant at the 1% probability level suggesting that control group pupils became:

- less likely to seek help when in difficulty (TOS Item 7, N = 30, Z = −2.76, p<0.01)
- less likely to listen to other pupils comments during class discussions (TOS Item 12, N = 30, Z = −2.85, p<0.01)
- less likely to arrive with appropriate equipment (TOS Item 17, N = 30, Z = −3.21, p<0.01).

More tentatively, there were two further results at the 5% probability level indicating control pupils became:

- more likely to switch off during class discussions (TOS Item 5, N = 30, Z = −2.33, p<0.05)
- less motivated toward classwork (TOS Item 6, N = 30, Z = −2.46, p<0.05).

Discussion

The findings reported in this section need to be treated cautiously. The Teacher Observation Schedule was not a sophisticated and statistically reliable instrument for assessing changes in pupil behavior over time. In view of this, no attempt was made to aggregate the scores. Instead, the 25 items were treated independently. As a result, many analyses were conducted and therefore some of the findings were bound to have occurred by chance.

It could be argued that the positive trends noted by the FIE teachers within the FIE classes were merely "halo" effects. The FIE teachers were knowledgeable about the expected outcomes of the program, and invested considerable time and energy in trying to achieve these outcomes. It is difficult, therefore, to know whether improvements in ratings by the FIE teachers related to a more optimistic and positive perspective of the pupils or to genuine objective changes in classroom behavior. Certainly, FIE teachers were more positive about their pupils at the beginning of the study than the non-FIE teachers.

In general the control group teachers did not know about the specific aims of the FIE program and there was a good deal of skepticism about the possibility of any positive effects transferring to other lessons and contexts. It could be argued that they might be more objective than the FIE teachers. While this may have been the case, there were other problems contaminating the data.

The control teachers were drawn from a wide range of subject domains. Quite a few of these teachers expressed difficulty in completing the schedules and experienced particular problems with items 12, 13, 14, 15, 21, 24, and 25. Further exploration revealed that many non-FIE teachers felt their lessons did not offer the opportunity to notice the kind of critical incidents that were being referred to in the Observation Schedule. As many of these teachers did not significantly alter their expectations of the low-achieving pupils or their teaching styles during the period of the study, it is not surprising that they failed to notice positive improvements in either the control or FIE pupils.

Summary and Conclusions

Bearing in mind the limitations in the data, the findings from both within and beyond the FIE classes suggest that FIE pupils, assessed by FIE teachers in FIE classes, showed significant behavioral improvements over the project period. Unfortunately, these behavioral improvements were not observed by non-FIE teachers who noted that a sample of the same FIE pupils deteriorated in their behavior in non-FIE classes over the same period. Surprisingly, the most significant, negative behavioral changes in non-FIE classes occurred among those FIE pupils who received theoretically the most effective (high-MLE) FIE teaching. Similar, negative behavioral trends over the same period were also noticed by the non-FIE teachers among the control pupils.

These data can be interpreted in many different ways. Changes on the Teacher Observation Schedule could reflect changes in teacher perceptions rather than pupil behavior. Certainly, this would concur with the findings in Chapter 5 which demonstrate positive, attitudinal changes over time toward low achieving pupils among FIE teachers, but not among the control teachers. Even if we accept that there were genuine behavioral changes in the FIE classes, there was little evidence of positive behavioral transfer from FIE to non-FIE classes and some evidence of negative behavioral transfer. The latter could be accounted for by pupils experiencing difficulty in switching from a rather novel interactive lesson activity geared around process issues to more familiar subject teaching emphasizing content. It was noted on more than one occasion that some pupils new-found enthusiasm for questioning, challenging, and discussion was regarded as threatening or unacceptable by some of the non-FIE teachers who were more formal and traditionalist.

CHANGES IN PUPILS' SELF-ESTEEM

Did FIE pupils gain in confidence during the period of the study as the FIE program predicted? This question was approached by administering the Anglicised Coopersmith Self Esteem Scale (Gurney, personal communication) to both FIE and control pupils at the beginning of the study, 10 months later, and again at the end of the study.

Analyzing the change scores over a 10-month period, only FIE pupils in School A showed a significant, positive improvement over time (N = 39, Wilcoxon Sign Rank Score = 155, p<0.01). FIE pupils in the three other schools (School B, N = 15; School C, N = 30; School D, N = 19) showed no significant self-esteem changes over a 10-month period. The two controls groups (from Schools B and D, N = 27) showed a negative trend (i.e., a deterioration in self-esteem over the same period) but this trend was not statistically significant. Nevertheless, analysis of the changes in self-esteem over 10 months by teaching group *within* each school, produced a consistent pattern. In all four schools, self-esteem changes were positively correlated with teacher effectiveness rated in terms of their MLE characteristics as shown in Fig. 4.1. Moreover, both control groups showed a deterioration in self-esteem over the same period.

Unfortunately, it was not possible to gather longer term follow-up data on any

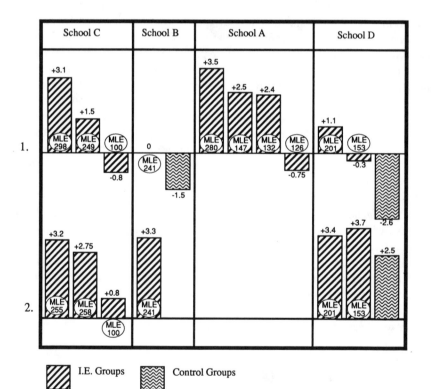

FIG. 4.1.   Changes in self-esteem over 10 months (1.) and 20 months (2.) in the experimental and control groups within the four project schools. The figures in circles illustrate the MLE scores for each teacher. The higher the score, the more effective the teacher in terms of the MLE profile (see chap. 3, Table 3.3).

pupils in school A nor on the control pupils in school B. Nevertheless, it can be seen from Fig. 4.1 that the consistent relationship within each school between teacher effectiveness and self-esteem enhancement was not maintained over the 20-month period in school D. Moreover, in this same school, self-esteem enhancements in the long term were almost as good in the control groups as in the FIE groups. In schools B and C, there was a slight but consistent improvement in the self-esteem scores of the FIE pupils.

In summary, it is difficult to draw any definite conclusions from these data, but the implication is that, in the short term, positive self-esteem changes did result from an interaction between teacher, school, and FIE program effects. There was no tidy relationship between self-esteem changes and teacher effectiveness across the four schools in the short or long term and over the total period of the FIE program there was no evidence to suggest that there were any long-term self-esteem enhancements peculiar to the FIE pupils.

CHANGES IN PUPILS' ATTITUDES TOWARD SCHOOL WORK

This section now turns to the less tangible topic of pupil attitudes and, in particular, to pupil feelings about their core subjects (maths, English, Physical Education (PE), Religious Education (RE), and careers) and Instrumental Enrichment. How did their feelings about these subjects compare with their attitudes toward FIE? Did their feelings change over the period of the study?

Individual Rating Scale

In an attempt to produce some systematic data on the aforementioned questions, I asked pupils to give a rating of 1–5 with respect to each core subject and FIE in the following areas:

- personal enjoyment
- personal relevance
- personal participation
- lesson format
- class cooperation.

The lower the rating, the more positive their response. Thus, for personal enjoyment, ratings of 1–5 were explained to the pupils as follows:

1 = thoroughly enjoy the subject

2 = quite enjoy the subject

3 = no marked feelings either way or sometimes enjoy it, sometimes don't

4 = don't enjoy the subject

5 = thoroughly dislike the subject

Personal relevance ratings were illustrated in relation to their current interests, hobbies, and schoolwork or future vocational intentions:

1 = highly relevant and useful

2 = quite relevant and useful

3 = sometimes relevant, sometimes not

4 = not very relevant or useful

5 = totally irrelevant and useless

For personal participation, pupils were advised to rate the extent to which they felt they participated in the lessons:

1 = take every opportunity to take part

2 = make an effort to participate

3 = sometimes participate, sometimes do not

4 = try to avoid participation

5 = take no part whatsoever in lessons

For lesson format, pupils rated the extent to which each lesson was organized to give them an opportunity to take part. More positive ratings were reserved for those lessons that gave pupils a chance to put forward their own ideas, discuss issues, and have a say in the content and pacing of the lesson. More negative (higher) ratings denoted formal, "chalk and talk" type lessons, where pupils felt they had little or no opportunity to participate in lessons.

1 = have many opportunities to discuss and share ideas

2 = have some opportunity to discuss and share ideas

3 = sometimes have opportunities to discuss, sometimes not

4 = have very few opportunities to discuss and share ideas

5 = have no opportunity to discuss and share ideas

For class cooperation, pupils were asked to rate the general behavior of the class, rather than consider their own behavior. Positive ratings were attributed to classes where all pupils were deemed to be highly cooperative and well-behaved in comparison to negative ratings for classes where many pupils were assessed as being uncooperative and disruptive much of the time.

1 = the class is exceptionally well-behaved
2 = the class is generally well-behaved
3 = the class is sometimes well-behaved and sometimes not
4 = the class is often poorly behaved
5 = the class is always poorly behaved

Results

Pupils rated each subject in each of the five areas during the first term of the project and toward the end of the fifth term, 20 months later. Mean ratings of each area across the core subjects and FIE at both points in time, are given for the FIE pupils in Table 4.15 and for the control pupils in Table 4.16.

The findings in Tables 4.15 and 4.16 show that there were no significant differences between the FIE and Control pupil ratings of their core subjects. Most pupils were either neutral or positive about their subjects with the exception of RE, which seemed to be given universally poorer ratings across all schools for enjoyment, relevance, personal participation, lesson format, and class cooperation. Interestingly, although FIE claimed to be more interactive and discussion

TABLE 4.15
FIE Pupil Mean Ratings of FIE and Their Core Subjects
at the Beginning and End of the Study

Subjects	Personal Enjoyment		Personal Relevance		Personal Participation		Lesson Format		Class Cooperation	
	Pre	Post	Pre	Post	Pre	Post	Pre	Post	Pre	Post
English	2.2	2.6	1.4	1.6	2.4	2.5	2.2	2.6	2.4	2.7
Maths	2.6	2.6	1.4	1.5	2.4	2.5	1.2	3.0	2.5	2.5
RE	3.6	3.0	3.9	3.1	3.3	3.0	3.2	2.9	3.0	2.9
FIE	2.3	2.8	2.3	2.5	2.4	2.4	1.9	1.9	2.4	2.5
PE	2.0	2.3	2.9	3.2	2.3	2.3	2.3	2.7	2.2	2.5
Careers	2.6	3.2	1.9	3.0	2.5	3.1	2.2	2.4	2.0	—

For pre-test:
N = 120 (English),
N = 119 (Maths),
N = 68 (RE),
N = 117 (FIE),
N = 116 (PE),
N = 64 (Careers),

For post-test:
N = 156 (English),
N = 156 (Maths),
N = 67 (RE),
N = 115 (FIE),
N = 152 (PE),
N = 90 (Careers),

TABLE 4.16
Control Pupil Mean Ratings of Their Core Subjects
at the Beginning and End of the Study

Subjects	Personal Enjoyment		Personal Relevance		Personal Participation		Lesson Format		Class Cooperation	
	Pre	Post	Pre	Post	Pre	Post	Pre	Post	Pre	Post
English	2.3	2.4	1.6	1.3	2.4	2.5	2.4	2.5	1.8	2.8
Maths	2.1	2.8	1.4	1.4	2.3	2.5	1.2	2.7	2.6	2.4
RE	3.7	2.6	4.2	3.3	3.7	2.5	3.3	2.6	4.0	2.8
PE	1.8	2.3	2.9	3.1	2.3	2.8	2.1	2.8	2.4	2.4
Career	2.6	3.5	2.1	2.8	2.4	3.2	2.4	2.0	2.2	—

For pre-test:
N = 26 (English),
N = 25 (Maths),
N = 18 (RE),
N = 25 (PE)
N = 16 (Careers)

For post-test:
N = 41 (English),
N = 41 (Maths),
N = 24 (RE),
N = 38 (PE),
N = 17 (Careers),

oriented than most other subjects, pupils rated the lesson format for FIE in very much the same way as they did for English, maths, PE, and careers.

For those pupils who were present at both the pre- and post-test, change scores were computed for each subject with respect to the enjoyment, relevance, participation, lesson format, and class cooperation. Pupils were divided into three groups (Control, low-MLE, and high-MLE) and the data was analyzed to check for the significance of any change scores within each group using the Wilcoxon Signed Rank test. Given the many analyses that were undertaken, only those findings significant at the 1% probability level or above will be discussed.

In terms of personal enjoyment, there were no significant changes in the control or FIE group pupil ratings of their core subjects. These findings applied to both the high- and low-MLE FIE groups. The low-MLE group did however show evidence of enjoying the FIE program more toward the end of the study than the beginning (N = 57, Z = -3.96, p <0.0001).

With respect to pupils' personal relevance ratings of their core subjects, there were no significant changes over time among the controls and only one significant change over time with respect to the FIE pupils. The high-MLE group became significantly more positive about the relevance of RE (N = 23, Z = -3.04, p <0.01). Only the low-MLE group became more positive about the relevance of FIE during the period of the project (N = 57, Z = -2.98, p <0.01).

There was no evidence of any significant changes over time with respect to the personal participation in core subjects by either the control, high-MLE, or low-MLE groups. Moreover, there were no apparent changes over time with respect to participation in the FIE classes by either the high- or low-MLE groups.

Pupils ratings of their classes from fairly formal and didactic through to informal and interactive changed very little over the period of the project. There were no significant changes in lesson format recorded by the control group and only one significant change recorded by the FIE pupils. The low-MLE group felt that their maths class became more interactive ($N = 56$, $Z = -2.57$, $p < 0.01$). The FIE lesson formats were regarded as remaining fairly stable over time with no significant changes in ratings by either the high- or low-MLE groups. Although many of the FIE teachers felt that they became more oriented toward discussion and interactive work as the project progressed, pupils did not seem to perceive those changes.

Finally, pupil ratings of class cooperation in their core subjects did not change in the control group, but did change in the two FIE groups. The low-MLE group felt that class behavior improved significantly in PE ($N = 53$, $Z = -3.14$, $p < 0.01$) and careers ($N = 25$, $Z = -3.86$, $p < 0.0001$). The high-MLE group felt that the class behavior improved in English ($N = 35$, $Z = -3.00$, $p < 0.01$) and careers ($N = 38$, $Z = -5.30$, $p < 0.0001$). The low-MLE group also indicated that class behavior improved in FIE over the period of the project ($N = 57$, $Z = -2.55$, $p < 0.01$).

Summary and Conclusions

Some attitudinal changes toward core subjects were to be expected over the period of the project with pupils growing older and teachers and teaching groups changing. Nevertheless, it was interesting to find that over the period of the study, there were no significant changes in either the control or FIE pupil ratings of any of their core subjects in terms of personal enjoyment and participation. Moreover, no significant changes were noted in the control pupils in terms of lesson format and personal relevance on any of the core subjects, whereas among the FIE pupils significant rating changes occurred on these dimensions in only two subjects. Significant and more widespread rating changes did however occur among the FIE pupils with respect to class cooperation in three core subjects. As far as the FIE pupils were concerned the behavior of their classmates improved over the period of the study, not only in FIE lessons but also in English, PE, and careers. Similar improvements in class behavior over time were not noted by the control pupils.

Anecdotal Evidence

Thus far, the evidence for pupil change is rather limited. Nevertheless, classroom observations of many classes suggested that the novelty of the FIE program and, in particular, its use of many visual tasks unassociated with previous failure experiences was beneficial to many pupils. For instance, it was noticed that many pupils with poor verbal skills and limited reading attainments were able to demonstrate sophisticated skills in the visual mode that had previously been unrecognized. Although this did not appear to lead to a general long-term benefit to pupils self-esteem within FIE groups as a whole, there were clear examples within the groups of individual pupils gaining in confidence. Moreover, the visual starting points provided by the materials often prompted pupils to reflect on the activities and participate in class discussions. Although relatively little quantifiable evidence was gathered in respect of changes in pupils oracy skills, the general impression of both the FIE teachers and visitors to the FIE classrooms was that most pupils improved in their ability and willingness to share their ideas with others and express them clearly. Some of these informal observations were confirmed by the individual comments of particular pupils. Nevertheless, it is only fair to add that some pupil comments implied that they remained, at best, curious onlookers, completely mystified by the FIE lessons.

A sample of the FIE pupils from two schools were given semi-structured interviews (see Appendix 1). A number of recurring themes emerged during these interviews. Pupils commented on:

(a) **their increased willingness to contribute to class discussions.** This was one area where there was general agreement among pupils of positive benefits of the FIE program.

> Before [FIE] I used to just sit down, even if I knew the answer I wouldn't put my hand up in case I was wrong. But with FIE teachers you have to have a go. . . .

> At the beginning of the year I could not talk in front of anybody. . . . I've changed because I've had more practice at talking in FIE and I'm more confident in other lessons.

> I'm much better at talking to the class now. . . . you can answer questions, think for yourself, know the right things to say. Without FIE you are still dumb.

(b) **the benefits of being in a small class.** Many pupils implied that their increased confidence in speaking in front of the class and sharing ideas was not so much a function of FIE but a benefit of being in a small group.

> Working in a small group makes it easier to speak up.

> The FIE class is a small group, you know everybody better. Everybody gets to say something. . . . This is the first time I've ever joined in discussions.

(c) **their acquisition of a wider range of words and concepts.** The majority of pupils indicated that they had learned new words but relatively few seemed to have made use of them.

I don't hardly use the [FIE] words in other subjects.

I forget most of the [FIE] words. You don't hear them in other lessons.

Other teachers don't seem to use the same [FIE] words.

However, several pupils highlighted the importance of the linguistic aspects of the FIE program.

Interviewer: "I see so you've learnt alot of new words in this program. Have they helped you?"

Interviewee: "No not really."

Interviewer: "Oh, why is that?"

Interviewee: "Well, the teachers don't use the words in other lessons."

Interviewer: "What kind of words are you talking about?"

Interviewee: "Well, words like—plan, anticipate, alternative."

Interviewer: "You don't use those words?"

Interviewee: "Well, I don't use the words but I do use the ideas."

Interviewer: "How do you mean?"

Interviewee: "I never used to plan anything. At the weekends I now have plans and alternatives in case things don't work out as I think they will."

(d) **improvements in thinking and planning skills.** Quite a few pupils gave the impression of being less impulsive in their approach to many problems. Some pupils commented on the need to slow down, take more time, look carefully, and make a plan rather than simply rushing into a problem.

I've learned never to go fast; take your time. Always look at things carefully. Make sure you understand it before you go ahead and do it. . . .

It makes me think more about questions, to look at them and read them carefully.

Think about what you do before you do it. If you have a lot to do make a plan first.

(e) **their ability to transfer the thinking skills and ideas developed in the FIE lessons to other contexts.** Qualitative impressions of individual pupils suggested that some were able to generalize from the FIE program to other settings.

> In wood work I used to hurry up and draw any picture and never stop to consider the joints carefully. Now I stop and think. . . .

> It helped me with spelling. I slow down and break the word up.

> I use the strategies on big sums in maths. . . . You break it down and work it out in sections.

> In English I use an elimination strategy; remembering to tick things off that you've done so you don't waste time.

However, it was not possible to quantify the range and extent of pupil generalization and there were some pupils who seemed totally unaware of the metacognitive aspects of the FIE program.

> In other lessons you learn about things. In this lesson [FIE] you just learn about your handwriting and drawing.

> Can't see the point of it [FIE]; it's boring. . . . It hasn't helped in other subjects.

> It's [FIE] a bit stupid. Joining dots, that's a bit ridiculous. What can you do with this lesson when you get out of school? I can't see the point of it.

Some pupils, while enjoying the activities, did not regard the FIE program as like "real" lessons. Pupils commonly asked: "When are we going to do some real work sir?"

CONCLUSIONS

The detailed findings in this chapter revealed little quantifiable evidence to suggest that the FIE program had a positive influence on the 14- to 16-year-old low-attaining pupils from the four project schools.

In particular, there was no evidence to suggest that the FIE program produced any improvements in childrens' cognitive abilities as assessed by the Word Definitions, Similarities, Block Design (Power), Matrices, and Recall of Design Tests from the British Ability Scales. Furthermore, the FIE program did not produce any significant improvements to childrens' work study skills, reading or maths attainments as assessed by the Richmond Test battery. It was hypothesized that positive treatment effects would be more likely to occur among those pupils who received the most FIE teaching time and the most effective mediation. Detailed analyses of covariance suggested that neither pupil attendance or the mediation characteristics of the teacher made any difference to pupil outcomes on the British Ability Scales or Richmond Tests.

There was no consistent relationship between the FIE program and self-esteem changes in the FIE pupils. There was some tentative evidence to suggest that in the short term (over a 10-month period) self-esteem changes did occur in certain schools with the more effective high-MLE teachers. In other words, self-esteem changes were as much a function of the whole school environment and the individual effectiveness of particular FIE teachers, as they were a function of the FIE program itself.

Less reliable data was presented concerning evidence of behavioral change among the FIE pupils. FIE teachers felt that their FIE pupils became more active contributors to class discussion work during the period of the project. FIE teachers also reported a number of other positive trends suggesting that FIE pupils became: more self-disciplined in class; more inclined to listen to other pupils comments in class discussions; more inclined to defend their opinions on the basis of logical evidence; more able to describe a number of different strategies for solving problems; more likely to spontaneously read and follow instructions carefully; more able to handle two or more sources of information simultaneously in problem solving and more able to make relationships between ideas and principles across different curriculum areas. It seems likely that at least some of these trends were more related to changes in teacher perceptions than genuine changes in pupil behavior.

Certainly, these positive behavioral improvements and trends were not observed outside the FIE classes. Indeed, there was some evidence to suggest a deterioriation in pupil behavior in non-FIE lessons over the 2-year period (among FIE and control pupils) especially among FIE pupils from the more effective high-MLE classes. This may have been associated with a clash between a change in pupil role (a desire to discuss and question) and teacher expectation (with some traditionalists regarding questioning as being challenging and even threatening).

There was some evidence to suggest that in spite of the observations of non-FIE teachers, the FIE pupils themselves felt that the behavior and cooperation of other pupils in certain other teaching groups (English, PE, and careers) improved over the period of the study. Similar improvements in class behavior were not noted in any of the core subjects by the control pupils.

Anecdotal evidence gathered from informal observations and semi-structured interviews suggested that the individual response of pupils to the FIE program was highly varied within and across the teaching groups. There were some teaching groups where the pupil responses were largely negative and others where the pupil response was generally positive. Within each group there were pupils who "opted out" or tried to participate but appeared to gain very little. On the other hand, pupil comments indicated that at least some FIE pupils became: more willing to participate in classroom discussions; more confident about speaking in front of the class; more fluent with a wider range of words and concepts related to the heuristics of problem solving; less impulsive; and, finally, able to give limited examples of the transfer of certain skills and techniques to other contexts.

The Teachers

This chapter is based on teachers' termly diary records, individual semi-structured interviews, informal discussions following classroom observations, and results from the pre- and post-assessment package referred to in Chapter 3 (i.e., Cattell's 16PF and the semantic differential scales shown in Tables 5.1, 5.5, and 5.8).

INITIAL REACTIONS TO TRAINING

FIE training courses took on an evangelical flavor with the majority of teachers enthused about the stimulating nature of the course and the potential of the materials. One teacher talked about feeling "fired up," another referred to herself as a "born again teacher." Another teacher said, "When I left the course I felt like a rocket ship leaving the launch pad." Many commented that the course had prompted them to examine their role and teaching style as well as attitudes toward pupils:

I have been teaching for 30 years. This was the first time I had been provoked into thinking about how pupils think. . . .

It's changed my views on thinking—made me more aware of the mental landscape.

If a pupil doesn't reply within a few seconds the answer is usually supplied by the teacher or another pupil calling out. We don't allow (pupils) enough time, and we don't listen well enough. The children don't have a moment to think. . . .

I had a pessimistic view of my role. I used to feel teaching was like sophisticated baby sitting. It seemed like a conveyor belt system and I had to make sure they (the pupils) stayed on the conveyor belt. Now I feel I have a more active role to play. . . . FIE opened up the importance of looking for and encouraging different approaches whilst helping pupils to realize that being right or wrong does not always matter.

In spite of this generally optimistic picture, most teachers expressed some reservations about training and a few teachers were very negative about the experience. In general, those teachers in their probationary years were less involved with the course as they were still primarily concerned with gaining fluency in their own specialist subject areas and coping with the everyday mechanics of being a teacher. Moreover, a few of the teachers that attended training were not obliged to teach FIE on their return to school. Perhaps not surprisingly, these teachers were less enthusiastic and committed and those that went on to year 2 training felt "lost" because of their lack of experience in teaching the program.

A common criticism of training was that too much time was spent on presentations of activities to the detriment of remaining instruments and issues on theory, lesson planning, and organization:

The training was too rigid; there wasn't enough on flexible classroom style. We came back with misconceptions, working slowly, and methodically losing the pupils as they got bored.

Overfocused on presentation. It was a bit like a sausage factory. There wasn't enough time to assimilate what was going on before you were onto the next instrument. Everybody did superb lessons but we fitted the last two instruments into one day.

The materials and the teaching approaches are overprescriptive. Taking parts of the program and adapting them to your children in your situation was discouraged. This seemed contrary to all my other secondment experiences.

The manual tries to be all things to all men. It is full of jargon and difficult to select out the key points. Eventually, I stopped using the manual; it didn't seem to relate to what I was trying to do in the lesson.

Underlying theoretical issues were largely ignored.

Several teachers, although enjoying the intellectual debate on the training course, doubted that the pupils would derive similar pleasures and benefits:

I think FIE has more impact on teachers than on pupils. Teachers already have the intellectual equipment to discuss, rationalize, explore, etc., in the way that many pupils can't.

Do teacher experiences with FIE mean that it can be so good with the pupils? Not necessarily; the range, breadth, and level of sophisticated discussion may not be so easy with pupils.

Summary

The majority of teachers very positive about the FIE training courses, were coming away feeling stimulated and optimistic about their potential role as teachers. A few teachers had specific concerns about the nature of the FIE training and some teachers were sceptical about the relevance of the FIE materials for classroom use. In general, those teachers that were not obliged to teach the program on their return to school were less enthused by the training.

REFLECTIONS ON FIE IN THE CLASSROOM

Most teachers appeared to leave the FIE training courses enthused in spite of some reservations. How did the realities of FIE in the classroom compare with training perceptions? Did their attitudes toward FIE change over time? These questions were explored via:

1. a specially constructed attitudinal scale (attitudes toward FIE Scale)
2. anecdotal evidence gathered from termly diary records, lesson observations, informal discussions, and a semi-structured interview with each FIE teacher at the end of the study.

Attitudes Toward FIE Scale

The *Attitudes Toward FIE Scale* (as shown in Table 5.1) was used with the FIE teachers only. It involved the teachers in recording their feelings by ticking one of seven positions between each of the two extreme statements listed in the table (e.g., "Undermines my confidence as a teacher" vs. "Improves my confidence as a teacher"). The proximity of each tick to one or other of the statements was taken to indicate the frequency with which that attitude was held to apply. Each position on each item was allocated a score between 1 and 7, with a high score indicating that the right statement more often applied and a low score that the left statement more often applied. A score of four was regarded as a neutral response. The right-hand statements generally reflected more positive attitudes toward the FIE course and its potential for both pupils and teachers. It should be noted that when the scales were administered, the positions of the statements for each item were randomized to avoid the teacher developing a response stereotype (i.e., not all the positive statements were located on one side of the schedule). Moreover,

TABLE 5.1
The Attitudes Toward FIE Scale Developed for the FIE Study.

ATTITUDES TOWARD FIE SCALE

School _____ Teacher _____

Age groups taught _____ Subject specialization _____

Number of years in teaching _____

INSTRUCTIONS: The following pairs of statements provide the opportunity to record *your* views about Instrumental Enrichment. Each pair of statements is separated by seven positions. Please rate yourself in each case by ticking the appropriate position. The closer you tick to the left statement the more often this applies, the nearer you tick to the right statement the more often that applies.

The Instrumental Enrichment . . .

1. Undermines my confidence as a teacher. — — — — — — — Improves my confidence as a teacher.

2. Provides little satisfaction for the teacher. — — — — — — — Provides great satisfaction for the teacher.

3. Offers very little in the way of stimulation for classroom discussions. — — — — — — — Provides ideal material for classroom discussions.

4. Involves learning irrelevant jargon. — — — — — — — Involves acquiring useful terminology for problem solving.

5. Is not altering my awareness of pupil capabilities. — — — — — — — Is altering my perception of pupil capabilities.

6. Does not have implications for my style in other teaching areas. — — — — — — — Has implications for my teaching style in my main subject area.

7. Invites a teaching style that I am uncomfortable with. — — — — — — — Invites a teaching style that I feel at home with.

8. Offers no potential in improving the motivation of adolescents. — — — — — — — Offers great potential in improving the motivation of adolescents.

9. Offers no possibilities for improving the problem-solving skills of adolescents. — — — — — — — Offers great possibilities for improving the problem-solving skills of adolescents.

10. Has nothing to offer different subject disciplines. — — — — — — — Has a great deal to offer all subject disciplines.

11.	Involves generalization which is extremely difficult to effect beyond my own subject discipline.	— — — — — —	Involves generalization which is easy to effect beyond my own subject discipline.
12.	Has attracted an extremely negative response from teaching staff in my school.	— — — — — —	Has attracted an extremely positive response from teaching staff in my school.
13.	Involves an interactive teaching style which is difficult to manage.	— — — — — —	Involves an interactive teaching style which is easy to manage.
14.	Is not improving my weak cognitive areas.	— — — — — —	Is improving my weak cognitive areas.
15.	Does not affect my work preparation.	— — — — — —	Causes me to prepare my work more thoroughly.
16.	Has no effect on pupils thinking for themselves.	— — — — — —	Helps pupils to think for themselves.
17.	Does not affect impulsivity amongst pupils.	— — — — — —	Has reduced impulsivity amongst pupils.
18.	Has not altered my effectiveness as a teacher.	— — — — — —	Has improved my effectiveness as a teacher.
19.	Does not affect my approach to solving everyday problems.	— — — — — —	Is improving my approach to solving everyday problems.
20.	Involves an uneconomical use of teacher time.	— — — — — —	Involves a reasonable return for teacher time and effort.
21.	Involves quite reasonable material costs.	— — — — — —	Involves quite unreasonable material costs.
22.	Involves a highly relevant teacher training element.	— — — — — —	Involves a teacher training element which is non-essential.

scores for each item were allocated by the evaluator and not by the teachers themselves.

As Table 5.2 shows, most teachers recorded neutral responses to the majority of the items. However, at the beginning and the end of the study, teachers recorded more positive responses on items 6, 10, 15, 16, and 22. Thus, at the beginning of the study most teachers felt that FIE:

- would involve implications for their teaching style in other areas of the curriculum (item 6)
- had much to offer other subject disciplines (item 10)

TABLE 5.2
Mean Pre- and Post-Test Scores for the FIE Teachers on the
Attitude Toward FIE Scale Together With Any Significant Changes
Over Time as Assessed by the Wilcoxon Sign Rank Test.

Attitudes Toward FIE Scale Items	FIE Teachers (N = 17)			
	Mean Pre-Test	Mean Post-Test	W	P
1	4.52	4.88	—	NS
2	4.71	4.52	—	NS
3	4.94	4.82	—	NS
4	4.35	5.12	—	NS
5	4.47	5.18	—	NS
6	5.29	6.06	—	NS
7	4.94	5.06	—	NS
8	4.41	4.88	—	NS
9	4.94	5.41	—	NS
10	5.06	5.52	—	NS
11	4.41	3.00	13	<0.01
12	4.00	3.47	—	NS
13	4.06	4.06	—	NS
14	4.52	5.12	—	NS
15	5.65	5.35	—	NS
16	5.12	5.17	—	NS
17	4.06	4.94	17	<0.025
18	4.41	5.23	—	NS
19	4.35	5.29	21.5	<0.05
20	3.76	4.53	—	NS
21	2.42	2.18	—	NS
22	5.76	6.10	—	NS

W = Wilcoxon sign rank score   P = probability levels

- would involve a lot of preparation (item 15)
- would help pupils to think for themselves (item 16)
- involved a highly relevant teacher training element (item 22).

These positive views were maintained during the study. At the same time, the majority of teachers at the beginning of the study felt that FIE involved quite unreasonable material costs (item 21). This finding also applied at the end of the study.

There were however, a number of additional attitudinal shifts over time which were significant on the Wilcoxon Sign Rank Test. In particular, teachers became *more optimistic* about FIE being able to (a) reduce the impulsivity of their pupils (item 17; p<0.025) and (b) improve their own approach to solving everyday problems (item 19; p<0.05). On the other hand, teachers became *less optimistic* about pupil ability to generalize the principles of FIE to activities beyond their own subject specialism (item 11; $p<0.01$).

Anecdotes and General Observations

Although teacher replies to the Attitudes Toward FIE Scale revealed mainly optimistic responses; lesson observations, termly diary records, and detailed discussions with each FIE teacher at the end of the study, revealed many areas of concern relating to:

- The nature of the materials
- Practical problems of implementation in the classroom
- Integration of the program with other curriculum areas.

As one teacher so clearly put it: "When I left the (FIE training) course I felt like a rocket leaving the launching pad. Now I feel as though I am burning up on re-entry."

The Nature of the Materials

In general the FIE teachers felt the materials were too expensive, too abstract and unfamiliar, too repetitive and poorly presented, and culturally inappropriate.

Too Expensive.   Most teachers indicated that the cost per pupil of the non-photocopiable materials would make them prohibitive to buy on their capitation allowances, once the special DES grant had expired—even if the materials were thought to be useful. This feeling was compounded by the fact that purchase of the materials was conditional on an expensive training program also deemed to be essential because of the unfamiliar and abstract nature of the materials.

Too Abstract and Unfamiliar.   Once the support and camaraderie of the training courses had dissipated and the realities of classroom implementation were on them, most teachers felt anxious about working with complex, abstract, and alien materials. There was a widespread feeling of insecurity stemming from a lack of familiarity with the materials, their mode of presentation, and styles of language. Teachers struggled to translate the abstract ideas embodied in the materials to make them meaningful and relevant to everyday situations. In reality, many teachers did not manage this and the FIE exercises were taught as a series of abstract work sheets that bore very little relationship to other areas of pupil or teacher experience. In the FIE jargon, it was difficult for both pupils and teachers to "bridge" from the FIE program to other curriculum areas and domestic experiences. Unfortunately, the majority of pupils and teachers found themselves "stuck" in the dots and the triangles:

> 50% of the pupils did not seem to want to think about "bridging." They were more interested in solving the abstract puzzles.

> They (pupils) see very little point in many of the activities. . . . You can give examples but they can't see what dot joining has to do with anything. . . . Establishing meaning and relevance is a major stumbling block in getting lessons going. . . .

> I prefer the second year materials. They have more familiar content making it easier for pupils to see everyday applications. The first year materials place a heavy reliance on your own resources for ideas and materials for bridging.

> It is difficult to keep track of the thread and purpose of the lesson when you are unfamiliar with the materials.

Too Repetitive and Poorly Presented. The result was that teachers reported that many pupils were bored with the activities. Each instrument does contain a range of tasks of increasing complexity and abstraction but the mode and content changes very little. Many mainstream pupils found the pace too slow and the materials insufficiently novel and challenging.

> Teaching FIE was very, very difficult. The materials were intrinsically unattractive and poorly presented. . . . Page after page of dots crucified them.

> In this modern multi-media age, where pupils are used to sophisticated graphics, I am embarrassed to use the FIE materials.

> With Organization of Dots the main problem was that the vast majority of pupils related this to dot to dot joining activities in simple puzzle books from their infant days, like "Find the Donkey."

Culturally Inappropriate. (with many Americanisms). Concerns here related to the lack of familiar content in many of the instruments and the inclusion of drawings and content areas more appropriate to the expectations and interests of young children rather than adolescents.

Practical Problems with Classroom Implementation

Interviews with individual teachers and termly diaries revealed a number of commonly recurring themes including: difficulties in establishing meaning and relevance; problems in managing classroom discussions; problems in meeting the needs of a disparate group of children; and developing suitable "bridging" materials.

Difficulties in Establishing Meaning and Relevance. Many teachers "stood on pirouettes" and engaged in all sorts of mental contortions in an attempt to make sense of the FIE program for themselves and the pupils. The most successful teachers spent an inordinate amount of time preparing lessons and materials to contextualize the program with varying degrees of success:

> I have never worked so hard in my life. Each FIE lesson took on average two hours preparation which, on top of other preparation and marking commitments, was an enormous workload.

> This year I have adapted FIE to suit my style of teaching rather than vice versa. I felt last year I had to do weird and wonderful things whereas my own style would have been appropriate anyway.

Problems in Managing Classroom Discussions. Many teachers felt that children's current and previous schooling experiences had not prepared them for real discussion work. They had not gained the confidence to speak in front of other pupils; listening skills were poor and many pupils found it extremely difficult to take turns in contributing. Some pupils simply seemed to lack the oracy skills to express a viewpoint clearly.

> They [pupils] have difficulty in understanding spoken English. Some panic if they have to speak in front of the class, let alone participate in class discussion.

> A major problem area is getting the pupils to discuss things. . . . They all talk together and it makes it difficult to exchange ideas in a group.

> Pupils find great difficulty in discussing in an adult way because the style encouraged in FIE has not been applied in other subjects. They are happy copying diagrams; answering questions from a book, but if it involves thinking and discussing they are not interested.

Moreover, the FIE program and the training courses provided very little help in fostering and managing class or small group discussion work. In a sense, the Rogerian "laid back" style on training courses lulled many teachers into thinking that a "safe, non-threatening" environment meant an informal, unstructured one and in some teachers' eyes, an environment free from traditional forms of discipline. In reality, there was a definite need for clear ground rules, standards, and disciplines, yet without the teacher constantly dominating the agenda and discussion. Many teachers found it very difficult to know when to adopt a neutral, distanced role and when to be assertive and take control in order to regulate behavior and focus pupils' attention on salient issues.

I do feel slightly apprehensive before an FIE lesson because you have to think so fast to keep the pupils together and make the work relevant to their activities. You need to orchestrate [pupil] attention very, very carefully. . . . You need to balance your own resources to the children's resources.

There is too much talking from me. I need to be more focused on children discovering for themselves through discussion. . . . It is partly a lack of confidence on my part.

Some teachers recognized deficiencies in themselves and felt the need for more training and guidance. Others felt that it was too late to change habits of a lifetime in either themselves or the pupils and continued to sacrifice real discussion in favor of a worksheet mentality where insufficient time was allowed to reflect on strategies, issues, and skills and their broad applicability.

I recognize now the powerful need for discussion but I need to know more about questioning skills. I must wait or ask another question to lead them [pupils] towards an answer rather than give answers.

With less able children you have to keep the pace moving for fear of boring or losing the children. You take a big risk if you have gaps of waiting. . . . It's a defensive stance—speed is an important thing and generally wins over waiting. . . . Most pupils have had a four year diet of speed at the expense of discussion. . . .

I think this work is too late with 14- to 16-year-olds. It should be started with much younger pupils before they become disenchanted with school.

Problems in Meeting the Needs of a Disparate Group of Children.   It was typical to find an enormous differentiation in response within a group of so called low-attaining pupils. Some pupils would complete tasks remarkably quickly and accurately, whereas others would need much mediation and guidance. Although clinical applications of FIE might involve selective use of particular instruments to suit pupils with particular problems, the classroom application of the program meant that all pupils went through the same activities irrespective of their individual abilities and needs. In practice, this meant that many pupils found the FIE exercises in the first few modules rather trivial and simple whereas others found them quite challenging. In some instances, teachers compensated for this by encouraging the faster pupils to support those in difficulty. In addition, the need to explain strategies and approaches rather than simply solve the exercises provided sufficient challenge for some pupils. Nevertheless, many teachers would have welcomed a more selective and flexible approach to using the program.

A lot of the activities were banal and boring because with 22–23 low-attaining adolescents you need to have an interesting topic. The danger is that only 3–4 pupils are having a really good discussion whilst the others are not involved at all.

Much of the work was below the level of my low-attaining pupils. For instance, the work on spatial referents was too easy for most pupils making discussions superfluous whilst the ones who had problems did not get a big enough range of activities to significantly change them.

There are difficulties in managing the group at different stages of cooperation and development. In most cases children enjoy PE and will have a go. But it is not always the case in the classroom.

Developing Suitable "Bridging" Materials.   These materials help pupils see the relationship between the skills and processes involved in the abstract activities and other areas of the curriculum. Apart from the time involved in preparing suitable activities, there was the additional problem of creating suitable examples. Many FIE teachers found they were able to bridge to their own subject areas but had insufficient knowledge of other subject disciplines to help pupils make cross-curricular links.

Organization is essential in the Workshop and bridges well into Organization of Dots. Comparisons fits well with identifying different tools. Analyzing and synthesizing processes are important in working out the parts and assembly of CDT work.

With a practical subject you have to work along FIE lines anyway. That sort of approach was part of my needlework training.

I integrated FIE work with examination technique by encouraging children to analyze questions, looking for explicit and implicit information, and deciding between relevant and irrelevant detail.

. . . in Orientation in Space—seeing things from different viewpoints leads onto more moral and social problems . . . character analysis—how do the characters see themselves/react in a new situation, etc.

I don't feel that bridging is as much value as the course seems to suggest. Giving examples to point out the relevance of FIE does not really transfer to other subjects.

Integrating FIE with Other Curriculum Areas

In general, teachers felt that FIE was a subject isolated on the school timetable, which was not integrated with other lessons. Although they tried to help pupils bridge from FIE lessons to other subjects, they felt that relatively few pupils made the kinds of connections they were hoping for. They suggested that more widespread transfer and generalization might have occurred if there had been an explicit attempt within other subjects to help pupils recognize the application of the FIE skills and processes. This, in turn, would have required the active involvement and commitment of teachers from across the full subject range. This was difficult to achieve as training was restricted to the chosen few and the artificial "IQ-like" materials were not easily understood by the uninformed. Although schools did mount awareness days, the absence of ready links into traditional subject matter led to many non-FIE teachers treating the FIE materials with feelings ranging from apathy to disdain, regarding it as yet another "bandwagon initiative":

> Who really has, or makes, the time to find out about something new unless it directly affects them? Very few.

> It all falls down through lack of Inservice training.

> Staff teaching different subjects in school aren't aware of the possibilities of FIE so don't reinforce bridging. Therefore I feel I am working a bit in isolation. Without better links it won't be used to its full potential.

> FIE stands on its own, it is not something that teachers feel they can get much from. A major PR job is still needed with the staff. Secondary schools are very departmentalized and FIE is just another department.

> . . . There are a lot of closed minds. . . . Some of the older teachers are reluctant to explore new ideas. . . . Others are keen so long as it does not disrupt or interfere with their timetable. It is very difficult to explain all of the notions involved in FIE. . . . You have to become involved to understand how it works.

Summary

In summary, although teachers felt that FIE helped pupils to think for themselves and become more reflective, classroom applications of the program revealed major concerns about the cost, format, and content of the materials. These concerns led to difficulties in establishing meaning and relevance and meeting the needs of a disparate group of children. Moreover, particular problems were experienced with transfer and generalization (i.e., helping the pupils to see the relationship between the skills and processes involved in the abstract FIE activities and other areas of the curriculum).

In addition, although teachers were generally positive about their FIE training experiences, classroom realities revealed that they were ill-prepared for the everyday practicalities of teaching the FIE course. In particular, teachers commented on their difficulties in managing small group and class discussion work.

Finally, the structured, sequenced nature of the FIE course meant that it was taught as a "bolt-on" package, which the FIE teachers tried to coordinate with other curriculum areas. Although there were a few non-FIE teachers across the schools who took a particular interest in the work, most regarded the artificial

"IQ-like" activities as irrelevant to their specialist subject areas and FIE remained an isolated subject on the timetable. Training restrictions and limited opportunities for dissemination meant there were few opportunities to challenge traditionalist teacher views.

PERSONALITY CHARACTERISTICS

Did the teachers selected for FIE show a personality profile different to the control teachers at the beginning of the study? Was there any evidence of FIE having an effect on teachers' personalities as well as their attitudes?

The Cattell 16 Personality Factor Questionnaire (16PF) was administered at the beginning of the study on 16 FIE teachers and 13 controls. The test was repeated 2 years later on the same teachers without them having recourse to their previous responses. The interpretation of each of the factors is summarized in Table 5.3 taken from Cattell (1956).

The distribution of the standardized (sten) scores for the pre-and post-test for both the FIE teachers and their controls is shown in Table 5.4. Very few of the mean standardized scores fell outside the average range. The FIE teachers showed an above average E factor score at both pre- and post-test indicating a tendency to be significantly more assertive than the average population of adults. They also showed below average N factor scores at both pre- and post-test indicating a tendency to be rather more forthright and direct in communications than the average adult. As one would expect, both the FIE and control teachers showed elevated B factor scores (at pre- and post-test) indicating superior intelligence. Finally, the control teachers only showed above average I factor scores at pre- and post-test, suggesting greater sensitivity than the average adult population.

Using t-tests, comparisons were made across groups (i.e., comparing control groups with FIE groups at pre-test and then again at post-test) and within groups (changes over time for FIE teachers and again for the control teachers). Dealing initially with differences across groups the control and FIE teachers were closely matched at pre-test with no significant differences emerging. At post-test, however, the following significant differences did emerge:

- The FIE teachers were more assertive than the controls (E factor, $p<0.01$: $t = +3.28$). During the period of the study the control teachers became less assertive and the FIE teachers became more assertive.
- The FIE teachers were significantly more tough-minded and realistic than their controls (I factor, $p<0.01$: $t = -2.85$).
- The FIE teachers were significantly more suspicious (i.e., less likely to take information at face value) than control teachers (L factor $p<0.02$: $t = +2.64$). This significant post-test difference emerged because of a combina-

TABLE 5.3
High and Low Score Interpretations of Each of the Factors
on Cattell's 16PF Taken From Cattell (1956).

Factor	Low Score Description	High Score Description
A	RESERVED, detached, critical, aloof	OUTGOING, warmhearted, easy going . . . participating
B	LESS INTELLIGENT, concrete thinking	MORE INTELLIGENT, abstract-thinking, bright
C	AFFECTED BY FEELINGS, emotionally less stable, easily upset	EMOTIONALLY STABLE, faces reality, calm, mature
E	HUMBLE, mild, accommodating, conforming	ASSERTIVE, aggressive, stubborn, competitive
F	SOBER, prudent, serious, taciturn	HAPPY-GO-LUCKY, impulsively, lively, gay, enthusiastic
G	EXPEDIENT, disregards rules, feels few obligations	CONSCIENTIOUS, persevering, staid, moralistic
H	SHY, restrained, timid, threat-sensitive	VENTURESOME, socially bold, uninhibited, spontaneous
I	TOUGH-MINDED, self-reliant realistic, no nonsense	TENDER-MINDED, clinging, over-protective, sensitive
L	TRUSTING, adaptable, free of jealousy, easy to get along with	SUSPICIOUS, self-opinionated, hard to fool
M	PRACTICAL, careful, conventional regulated by external realities, proper	IMAGINATIVE, wrapped up in inner urgencies, careless of practical matters, bohemian
N	FORTHRIGHT, natural, artless, unpretentious	SHREWD, calculating, worldly, penetrating
O	SELF-ASSURED, confident, serene	APPREHENSIVE, self-reproaching, worrying, troubled
Q1	CONSERVATIVE, respecting established ideas, tolerant of traditional difficulties	EXPERIMENTING, liberal, analytical, free thinking
Q2	GROUP-DEPENDENT, A "joiner" and sound follower	SELF-SUFFICIENT, prefers own decisions, resourceful
Q3	UNDISCIPLINED SELF CONFLICT follows own urges, careless of protocol	CONTROLLED, socially precise, following self-image
Q4	RELAXED, tranquil, unfrustrated	TENSE, frustrated, driven, overwrought

TABLE 5.4
**Mean Sten Scores on Cattell's 16PF for FIE Teachers and Control
Group Teachers at Pre-Test and Again at Post-Test**

16PF Items	FIE Group (N=16)		Control Group (N=13)	
	Pre-Test	Post-Test	Pre-Test	Post-Test
A	5.87	5.06	5.69	5.23
B	8.50*	8.75*	8.90*	8.62*
C	5.00	5.50	6.20	5.38
E	7.44*	7.56*	6.08	5.23
F	6.06	6.06	5.46	5.69
G	5.25	5.81	5.69	5.38
H	6.25	6.25	5.92	5.69
I	5.63	4.44	6.85*	6.69*
L	5.44	5.75	4.92	3.85*
M	6.69	7.19	6.54	6.62
N	3.94*	4.00*	4.23	4.46
O	5.06	5.19	4.92	4.85
Q1	5.69	5.94	4.85	4.54
Q2	5.31	5.63	4.46	5.23
Q3	5.50	5.00	5.69	5.46
Q4	5.69	5.75	5.31	5.92

NE Sten scores range from 1–10; scores 4.5–6.4 are within the average range.
* starred items fall outside the average range.

tion of an increase in the L factor scores for the FIE teachers over time, compared with a decrease in the L factor scores over time for the control teachers.

In terms of within group comparisons there was only one significant change over time: The FIE teachers became significantly more tough minded, realistic and self-reliant as reflected by a decrease in the mean I factor score ($p<0.01$; t = -3.70). No other significant changes over time were noted for either the FIE or the control group teachers.

These findings were explored informally with the FIE teachers. The majority confirmed that the shifts on their test profiles reflected genuine changes in their behavior, largely associated with their higher public profile within the school and LEA as a result of becoming involved with the FIE project. They commented on their increased recognition in school and the peculiar feeling of suddenly finding themselves in the role of expert having to give talks to groups of high status educationalists:

I am no longer a forgotten person in the school. I feel in the forefront of an initiative. When HMI come in and comment favorably, the head teacher comes over and makes you feel good. I had a visitor last week. Three years ago I would have been paralytic with fear . . . I was slightly apprehensive but no more than that.

When I talked about FIE to the secondary heads I felt like an expert for a change which has made me feel more confident in myself.

All of the teachers were subjected to regular classroom visits by HMI, Psychologists, Advisers, and LEA officials. Many visitors were curious about the program but skeptical about its potential to change pupils. Indeed, skepticism was not confined merely to the visitors but was also widespread throughout the schools among those staff not directly involved in the FIE program. Thus, FIE teachers were not only given extra recognition and attention but also were constantly put in a position of needing to justify their work. In these circumstances, it is perhaps not surprising that many teachers became more assertive, self-reliant, and suspicious.

Summary and Conclusions

In summary the IE and control teachers were generally well-matched in terms of personality profiles on Cattell's 16PF. There was no evidence to suggest that those teachers selected for the project showed an atypical personality profile. T-test analyses across and within groups provided modest evidence to suggest that FIE teachers became:

- more assertive
- more tough-minded, self-reliant, and realistic
- more suspicious and self-opinionated.

These changes may not have been a function of the FIE program alone but also an outcome of being involved in a high profile curriculum innovation that was being closely monitored and evaluated.

ATTITUDES TOWARD TEACHING

Many features of Instrumental Enrichment work challenged teachers' traditional views. The program involves an optimistic view of cognitive development. Feuerstein, like Vygotsky, views intellectual development as an outcome of education rather than a necessary prerequisite for it. In other words, the teacher does not merely have a passive role offering appropriate experiences as the child's development unfolds, but rather has an active transformational role ensuring that the child's world is organized and mediated in a way that promotes and enhances intellectual development. This philosophy obligates teachers to reflect on their own attitudes and beliefs. So, in comparison to the controls, did the FIE teachers change their attitudes toward teaching?

This question was investigated using the "Myself as a Teacher" Questionnaire as shown in Table 5.5. The scale was similar in form to the Attitudes Toward FIE Questionnaire. As before, teachers were required to record their feelings by ticking one of seven positions between two extreme statements for each of the items listed (e.g., "As a teacher I do not gain much satisfaction from my work" vs. "Gain great satisfaction from my work"). As before, the proximity of each tick to one or other of the statements was taken to indicate the frequency with which that attitude was held to apply. Each item scored between 1 and 7, with a high score indicating that the right statement more often applied and a low score that the left statement more often applied. A score of 4 was regarded as a neutral response. The statements illustrated on the right side of each item generally reflected more positive attitudes in tune with the philosophy of the FIE project. It should be noted that when the scales were administered to the teachers the positions of the statements for each item were randomized to avoid a response stereotype (i.e., not all the positive statements were located on one side of the schedule). Scores for each item were allocated by the evaluator and not by the teachers themselves.

As the Myself as a Teacher Scale was not factor analyzed, each item was treated independently (i.e., no attempt was made to summate the scores on the scale). Initially, group mean scores were calculated for each item at pre- and post-test for the FIE teachers (N=17), the TVEI teachers (N=5), and the non-FIE teachers (N=8). As the mean scores on each item of the Myself as a Teacher Scale at pre-test and post-test for the TVEI controls and non-FIE controls revealed no significant differences on the Mann-Whitney test, the two samples were combined to form one control group for all further analyses on this schedule. The results are summarized in Table 5.6.

A superficial glance at the group mean scores for the FIE and controls at pre-test suggests that both groups of teachers were initially neutral or marginally in favor of the statements shown on the right side of each item. There was only one exception to this (item 5), which suggested that teachers were, in general, not very optimistic about their ability to influence pupils' lives outside their lessons.

Using the Mann-Whitney and Wilcoxon rank tests comparisons were made across groups (i.e., comparing IE with controls at pre-test and then again at post-test) and within groups (looking for changes over time within the FIE group and again within the control group).

Dealing initially with differences across groups, the control and FIE teachers were closely matched at pre-test with only 1 significant difference emerging out of 14 (item 8). This suggested that the control teachers were more committed to

TABLE 5.5
The Attitudes Toward Myself as a Teacher Scale Developed
for the FIE Study

MYSELF AS A TEACHER

School _____ Teacher _____

Age groups taught _____ Subject specialization _____

INSTRUCTIONS: The following pairs of statements provide the opportunity to record *your* feelings about your role as a teacher. Each pair of statements is separated by seven positions. In each case tick the appropriate position according to the following guide: The closer you tick to the left statement the more often this applies, the nearer you tick to the right statement the more often that applies.

As a teacher I . . .

1. Do not gain much   — — — — — — —   Gain great satisfaction
    satisfaction from my work.   from my work.

2. Have doubts about my   — — — — — — —   Am confident in my ability.
    ability.

3. Prefer a formal approach — — — — — — —   Prefer an informal
    to pupils.   approach to pupils.

4. Do not feel the need for les- — — — — — — — Feel the need to prepare les-
    son preparation.   sons thoroughly.

5. Do not feel that I have   — — — — — — —   Feel that I have an impor-
    much influence on pupils'   tant influence on pupils'
    lives outside my lessons.   lives outside my lessons.

6. Prefer a very directive ap- — — — — — — —   Prefer a more open-ended
    proach to teaching.   approach to teaching.

7. See the content of lessons — — — — — — —   See the process of teacher-
    as most important.   pupil interaction as most
                                                important.

8. Have doubts about my   — — — — — — —   Feel a strong sense of
    level of commitment to   commitment to teaching.
    teaching.

9. Believe in keeping a dis- — — — — — — —   Try to develop a close
    tance between myself and   personal relationship with
    pupils.   pupils.

10. Prefer to be directive in my — — — — — — — Take a less directive ap-
    teaching.   proach to pupil learning.

11. Do not bother much about — — — — — — —   Keep strict control of my
    discipline.   classes.

12. Do not have much to learn. — — — — — — —   Still have a lot to learn.

13. Often find it difficult to — — — — — — —   Have no difficulty in
    arouse pupils' interest.   arousing pupils' interest.

14. Have doubts about the   — — — — — — —   Feel that I make a very
    value of my contribution to   valuable contribution to
    teaching.   teaching.

TABLE 5.6
The Mean Scores for the FIE and Control Teachers on Each Item
From the "Myself as a Teacher" Rating Scale Both at the Beginning
and End of the Study.

Myself as a Teacher	FIE (N = 17) vs. Controls (N = 8)			
	Pre-Test Means		Post-Test Means	
	FIE	Control	FIE	Control
1	5.24	5.77	6.06	5.46
2	5.00	5.23	5.65	4.92
3	4.00	4.77	4.88	4.85
4	4.76	5.08	5.29	5.08
5	3.65	4.00	3.76	3.92
6	4.94	4.54	5.12	4.62
7	4.59	4.46	5.00	5.31
8	4.35	5.69	5.12	5.08
9	4.82	5.31	4.65	4.85
10	4.12	4.23	4.94	4.15
11	4.76	4.92	5.76	5.08
12	5.82	5.92	6.18	5.77
13	4.35	4.62	5.00	4.15
14	4.12	4.62	5.00	4.00

teaching at the start of the study than the FIE teachers. The difference between the groups, however, was only significant at the 5% level (Mann-Whitney score 55.5; $p<0.05$).

At post-test, two significant differences emerged on items 2 and 14 (but again, only at the 5% level) suggesting that FIE teachers at the end of the study were: (a) more confident in their teaching ability (item 2, Mann-Whitney Score 69.5; $p<0.05$) and (b) more optimistic about their ability to make a valuable contribution to teaching (item 14, Mann-Whitney Score 69.5; $p<0.05$).

Exploring differences within groups using the Wilcoxon rank test there were significant, positive attitudinal shifts among the FIE teachers on seven items suggesting that over the 2-year period of the study the FIE teachers felt they:

- gained greater satisfaction from their work (item 1, N=11, Wilcoxon rank score = +7; $p<0.01$)
- became more confident about their teaching ability (item 2, N=14, Wilcoxon rank score = +20.5; $p<0.025$)
- developed a more informal approach to pupils (item 3, N=10, Wilcoxon rank score = +5; $p<0.01$)
- became more committed to teaching (item 8, N=9, Wilcoxon rank score = +5; $p<0.025$)

- became less directive in their approach to pupil learning (item 10, N=10, Wilcoxon rank score = +6; p<0.025)
- found it easier to arouse pupil interest (item 13, N=14, Wilcoxon rank score = +26; p<0.05)
- made a more valuable contribution toward teaching (item 14, N=12, Wilcoxon rank score = +15.5; p<0.05).

In view of the number of comparisons made both across and within groups, some of the findings at the 5% significance level could be spurious. In addition, items 3 and 10 are probably assessing the same issue. Nevertheless,the general pattern of the attitudinal changes over time among the FIE teachers was encouraging and was not matched by similar patterns and trends in the control teachers. Indeed, in contrast there was one significant negative trend in the control group, suggesting that the non-FIE teachers became less committed to teaching during the period of the study (item 8, N=8, Wilcox rank score = −4; p<0.025). The within-group trends over time are diagrammatically represented in Table 5.7.

Summary and Conclusions

The Myself as a Teacher Questionnaire used with both FIE and control teachers at the beginning and end of the study produced substantial evidence to suggest that FIE teachers became more positive and optimistic about their role as teachers. During the course of the study, they reported that they: became more committed to teaching; gained increased satisfaction from their work; became more confident in their teaching ability; felt they made a more valuable contribution toward teaching; became more informal and less directive in their approach to pupils and found it easier to arouse pupil interest. These findings were not duplicated in the control group, even though many of the control teachers were involved in another high profile, educational initiative (TVEI).

ATTITUDES TOWARD LOW-ACHIEVING ADOLESCENTS

This next section explores teachers attitudes further, and in particular considers their perspectives on low-achieving adolescents. A prerequisite to becoming an effective FIE teacher involves adopting an optimistic stance on the enormous plasticity of the human intellect and greater personal responsibility for pupil cognitive development. Thus, in comparison to the controls, did the FIE teachers change their attitudes toward low-achieving adolescents? This question was investigated using the "Characteristics of Less Academic Pupils" Questionnaire as shown in Table 5.8.

TABLE 5.7
Diagrammatically Illustrating the Direction of Significant Attitudinal Changes Over 2 Years Among FIE and Control Teachers on "Myself as a Teacher" Schedule.

As a teacher I . . .

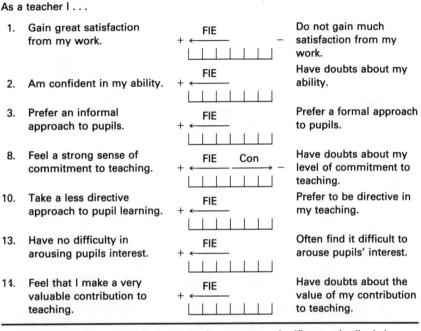

1. Gain great satisfaction from my work. — Do not gain much satisfaction from my work.

2. Am confident in my ability. — Have doubts about my ability.

3. Prefer an informal approach to pupils. — Prefer a formal approach to pupils.

8. Feel a strong sense of commitment to teaching. — Have doubts about my level of commitment to teaching.

10. Take a less directive approach to pupil learning. — Prefer to be directive in my teaching.

13. Have no difficulty in arousing pupils interest. — Often find it difficult to arouse pupils' interest.

14. Feel that I make a very valuable contribution to teaching. — Have doubts about the value of my contribution to teaching.

NB: For questions 4, 5, 6, 7, 9, 11, 12, there were no significant attitudinal changes in the teachers from either the FIE or control groups.

The scale was similar in form to the two attitudinal scales already mentioned in this chapter (Tables 5.5 and 5.7). The same principles of completion, scoring, and interpretation applied. As before, the statements illustrated on the right side of each item generally reflected more positive attitudes in tune with the philosophy of the FIE project. As on previous occasions, the positions of the statements for each item were randomized during administration to avoid a response stereotype.

In common with the two earlier attitudinal scales this present scale was not factor analyzed and so once again, each item was treated independently. Group mean scores were calculated at pre- and post-test separately for the FIE teachers (N=17) and the control teachers (N=13). The summarized mean scores for each item on the Characteristics of Less Academic Pupils Questionnaire are recorded in Table 5.9 for both FIE and control groups at the beginning and end of the study. At the beginning of the study both the FIE and control teachers recorded neutral responses on each item with the exception of marginally positive responses on items 6 and 7 and more negative responses on items 8, 9, and 13. These results

TABLE 5.8
**The Attitudes Toward the "Characteristics of Less
Academic Pupils'" Scale**

THE CHARACTERISTICS OF LESS ACADEMIC PUPILS

School _____ Teacher _____

Age groups taught _____ Subject specialization _____

Number of years in teaching _____

INSTRUCTIONS: The following pairs of statements provide the opportunity to record your feelings about less academic pupils. Each pair of statements is separated by seven positions. In each case tick the appropriate position according to the following guide: The closer you tick to the left statement the more often this applies, the nearer you tick to the right statement the more often that applies.

Less academic pupils . . .

1. Are difficult to teach.   — — — — — — Are easy to teach.

2. Usually lack intellectual ability.   — — — — — — Often have good (but un-realized) intellectual ability.

3. Tend not to be interested in learning.   — — — — — — Desperately want to learn.

4. Are not good at thinking for themselves.   — — — — — — Are very capable of thinking for themselves.

5. Are not much of a pleasure to be with.   — — — — — — Are a pleasure to be with.

6. Have mainly themselves to blame for their lack of success.   — — — — — — Owe their lack of success to circumstances beyond their control.

7. Have nothing to teach me.   — — — — — — Have something to teach me.

8. Show marked behavior problems.   — — — — — — Do not show behavior problems.

9. Cannot generalize what they have learned.   — — — — — — Are perfectly capable of generalizing what they have learned.

10. Provide little satisfaction to a teacher.   — — — — — — Provide great satisfaction to a teacher.

11. Have very limited capabilities.   — — — — — — Are far more capable than teachers realized.

12. Gain a limited amount from my lessons.   — — — — — — Gain a great deal from my lessons.

13. Tend to get too bored very quickly.   — — — — — — Can maintain high levels of interest for long periods.

14. Seem incapable of participating in classroom discussions.   — — — — — — Are very capable of good classroom discussions.

TABLE 5.9
Attitudinal Ratings of FIE and Control Teachers on the "Characteristics of Less Academic Pupils" Questionnaire at Pre-test and Post-test.

| Characteristics of Less Academic Pupils | FIE (N = 17) vs. Controls (N = 13) | | | |
| | Pre-Test Means | | Post-Test Means | |
	FIE	Control	FIE	Control
1	3.47	3.38	3.53	2.85
2	4.10	4.62	5.10	3.54
3	3.47	4.31	4.00	3.92
4	3.24	4.00	4.41	3.85
5	4.88	5.00	4.59	4.77
6	5.18	5.62	5.35	5.31
7	5.24	5.85	5.35	5.85
8	2.29	2.92	2.65	2.85
9	2.41	3.00	3.88	3.54
10	4.53	5.77	4.88	5.31
11	4.59	5.00	5.71	5.00
12	4.06	3.92	4.95	3.62
13	2.94	2.54	3.94	2.46
14	3.65	4.00	4.71	4.77

suggested that at the beginning of the study most teachers regarded low-attaining pupils as owing their lack of success to circumstances beyond their control and as having something to teach them. On the other hand they also viewed low-attaining pupils as: (a) presenting behavior problems, (b) finding difficulty in maintaining high levels of interest for long periods, and (c) being unable to generalize what they had learned in particular lessons.

Using the Mann-Whitney and Wilcoxon Rank tests, comparisons were made across groups (comparing FIE with controls at pre- and then again at post-test) and within groups (looking for changes over time within the FIE group and again within the control group).

Dealing initially with differences across groups, the control and FIE groups were extremely well-matched at pre-test with no significant differences emerging on any of the items. At post-test however, four significant differences emerged on items 2, 11, 12, and 13. This indicated that the FIE teachers at the end of the study were significantly more optimistic about low attainers than the control teachers with respect to the pupils:

- having good but unrealized intellectual ability (item 2, Mann-Whitney Score 36; $p < 0.005$)

- being far more capable than teachers realized (item 11, Mann-Whitney score 66.5; $p < 0.05$)

- gaining a great deal from their lessons, (item 12, Mann-Whitney Score 61; $p<0.025$)
- being able to maintain high levels of interest for long periods (item 13, Mann-Whitney Score 45.5; $p<0.005$).

Exploring differences within groups using the Wilcoxon Sign Rank test a number of significant changes over time were recorded for both the FIE and control teachers. In general, the FIE teachers became more positive about the potential of low-attaining pupils, whereas over the same period the control teachers became more negative. In particular, the FIE teachers became more optimistic about low-attaining pupils:

- having good but unrealized intellectual ability (item 2, $N = 16$; Wilcoxon Sign Rank score $= +24.5$; $p<0.025$)
- being very capable of thinking for themselves (item 4, $N = 13$; Wilcoxon Sign Rank score $= +14$; $p<0.025$)
- being perfectly capable of generalizing what they have learned (item 9, $N = 14$; Wilcoxon Sign Rank score $= +7$; $p<0.005$)
- being far more capable than most teachers realize (item 11, $N = 11$; Wilcoxon Sign Rank score $= +3$; $p<0.005$)
- being able to maintain high levels of interest for long periods (item 13, $N = 12$; Wilcoxon Sign Rank score $= +13$; $p<0.025$)
- being very capable of holding good classroom discussions (item 14, $N = 16$; Wilcoxon Sign Rank score $= +27.5$; $p<0.025$).

In contrast, the control teachers showed only two statistically significant effects and these both indicated negative trends showing an increased feeling that low attainers:

- usually lack intellectual ability (item 2, $N = 11$; Wilcoxon Sign Rank score $= -7$; $p<0.01$)
- provide little satisfaction for the teacher (item 10, $N = 11$; Wilcoxon Sign Rank score $= -10,5$; $p<0.025$).

These changes over time are diagrammatically represented in Table 5.10. Although the individual items on the attitudinal scale are probably not independent of one another, the positive attitudinal shifts for the FIE teachers are encouraging. The fact that they were not duplicated by the control teachers does suggest that the changes are the result of participating in the FIE project.

TABLE 5.10
Diagrammatically Illustrating the Direction of Significant Attitudinal Changes Over 2 Years Amongst FIE and Control Teachers on "The Characteristics of Less Academic Pupils'" Schedule.

Less academic pupils . . .

2. Often have good (but unrealized) intellectual ability.	+ FIE ← → Con −	Usually lack intellectual ability.
4. Are very capable of thinking for themselves.	+ FIE ←	Are not good at thinking for themselves.
9. Are perfectly capable of generalizing what they have learned.	+ FIE ←	Cannot generalize what they have learned.
10. Provide great satisfaction to a teacher.	+ Con → −	Provide little satisfaction to a teacher.
11. Are far more capable than most teachers realize.	+ FIE ←	Have very limited capabilities.
13. Can maintain high levels of interest for long periods.	+ FIE ←	Tend to get too bored very quickly.
14. Are very capable of good classroom discussions.	+ FIE ←	Seem incapable of participating in classroom discussions.

NB: For questions 1, 3, 5, 6, 7, 8, 12, there were no significant changes in teacher attitudes in either FIE or control groups.

Summary and Conclusions

Teacher replies to the "Attitudes Toward Less Academic Pupils" Questionnaire at the beginning and end of the study suggest that, over the period of the study, FIE teachers became more optimistic about the potential for change among low-achieving adolescents. In particular, they came to believe that the majority of their low attainers: showed unrealized intellectual ability; were far more capable than most teachers realized; were able to maintain high levels of interest for long periods; were capable of holding good classroom discussions; and were capable of generalizing what they had learned. They also felt that low achievers gained a great deal from their FIE lessons. None of these positive attitudinal shifts were duplicated among the control teachers. Indeed, the control teachers became more negative about low achievers, feeling that they generally lacked intellectual ability and provided little satisfaction for the teacher.

CHANGES IN TEACHER BEHAVIOR

So far, this chapter has reported some encouraging evidence of attitudinal change among the FIE teachers toward themselves as teachers and also toward low-achieving adolescents. Were these attitudinal changes reflected in behavioral changes? It was not within the scope of this study to quantify, monitor, and measure behavioral change in teachers. However, some tentative comments can be made about this topic, based on observations and informal interviews with FIE teachers and the senior management in the four project schools.

Undoubtedly, there were some FIE teachers who appeared to be transformed during the period of the project. Of the eight teachers trained in the first year, six have subsequently made significant career progress. Four have gained heads of department in their own specialist areas and four have been seconded for periods to work on the Somerset Thinking Skills Course. Head teachers commented on the increased confidence and assertiveness of many of the project teachers. Over and above these general behavioral changes, which were also reflected in slight shifts on the Cattell 16PF profiles, many teachers felt that they had changed their classroom behavior as a result of becoming involved in FIE. Their comments suggested that they had become:

- more aware of the kinds of skills and strategies being called for in their own subject areas
- more aware of the dangers of making assumptions about pupils' abilities
- more sensitive to pupil involvement and participation as a prerequisite to developing understanding.

In general, teachers reported that they had become more interested in how children were learning and the kinds of barriers that could undermine understanding. They began to feel more responsible for children's progress and claimed to take more care in analyzing the skills and processes required by pupils to enable them to benefit from particular lesson topics. For instance, Geography teachers often commented that they had previously made too many assumptions about children's competences.

> In Geography lessons I'm more conscious of pupils gathering information together before starting and checking back to see that the work is . . . appropriate. . . . Previously, I expected this (pupil understanding) to be automatic. . . . In map drawing with a first year group, we talk about maps; what needs to go into a map; what is the purpose of a map etc. . . . then we criticize existing maps before designing our own. . . .

English teachers became more conscious of the need to equip children with a better understanding of the structure of different forms of writing rather than concentrating almost exclusively on more affective and creative objectives. Many had come to feel that some pupils' creativity was being restricted by a limited repertoire of cognitive resources.

> I like making things explicit that are often left at an implicit level. How do you create suspense in a story? We analyze that. A story is not a story until the reader is involved, how do you go about enhancing that?

> In my English lessons, I am much more aware of structure . . . even to talking about the structure of story. Instead of relying on "inspiration" after chucking ideas about I now work a little more on craft/structure. This fits in well with drafting work from the first, second, and third drafts. If you are going to improve your work you have to have some notion of how to go about it. Children who write well seem to have an intuitive/instinctive understanding of story structure . . . but what of the many who do not have that. . . . Some say that structure can stifle creativity. On the other hand 99% of us will not be authors, but there is no reason why most of us cannot write competently.

Similar observations were made by Geography teachers who felt they had been making unrealistic assumptions about children's conceptual development. There was a general appreciation that many children simply did not understand north, south, east, and west as a universal reference system. Moreover, many of the younger children in the groups did not even understand left, right, front, and back as a relative reference system:

> Many children just don't understand the idea that as you change your own orientation north, south, east, and west remain constant. This situation is compounded in map work because the convention normally dictates that north is at the top of the map which means that pupils have to mentally orientate the map so that map north matches true north and then orientate themselves with respect to where they want to move on the map. I now start at a much lower level and build up the elements of the concepts, piece by piece.

Teachers across a range of curriculum areas reflected that in the past their transmissive teaching styles had minimized pupil involvement and prevented many from developing a genuine understanding of the principles and ideas of the lesson. Most teachers had come to appreciate the importance of pupils having some say in the agenda of the lesson and of checking what pupils had gained at the end of the lesson:

> I think I listen more to the children now.

> I used to rely on explicit instructions. Now I make much stronger use of implicit instructions as a way of setting them [pupils] thinking more. . . . I am far less interested in teaching science as opposed to teaching anything that the pupils find

useful. For example, I am doing magnetism. . . . This had led to exploring pupil understanding of direction and spatial relationships. This seems more important than magnetism per se.

Nowadays I try not to lead the children to the answer I have in my mind. I make less use of closed questioning. . . . I place an increased emphasis on oracy and less emphasis on my old style of outlining the aims, apparatus, method, results, and conclusion for each experiment.

Now I always ask what they [pupils] have learned from the lesson. I should have asked that before but didn't. . . .

Even teachers who felt that they were already highly skilled in interactive teaching styles remarked on their increased awareness of the need for more structure and organization in class and small group discussion work.

I used to pride myself on my ability to promote and manage lively class discussions. In retrospect, these were often no more than heated exchanges of prejudiced positions. Pupils didn't listen to the different points of view or even consider coming to some shared agreement.

Although many teachers were able to supply examples of ways in which they had changed their teaching style, they often commented that extensive changes had been minimized by:

1. A lack of time to prepare adequately because of too many competing management and teaching demands.
2. The pressure of covering the content of particular curriculum areas.
3. A feeling of hopelessness about not being able to make sufficient impact because of working in isolation:

    Your awareness of the child's ability to change, moves more rapidly than your own ability to do something about it. Once you realize that a child isn't unintelligent but rather illiterate and innumerate you think—my God, what can I do about it?—you may not be able to do very much, and then disillusionment sets it.

In addition, teachers who had only just joined the profession were less willing to embrace the philosophy and issues underlying FIE, being more concerned about becoming fluent in their own specialist subject area and confident in their dealings with pupils and staff.

Summary and Conclusions

Anecdotal evidence suggests that teachers involved in the FIE program benefited personally from the experience to the extent that they began to alter the way they taught their own specialist subject area. In particular, they became more sensitive to potential pupil deficiencies likely to prevent understanding and learning and more conscious of the need to take a more structured, but more interactive, approach to their teaching. Most teachers indicated that teaching style changes were nevertheless limited by insufficient time created by competing management and curriculum content demands. In general, teacher comments suggested that experienced teachers benefited more from the FIE program than teachers new to the profession.

CONCLUSIONS

Above all else, Instrumental Enrichment has prompted teachers to think about how pupils think and learn. There is no doubt that the vast majority of teachers were enormously stimulated by the training courses that prompted them to examine their role as mediators of childrens' intellectual development.

Nevertheless, although teachers were enthused by the underlying philosophy of the FIE program and the implications for their own teaching, they expressed consistent and widespread concern about the cost, format, and content of the FIE materials. Although they and some of the pupils enjoyed the initial novelty of the program, the abstract "IQ-like" nature of the materials created problems in establishing the meaning and relevance of the program. Furthermore, most pupils and teachers experienced problems with the key area of transfer and generalization. Although many pupils became good at certain abstract tasks and could even begin to articulate the cognitive skills involved, they were typically unable to relate them to other curriculum areas in everyday life. Very often, the teachers were only one step ahead of the pupils. In most cases, they were insufficiently familiar with the program and its possibilities to guide pupils toward appropriate bridging activities. In other words, both the pupils and the teachers became "stuck in the dots and triangles."

Feuerstein's insistence that the FIE course should be mediated to the pupils in a particular set sequence (irrespective of the varying abilities of the pupils) for so many hours each week meant that it was timetabled and taught as a "bolt-on" package. Given the contextually bare and abstract nature of the materials, the uninformed non-FIE teachers saw little point or relevance in the activities. Consequently, in most schools it was very difficult to establish comprehensive, cross-curricular links. Despite the expressed shortcomings in the materials, FIE teachers nevertheless consistently indicated that the course had the potential to reduce the impulsivity of their pupils by making them more aware of problem-solving processes and the need to take time to stop and think. The teachers even suggested that the FIE course had applications for their own (teachers) personal lives, helping them to become more systematic in their approach to their own everyday problems.

The study did reveal substantial evidence to suggest that teachers attitudes and behavior had changed during the period of the study. In particular, psychometric testing using Cattell's 16PF substantiated informal observations by senior management that FIE teachers had become more assertive, confident, and self-reliant. The 16PF also indicated that FIE teachers had become more suspicious and difficult to fool. FIE teachers implied that these personality changes were related to their involvement in a high-profile education initiative, rather than to the FIE course per se. Nevertheless, similar personality trends were not noted in the control teachers even though the majority of these teachers were involved in another education initiative (TVEI).

Undoubtedly, the most beneficial effects of the FIE program related to the development of more positive attitudes in teachers in terms of their professional role and their perspectives on low-achieving adolescents. Substantial evidence was presented to demonstrate that FIE teachers during the period of the project became more satisfied, confident, commited, and valued in their work. In addition, they came to believe that most low attainers were mislabled, being far more capable than most teachers realized in terms of their: intellectual capabilities; concentration skills; discussion skills; and ability to generalize. None of these changes were noted among the control teachers who became more negative about low achievers during the period of the study.

Some anecdotal evidence was presented to suggest that these positive attitudinal changes among FIE teachers translated into changes in teaching style, not only in FIE lessons, but also in mainstream specialist areas. Thus, FIE teachers stated that they had become more informal and less transmissive in their approach to pupils while at the same time, realizing the need to orchestrate and organize lessons to compensate for potential barriers to learning and understanding. In general, the FIE teachers became far more analytic in their work but admitted that changes in teaching style were limited by time restrictions created by competing management and curriculum content demands. Many teachers became despondent about the plight of low achievers, being aware of their potential for development, but unable to facilitate significant changes because of limited time and resources.

Chapter 6

Review and Discussion of the Main Findings

This comprehensive study has presented a mass of observations and statistics concerning the effects of Instrumental Enrichment on teachers and mainstream low-achieving adolescents. So many detailed issues have been explored, that it may be difficult for the reader to digest all of the relevant information and identify common threads and implications. Accordingly, this chapter will review and discuss the overall findings, which can be best organized within Stufflebeam's CIPP model, outlined in Chapter 3.

THE CONTEXT

The evaluation of Instrumental Enrichment was part of a major government initiative (the Low Attaining Pupil Project—LAPP) which was set up by Lord Keith Joseph in 1982 as a means of exploring ways of providing a more effective education for those pupils, in their final 2 years of school, who were not benefiting from the traditional system of public examinations. Thus from the outset the target group of 14- to 16-year-old low-achieving mainstream adolescents was determined by the Department of Education and Science. As a consequence, the project findings cannot be generalized to younger pupils or those in special schools.

LAPP was introduced to Somerset as a "top downwards initiative." The funding was organized centrally and controlled throughout by administrative officers and advisers. The location of the project (i.e., four mainstream secondary schools in a large industrial town in a rural setting) was also centrally determined. In other words LAPP and the Instrumental Enrichment Program did not arise out of a 'grass roots' need or commitment. This meant that the project outcomes were unlikely to be artifacts of the enthusiasm and commitment of an atypical group of schools and teachers.

The "top downwards" aspect of the project did bring with it some problems. Schools were generally ill-prepared for the project with the funding arriving late. As a consequence, implementation was hastily arranged rather than carefully planned. During the first year of the project, pupils were in some cases withdrawn from chosen options to pursue a course referred to variously as "extra English" or thinking skills.

From the outset, the FIE program appeared to be cloaked in psychological mystique. Feuerstein emphasizes the universality of mediation as the basis of cultural transmission. He points to the way in which parents act as natural mediators using all kinds of everyday objects, events, and experiences to extend and transform the child's understanding of the world. Nevertheless, while acknowledging this infinite variety of mediation vehicles, Feuerstein promotes the FIE program as a uniquely useful mediation tool and vigorously protects it against any form of alteration, adaptation, and development. For instance:

- the FIE materials were only available to those selected for training
- inspection copies of the materials were not available beforehand
- the manner in which the program should be delivered, its sequence, and even the minimal number of hours necessary for positive effects are prescribed.

The "black box" nature of the FIE materials and training meant that teachers in the project schools knew little about the program at the beginning of the study. Moreover, the dissemination of the FIE program and teaching philosophy to a wider audience was hampered by:

- training restrictions (trained FIE teachers were not allowed to train others, without formal trainer qualifications)
- the lack of face validity in the materials (i.e., they look more like psychological tests than typical teaching materials).

To some extent these difficulties were mitigated by beginning the formal evaluation of Instrumental Enrichment at the start of the second year of the LAP Project. At this stage, most of the project teachers were becoming more familiar with the work, and timetabling arrangements were in general more satisfactory. However, in the two schools operating, clearly defined streaming arrangements (where FIE was timetabled as a core subject) "think skills" became known by some pupils as "thick skills." In the two remaining schools, timetabling was more flexible; FIE was offered as a guided option and the project pupils had a less definable identity. Negative labeling effects associated with the FIE program were less obvious in these schools.

Finally, it should be mentioned that the project was conducted against a background of industrial action which limited opportunities for planning and discussing ways of establishing cross-curricular links and a better school environment for the project.

THE INPUT

Teachers

The status and experience of the teachers selected for the project was also a further factor contributing to difficulties in establishing cross-curricular links and adequate dissemination of the FIE philosophy. Although the FIE teachers were mainly experienced staff drawn from a wide range of subject disciplines, the majority were only scale 1 or scale 2 teachers who were unable to significantly influence senior management in the schools.

Instrumental Enrichment involves a series of psychometrically based modules, loosely linked to an eclectic web of psychological models and conceptual frameworks. Perhaps not surprisingly, the material is more the "stock in trade" of clinical and educational psychologists than teachers. In view of these issues, one could criticize the level of training and support for the teachers as being insufficient. Nevertheless, in comparison to most other educational initiatives, teacher training was extensive: for example, all FIE teachers received at least 2 weeks training over a 2-year period and quite a number of FIE teachers received 3 and 4 weeks training.

Although the level of support within and between the schools was variable during the project, FIE teachers had access to:

- monthly discussion groups (for all FIE teachers) within their schools.
- Inservice Training days with their Oxfordshire colleagues (for the most experienced FIE teachers the majority of whom were directly involved with the project pupils).

In addition, the four project schools were well-funded with:

- extra resources for equipment and materials
- scale points for teachers in charge of FIE
- extra staffing to enable smaller teaching groups.

In summary, although Instrumental Enrichment was probably not evaluated under optimal conditions, the context was certainly very favorable. Indeed, without special funding, it would be difficult for other schools to match the training and resourcing levels possible within the project.

Beyond these issues, it was felt important to make some assessment of teacher effectiveness in terms of Feuerstein's mediation framework so that pupil outcomes could be considered in relation to mediation characteristics of the teacher. A comprehensive classroom observation schedule was developed as an aid memoir to help systematize and record aspects of teacher classroom behavior. This was eventually recoded and reorganized in terms of Feuerstein's parameters for mediation with teachers' effectiveness being judged in terms of Feuerstein's three universal mediation characteristics (intentionality/reciprocity, meaning, and transcendence).

Pupils

The pupils selected for the program were 14-year-old, low-achieving adolescents. Although the selection procedures were slightly different in each of the four project schools, the ability and attainment characteristics of the pupils as assessed by a range of standardized tests (see chap. 4) were remarkably similar across and within the schools. In general, the project pupils showed:

- a normal distribution of ability on certain spatial reasoning and visual memory tasks. Indeed, there were some so-called low attaining pupils with quite remarkable abilities in these areas;
- below average verbal reasoning and vocabulary skills;
- depressed reading and maths attainments;
- poor work study skills.

A critical incident observation schedule (Teacher Observation Schedule— Table 4.13) was designed to record evidence of pupil behavioral change over the period of the study. The initial screening of all project pupils (at the beginning of the study) revealed that within FIE lessons most pupils showed problems in:

- a failure to use precise problem-solving vocabulary;
- an inability to make links across different curriculum areas;
- a failure to make spontaneous use of the dictionary to check the meanings of unknown words.

Outside the FIE lessons, the same pupils demonstrated these and many other behavioral difficulties likely to hinder their ability to learn (see chap. 4).

In the four project schools:

- the FIE program was taught as a separate subject;
- most pupils were offered approximately 2 hours FIE teaching per week;
- the majority were Easter leavers so that they received only five terms of FIE teaching;
- the actual number of hours of FIE teaching each pupil received was quite variable bearing in mind such factors as common interruptions to the timetable (work experience, sports days, speech days, and so on) as well as pupil and teacher absenteeism;
- the average number of hours of FIE teaching each pupil received was 112.

Each FIE class covered 10 of the 14 FIE instruments available at the time:

Organization of Dots

Orientations in Space 1

Comparisons

Analytic Perception

Categorization

Family Relations

Temporal Relations

Numerical Progressions

Instructions

Cartoons.

THE PROCESS

During the study, one thing became very clear; from the teachers' viewpoint, FIE appeared to generate more careful thought and analysis about the nature of teaching and learning than most other educational initiatives had hitherto achieved. For most, the first-year training course was an open rehearsal of coming to grips with an alien, abstract curriculum. Highly experienced teachers felt as though they were back on teaching practice, not fully understanding the syllabus, unsure of how it would be received, and unfamiliar with a different teaching style. The relevance of Feuerstein's ideas were underlined by an awareness of their own problems in managing certain aspects of the FIE course and the kind of processes required to correct their misconceptions. For many teachers, this was a humbling experience that gave them insight into the kind of problems pupils might be experiencing in the classroom.

Some teachers adapted remarkably well and with each year's experience became more confident with the course. These FIE teachers were able to apply the materials in a creative manner consistent with Feuerstein's mediated learning experience parameters. In general, the involvement and commitment of their pupils was more positive. Regular visits to these more successful (high-MLE) classes were a delight. The quality of discussion in one particular class was reminiscent of able sixth-year formers rather than fifth-year low attainers. In many classes, it was surprising to hear so-called low attainers using the sophisticated vocabulary encouraged in the FIE program. It was also apparent that the visually based tasks enabled many reticent pupils with poor language skills to demonstrate previously unnoticed abilities. This led to higher teacher expectations and increased confidence in the pupils.

However, like most educational innovations, the processes of dissemination and implementation often eroded the originator's intentions and ideas:

- some teachers did not fully appreciate the theoretical underpinnings of the program;
- some were not comfortable with the teaching style required;
- a few relied too heavily on the task pages, using them like worksheets.

Finally, it was only toward the end of the project that teachers became aware of the deeper issues. In particular, the kinds of mediation necessary to ensure that the lesson transcends the immediate activity. Without that understanding, it was difficult to facilitate pupil ability to make meaningful and spontaneous applications to real life.

In many ways, disseminating an educational initiative is rather like a game of Chinese whispers. Sometimes the messages remain clear and intact, but more often at the end of the communication chain, the message received is very different from the original one. In certain respects, this applied to the FIE course. We can illustrate this by using a visual analogy as shown in Fig. 6.1.

If we imagine the original FIE program as a tree growing in Israel, deeply rooted in Feuerstein's beliefs and theories and well-supported by the originator, we can see how the processes of marketing, packaging, and dissemination can distort theory and practice. Although the time allowed for training was generous, it may have been insufficient given the abstract and unfamiliar nature of the course.

Implementing FIE also involved some compromises. The very nature of the course with its prescribed format and sequence established it as a "bolt on" program. Indeed, FIE proponents argue that pupils will only benefit from carefully controlled exposure to the exercises in four, approximately 1-hour sessions each week. In reality, the project schools could only manage 2 hours FIE teaching per week and regular classroom support was limited.

During the final 2 years of schooling, it is common to find all manner of

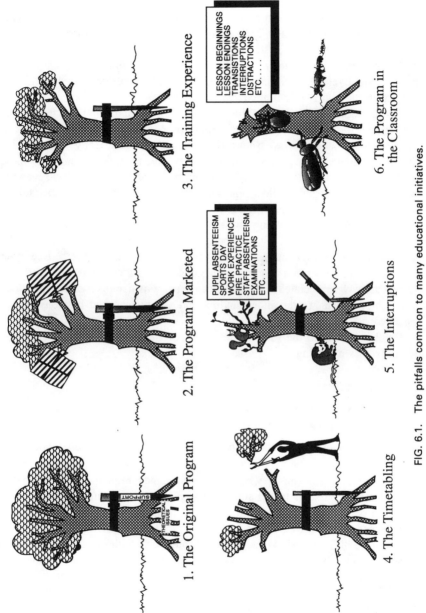

1. The Original Program

2. The Program Marketed

3. The Training Experience

4. The Timetabling

5. The Interruptions

6. The Program in the Classroom

SUPPORT

THEORETICAL ISSUES

PUPIL ABSENTEEISM
SPORTS DAY
WORK EXPERIENCE
FIRE PRACTICE
STAFF ABSENTEEISM
EXAMINATIONS
ETC. . . . . . .

LESSON BEGINNINGS
LESSON ENDINGS
TRANSISTIONS
INTERRUPTIONS
DISTRACTIONS
ETC. . . . . .

FIG. 6.1.   The pitfalls common to many educational initiatives.

interruptions to the timetable. Quite apart from the familiar problems of pupil and staff absenteeism, lesson time is further restricted by the cumulative impact of such events as sports days, speech days, fire practice, examinations, and work experience. In some cases, FIE pupils received less than half the FIE lessons they were timetabled for. Finally, not all FIE teachers were able to manage their lessons effectively. In these classes, pupils were often "off task" so that the final impact on the pupils was limited.

The cartoons are meant to illustrate the realities and problems facing any educational initiative as well as the weaker process aspects of the FIE work in certain schools and classes. Naturally, there were more effective and positive teachers in more supportive schools who were able to transcend many of these problems. Freed from the constraints of a normal examination syllabus, even the weaker teachers began to allow time for pupils to think and share ideas. Quite a number commented on the fascinating outcome of adopting open questioning tactics. Instead of encouraging and searching for specific solutions/answers to particular questions, some teachers became more interested in exploring pupils' own ideas: "That's an interesting answer. Why do you say that?" Exploring unexpected answers often revealed pupil conceptual difficulties that teachers had not previously appreciated. On other occasions, sensitive open-ended questions highlighted much greater understanding and ability than had previously been assumed.

Pupil reactions to the FIE course were extremely varied and influenced by many factors including:

- perceived status of the teacher;
- perceived status of the program;
- the level of the control in the classroom;
- the ability of the teacher to understand the program and use it effectively.

There were some pupils who had closed minds from the very beginning regarding the course as trivial and boring—clearly associating it with remedial activities or the sorts of simple puzzles that younger brothers and sisters enjoy. Others obviously enjoyed the novelty of the program and the challenge of some of the more difficult task pages. Informal interviews with pupils at the ends of lessons commonly revealed that they had learned lots of new words. However, they often added that they were useless because they weren't used in other lessons. Nevertheless, a few pupils implied that although they did not use the words (e.g., plan, anticipate, alternative), they did use the ideas in their everyday life.

In general, however, the majority of pupils found it extremely difficult to bridge from the FIE activities to real life, even when prompted by the FIE teacher. Beyond the FIE lessons, very few were able to transfer and generalize. FIE pupils themselves felt that the course had helped them to become less impulsive and generally better behaved in a number of other lessons. Non-FIE, teachers, however, did not confirm that these positive pupil self-perceptions had translated into improvements in behavior.

Some of the difficulties experienced by both pupils and teachers throughout the project were attributed to the content and nature of the FIE materials. Apart from concerns about cost, the FIE teachers consistently reported that the materials were:

- too abstract and unfamiliar;
- too repetitive and poorly presented;
- culturally inappropriate;

making it very difficult to establish meaning and relevance to the wider curriculum.

THE PRODUCT

Pupil Outcomes

Some of the apparently positive benefits observed over the period of the study were confirmed by measurable changes on the teacher observation schedule (Table 4.13). Within FIE classes teachers indicated that pupils became more active contributors to class discussions.

There were less significant trends in the data suggesting that, again, within FIE classes pupils became:

- more self-disciplined;
- more inclined to listen to other peoples' comments;
- more likely to defend their opinions on the basis of logical evidence;
- more able to describe different strategies for solving problems;
- more likely to spontaneously read and follow instructions carefully;
- more able to handle two or more sources of information simultaneously;
- more able to make spontaneous links between ideas and principles in different curriculum areas.

These results should be treated with caution because of the unknown characteristics of the observation schedule and the fact that since so many investigations were conducted, some were bound to be statistically significant.

Unfortunately, these positive behavioral changes did not appear to generalize to other subject areas. At least, they were not observed by the non-FIE teachers.

Indeed, completion of the same observation schedules by these teachers at the beginning and end of the study suggested a deterioration in pupil behavior among FIE and control pupils over the study period. These findings applied to pupils taught by both high-MLE and low-MLE teachers. In other words, pupils who had more effective FIE teachers showed no greater behavioral improvements beyond the FIE classes than those who had the less effective FIE teachers. There was even some evidence to suggest a greater deterioration in pupil behavior among the high-MLE pupils—possibly associated with difficulties in coping with dramatically different teaching styles and teacher expectations.

It is difficult to know the extent to which changes on the teacher observation schedule reflected changes in teacher perceptions or pupil behavior. Certainly, FIE teachers were more optimistic about the potential for change among the FIE pupils. They were also anticipating potential benefits and were sensitive to the areas in which change was expected. In contrast, the non-FIE teachers were in general skeptical about the potential benefits of the FIE program. They also found some of the items on the schedule difficult to complete, because their traditional methods of teaching denied them the opportunity of noticing certain aspects of pupil behavior.

Informal observations of the pupils did suggest that many gained in confidence, at least in the early stages of the project. The picture was, however, very inconsistent within and across the schools. Nevertheless, the data did suggest that there were some fairly widespread short-term (over a 10-month period) self-esteem benefits to the pupils. Short-term self-esteem enhancements were particularly noticeable in the two schools that offered more flexible timetabling arrangements where the pupils were not seen to be clearly identified with LAPP. Moreover, the most dramatic improvements in self-esteem occurred in the high-MLE classes. These trends disappeared in the long term (over the period of the project).

In terms of hard data, the study revealed no real evidence of positive benefits of the FIE program. As Chapter 4 reports, over the period of the project there were no significant improvements (relative to the controls) in FIE pupils in the following areas:

- reading skills (Edinburgh Reading Test);
- mathematics skills—concepts and problem solving (Richmond Mathematics Skills Tests, M1 and M2);
- work study skills—map reading, reading graphs and tables and knowledge and use of reference materials (Richmond Work Study Skills Tests, W1, W2 and W3).

In fact, a negative treatment effect (significant at the 5% level) was noted with respect to FIE pupils' work study skills (map reading). Although the FIE pupils made some marginal gains in this area, the controls showed significantly greater improvements.

Moreover, there was no hard evidence to suggest that FIE improved pupils' cognitive abilities as assessed by the British Ability Scales (BAS). In particular, there were no significant differences between the FIE pupils and the controls in terms of changes in their BAS IQs or their BAS scaled scores on the Word Definitions, Similarities, Matrices, Block Design (Level), and Recall of Designs Tests. There was a general improvement in the Block Design (Power) scaled scores in the FIE groups compared to the controls. However, this was only significant at the 5% level and given the number of procedures undertaken, this may have been a chance finding. On the other hand, this test assesses pupil efficiency in tasks that involve the use of spatial imagery—an area closely related to the FIE program.

These disappointing findings applied to all four schools, suggesting that differences in setting, banding and timetabling made no differences to pupil outcomes. The data was also analyzed to check for the influence of pupil attendance and teacher mediation characteristics. There was no evidence to suggest that either factor made any significant difference to the outcome. Good attenders did no better than poor attenders and pupils who were taught by teachers more effective in terms of Feuerstein's mediation framework (high-MLE teachers) could not be differentiated from those taught by the least effective (low-MLE) teachers.

Teacher Outcomes

Although the measurable effects of FIE on pupil abilities, attainments, and behavior were rather disappointing, there were much more encouraging outcomes with respect to attitudinal and behavioral change in the teachers.

Psychometric testing using Cattell's 16PF substantiated informal observations by the senior management in schools that, in general, FIE teachers had become:

- more assertive
- confident
- self-reliant

during the period of the study. Discussions with the teachers revealed that these beneficial effects were as much related to their involvement in a high profile educational initiative as to the FIE course per se. Nevertheless, similar personality changes did not occur among the control teachers, many of whom were involved in another educational initiative (TVEI).

Two self-assessment schedules were constructed for the purposes of the study to assess changes in attitudes toward: teaching (Myself as a Teacher Scale, Table 5.5) and low-achieving adolescents (Attitudes Toward the Characteristics of Less

Academic Pupils Scale, Table 5.8). Significant changes over time were noted in FIE teachers ratings of themselves on a number of dimensions within each scale. In particular, FIE teachers became more positive about their role as teachers, feeling:

- more satisfied with their job
- more confident in their teaching abilities
- more committed to their profession
- more valued in their work.

Moreover, they became much more optimistic about low achievers, considering that many of these pupils were mislabeled and were far more capable than most teachers realized in terms of:

- intellectual abilities
- concentration skills
- discussion skills
- the ability to generalize.

Similar attitudinal changes were not noted among the control teachers over the same period.

Summary

In summary, the implementation of Feuerstein's Instrumental Enrichment Program, combined with a detailed analysis of his theories and beliefs, has pointed up the potential of cognitive skills work and exposed many important issues at the heart of "learning to learn." The principles and ideas in the FIE program have major implications for teacher development with respect to enhancing more positive teacher attitudes and facilitating a more interactive, process-orientated approach to teaching.

Undoubtedly, large numbers of pupils in mainstream secondary schools have significant gaps in their cognitive makeup. Teachers commonly observe that pupils are deficient in cognitive skills such as the ability to analyze or compare. Therefore, it is not surprising that many are unable to make effective use of their past experiences in tackling fresh problems. Even those pupils who possess the basic skills and resources often seem unable to know when to use them. Instrumental Enrichment exposed many of these problems and offered the potential of providing the pupils with a nucleus of generic transferable skills. Unfortunately, while pupils became more conscious of these skills, relatively little evidence was amassed to suggest that they became more able to apply them in real life.

It would seem that FIE's abstract format does have major drawbacks for pupils, teachers, and the mainstream school curriculum. In spite of its enormous attractions, one is left wondering whether some of the strengths of FIE are also its weaknesses. Its abstract nature and potential broad applicability also mean that it lacks specificity for particular population groups. Although FIE may have provided an ideal "set of tools" for clinical work with linguistically deficient and emotionally disturbed immigrants coming to Israel after the holocaust, it appears that it is not an ideal program for integration within mainstream UK secondary schools today.

The major stumbling block with FIE appears to be its failure to teach for transfer. There is good evidence that working with familiar everyday examples and concrete materials does not necessarily lead to transfer and generalization. Children and adults often find it difficult to generalize from particular examples to fresh contexts—in other words, "they get stuck in the concrete." Perkins and Salomon (1988) cite many examples of "inert" knowledge in both students and young adults involved in different learning tasks. They instance Barrows and Tamblyn's (1980) work illustrating the difficulties student physicians experience in applying technical knowledge acquired on courses to real-life diagnostic contexts. In a previous review (Salomon & Perkins, 1987) also highlight the minimal impact of computer programing instruction on cognitive skill development despite the richness, rigor, and wide applicability of the procedures involved. Similar findings permeate studies that have attempted to teach strategies to aid memorizing. As Belmont, Butterfield, and Ferretti (1982) show, memory strategies become "contextually welded" to the circumstances of their acquisition.

On the other hand, Feuerstein's attempt to teach prerequisites to thinking via the medium of contextually bare, abstract tasks also seems to have limitations. During the course of this study, pupils certainly became more competent in tasks, like searching for geometric shapes in amorphous clouds of dots. Unfortunately, the skills and strategies exposed by these tasks often remained steadfastly tied to those artificial contexts. The bridging process at the end of each lesson did not always work. Even with appropriate provocation and help, some pupils were unable to identify important elements in their learning and consider where else they might apply. Moreover, some teachers were less resourceful in prompting pupils to think of various literal or figural transfer situations. In other words, some pupils and teachers were "stuck in the dots and the triangles."

CONCLUSIONS

The educational world is indebted to Feuerstein for his pioneering work. Faced with enormous clinical challenges and armed with a powerful belief in the potential to change the human intellect, he has drawn from the depths of psychological theory, research, and practice to create a complex series of overlapping conceptual frameworks and theoretical models. His model of the intellectual act (the cognitive map); his list of deficient cognitive functions (at the phase level of the cognitive map); and his theoretical ideas on mediated learning experience, are incomplete and imprecise but extremely useful in providing vantage points from which to understand children's learning problems and starting points for intervention.

Some psychological models restrict their application to rather narrow aspects of human behavior. Feuerstein's work is more holistic and ambitious—attempting to understand and explain the many nuances of thinking, learning, and development. He goes beyond the limits of psychological knowledge and thus, it is not surprising that his theoretical ideas are constantly evolving as he seeks to extend, clarify, and operationalize aspects of his work.

Nevertheless, although Feuerstein's ideas and theories are dynamic, his intervention program remains fairly inflexible and unchanging. Many of the tasks included within the FIE program were selected and adapted from existing aptitude and ability tests to meet a particular clinical need (i.e., the assessment and rehabilitation of holocaust victims). Although FIE has now been used for many different purposes and applied to a wide range of population groups, the originators have vigorously resisted any form of adaptation and development to suit different needs. Although Feuerstein rejects IQ tests as predictors of learning potential, his objections are based on their static, standardized, and restricted mode of delivery rather than the content and relevance of the items. Thus, he still places great value on a whole range of abstract psychological test items "as tools for mediation," arguing that their remoteness from everyday life and other curriculum areas is a strength by enabling the child to become aware of essential process issues without being distracted by subject matter content. Although the original selection of items for FIE was based on the intuitive selection of tasks to meet a particular clinical need, it has been the many subsequent research studies that have helped to keep the program intact and relatively unchanged.

Feuerstein's FIE has probably provoked more research than any other cognitive skills intervention program. As Chapter 2 implied, much of this has been of questionable value because of the difficulties of finding adequate ways of assessing the transfer of skills from the program to real-life contexts. Ironically, Feuerstein cites changes in IQ scores as major evidence to support the application of FIE. This is not only inconsistent with his rejection of IQ tests as predictors of learning potential, but highly questionable because of the similarity between many IQ test items and FIE task types. While the psychological world realizes that the theoretical and empirical basis of Feuerstein's work remains unproven, the popularist media sometimes assume that changes in IQ scores equates with raising intelligence.

The Somerset study was intended as a highly detailed and searching evaluation of the application of FIE to mainstream, low-achieving, UK adolescents. Intriguingly, this present study failed to confirm any rise in IQs associated with FIE.

Moreover, there was no evidence to imply that FIE had a positive influence on attainments or work study skills. However, as Chapter 6 summarizes, there was some basis for mild optimism about positive attitudinal and behavioral change in the pupils and clearer evidence of positive benefits for the teachers. In many ways, the positive outcomes of the work were more related to the underlying philosophy of FIE than the FIE materials. Indeed, the materials themselves posed many problems in interpretation, implementation, and application. Reflecting on Barry Taylor's opening quote:

> Certainly, the (FIE) 'instruments' seem to have universal appeal. . . . Whether it (FIE) has staying power remains to be seen . . .
> (Barry Taylor, quoted in Weller & Craft, 1983, p. i)

it would seem that while Feuerstein's clinical and theoretical contributions have long-lasting implications, FIE has a more restricted and limited use.

Chapter 7

Wider Implications

*The task is to produce a changed environment for learning—an environ-
ment in which there is a new relationship between students and their
subject matter, in which knowledge and skill become objects of interroga-
tion, inquiry and extrapolation. As individuals acquire knowledge, they
should also be empowered to think and reason.*

R. Glaser (1984, p. 26)

Glaser's quote returns us to issues raised at the beginning of this book. Is the
idea of teaching thinking skills a kind of timeless delusion or are there grounds
for assuming that teaching thinking is a practical reality? Although the results of
this present study are in some ways disappointing, they need to be viewed within
the context of the wider literature.

Much of the existing research supporting the application of FIE and other
widely used programs is fundamentally flawed (Bradley, 1983; Sternberg &
Bhana, 1986). However, as these latter authors point out, methodological inadequacies are not uniform across studies, so that a cumulative picture can be
discerned demonstrating that thinking skills can be improved by a variety of
interventions. However, we are clearly a long way from knowing the most
efficient ways of promoting cognitive growth in particular population groups. As
Chapter 1 demonstrated, many exciting theoretical developments and empirical
findings are emerging in the psychological world that can help to inform the
design of new cognitive skills courses. Moreover, lessons can be learned from
testing and trialing existing programs such as Feuerstein's FIE.

This final chapter will briefly consider some of the recurring issues of this
study and their implications for the design of future cognitive skills programs. It
will conclude by illustrating how these design implications have shaped the

nature, organization, and content of the Somerset Thinking Skills Course (Blagg, Ballinger, Gardner, Petty, & Williams, 1988a, 1988b; Blagg, Ballinger, Gardner, & Petty, 1988a, 1988b; Blagg, Ballinger, & Gardner, 1988, 1989, 1990, and in preparation-a) which has built on the theoretical and empirical lessons of the FIE evaluation.

RESEARCH ISSUES

The Somerset evaluation of FIE illustrates that successful teaching of thinking skills does not depend simply on program design. It also depends on many school system issues, teacher behavior, and personality factors, training, implementation, and support issues. It probably depends also on selecting the cognitive skills program that is most appropriate to meet the needs of the particular target population. However, determining which program (or parts of a program) best suits specific age and/or ability groups is in itself a massive research question.

Indeed, the number of critical factor combinations likely to effect program outcome are so numerous, that evaluation studies in the future will need to be far more comprehensive and complex than most studies reported thus far. Sternberg and Bhana (1986) reviewed the evidence favoring Feuerstein's FIE, Lipman's Philosophy for Children, the SOI Program developed by Mary Meeker (1969), Whimbey and Lochhead's (1979) Problem Solving and Comprehension Course and the Odyssey Project. Their findings were somewhat disconcerting. The quality of the research studies left much to be desired. In particular, they were concerned that:

1. The majority of studies were potentially biased as they were either sponsored by the program developers or conducted in collaboration with them. Only a very small proportion of studies were published in independent, refereed journals while many were published in journals and magazines sponsored and controlled by the program developers.
2. Typically insufficient details were supplied making it impossible to replicate the conditions of the study.
3. Most studies lacked control groups or used inadequate controls.
4. Very few studies attempted to compare the efficacy of one program with another or judge the effectiveness of individual elements within each program.
5. The kind of outcome measures used to support various programs was wholly inadequate. They often amounted to no more than "user testimonials." On other occasions, measures were so closely related to the program, that they were almost bound to show some favorable results. In general,

insufficient attention was given to "transfer of training and to durability of training over the long term."

6. None of the studies assessed or commented on the extent to which improvements on tests of intellectual skill were due to improved motivation and/ or the desire to impress the examiners.

Clearly, Sternberg and Bhana's (1986) observations underline the need for independent, comprehensive studies, that can meaningfully inform potential program users. This present study goes some way toward meeting Sternberg and Bhana's critical points. Stufflebeam's CIPP framework does provide a useful model within which illuminative and more traditional experimental designs can be incorporated into a complex research design. However, as Chapter 3 highlighted, there is a desperate need for the development of new, reliable, and valid procedures that can more sensitively assess and monitor attitudinal, behavioral, and cognitive changes in both pupils and adults. Dynamic approaches to assessment such as those advocated by Feuerstein provide additional vantage points for the clinician but problems of time constraints, reliability, and validity would limit their use as research tools.

Some of the questionnaires and observation schedules used in the present study could be developed into useful research tools with further elaboration and study. Indeed, Lake (1987) has experimented with the Teacher Observation Schedule (Table 4.13) used in the present study and produced a shortened factor analyzed version with norms for 10- to 12-year-olds, based on 224 pupils from six schools in Milton Keynes, Buckinghamshire, England. Details of the revised schedule known as the Gatehouse Observation Schedule for Teachers (GHOST) is given in Appendix 31. On the basis of a hierarchical linkage analysis backed by a principal components analysis, Lake found that the schedule distinguished between two separate factors (factor A covered by items 1 to 9 and factor B by items 10 to 18). The factors have not been named, but factor A appears to relate to pupil behaviors with respect to routine aspects of classroom life, whereas factor B seems more concerned with pupil ability to initiate and monitor their own work and respond appropriately to complex, non-routine tasks.

PROGRAM DESIGN AND IMPLEMENTATION ISSUES

Content Free or Knowledge Rich?

While many teachers and educationalists were excited about Feuerstein's ideas, they questioned the relevance and applicability of the FIE program to UK mainstream British adolescents. As Chapter 5 showed, there were enormous implementation difficulties, which related in part to the design of the FIE program. In particular, there were concerns about the artificial, abstract, contextually bare nature of the materials—making it difficult to establish meaning and relevance at the beginning of the lesson and hard to bridge to interpersonal and curriculum areas at the end of the lesson.

In other words, there were problems with transfer and generalization that seemed to relate to the "content free" nature of FIE. These concerns draw attention to the dilemmas between programs like FIE, that attempt to teach transferable skills independent of particular domains, and those that teach reasoning skills within the context of specific domains. In a useful review, Glaser (1984) illustrates a number of central issues concerning the "transferability of acquired skills and knowledge" that theory and experiment have yet to resolve. In teaching thinking skills, should we:

- use general methods programs remote from familiar subject matter?
- rely on the essential processes being covered within traditional subject teaching?
- attempt some fusion of these two approaches by encouraging a greater emphasis on general processes such as self-regulatory skills alongside the acquisition of specific declarative knowledge?

In the real world, problems are embedded in complex contexts so that even if pupils acquire general heuristics in a decontextualized way, they may still fail to solve everyday problems because of: deficiencies in essential knowledge peculiar to each fresh problem and/or inadequacies in higher level control processes responsible for the selection, coordination, and organization of skills and procedures.

Thus, Glaser (1984) argues for a fusion of approaches in which specific knowledge domains are taught in "interactive, interrogative ways so that general self regulatory skills are exercised in the course of acquiring domain related knowledge" (p. 25). On the other hand, Feuerstein would argue that attempting to teach thinking skills in knowledge-rich contexts would not work as the content of real-life problems would merely serve to distract pupils from becoming aware and in control of their cognitive processes. In other words, they would be more concerned about solving problems or acquiring new information than they would be about thinking about thinking.

On the other hand, Shayer and Beasley (1987) point out that while Feuerstein chose psychometric-like tasks for FIE, there is no good reason why other types of content should not serve equally well as suitable vehicles for achieving the underlying aims of FIE. Indeed, Mehl (1985) carried out a fascinating study with culturally deprived undergraduate physics students in Capetown University. Although rejecting the use of the FIE program, Mehl used Feuerstein's theoretical models, especially the deficient functions list and the MLE parameters to modify the existing nuclear physics program with the result that there was significant improvements in students' understanding and a greatly improved pass rate in the end-of-year examinations.

Teaching Style

Glaser (1984) emphasizes the sensitive use of Socratic dialogue. Analyzing and operationalizing this approach, it reduces to the kinds of teacher behaviors that can also be framed within mediated learning experience theory. It was interesting that when I tried to operationalize Feuerstein's MLE parameters in terms of a series of behavioral descriptors (see Table 3.3), certain aspects of teacher behavior seemed more critical than others. In particular, the sensitive use of open-ended and relational questioning seemed not only to mediate for intentionality/reciprocity, meaning, and transcendence, but also for many other aspects of mediation including individuation/differentiation, sharing behavior, and challenge. In other words, both Glaser and Feuerstein address overlapping teacher behavior issues but using slightly different linguistic frameworks and technical terms. Probably, the most critical and important aspects of mediation are contained within the elements involved in Socratic dialogue.

Hence, although the "content-free" nature of FIE denies the opportunity for Glaser's fusion approach, the FIE teaching style is not inconsistent with his teaching philosophy. Interestingly, the FIE program did seem to promote the kinds of teacher behaviors essential to create a better balance between acquiring subject-specific information and general problem-solving skills. Anecdotal information and informal observations suggested that, outside FIE lessons, FIE teachers were beginning to move toward Glaser's (1984) challenge. Many had taken on a more interactive, interrogative teaching style in their own specialist subject areas. Nevertheless, it is reasonable to ask whether these benefits could have accrued, been maintained, or even enhanced had the content of the FIE program included activities and tasks more closely related to interpersonal and curriculum issues. Certainly, if such tasks had been explicitly incorporated into the program, it might have assisted both pupils and teachers with transfer.

Accessibility and Dissemination

Shayer and Beasley (1987) make some useful points about the wider implications of Feuerstein's ideas and FIE. They draw a parallel between FIE and the humanities curriculum "Man, A Course of Study" (MACOS), comparing this with the fate of Nuffield Science Courses. Like FIE, the purchase of MACOS was conditional upon training, and its copyright was closely guarded. Nuffield Science was available to all without restrictions on copyright or development. MACOS remained "fossilised in its present form" (Shayer & Beasley, 1987, p. 117) and reached only a small proportion of those professionals who might have benefited from it. However, Nuffield Science had a major impact on schools. In conclusion, Shayer and Beasley (1987) argue:

> The experience, theory and fruitfulness of the Feuerstein team is too valuable to remain locked up in a commercial agreement. (p. 117)

They go on to suggest that:

> . . . learning materials be generated by those concerned with remedial education, free of existing copyright so that the professional skills underlying IE can be clarified. (p. 117)

In the UK, Shayer and Beasley's (1987) suggestions are already being realized. Many teachers are now using Feuerstein's theoretical models to adapt existing curricular programs or develop new ones.

Bolt-on versus Infusion Approaches

The recent Education Reform Act (1988) and in particular, the constraints and demands of the National Curriculum now create new needs and challenges:

> So far, DES Publications have emphasised the importance of promoting understanding alongside the acquisition of knowledge. . . . Pupils will be assessed not only on facts and information, but also on a wide range of conceptual, linguistic and procedural knowledge. They will require the skills necessary to study a wide variety of evidence, comprehend and extract information from it, notice gaps and inconsistencies and detect bias. Moreover, they will need to be fluent in a range of basic techniques for classifying and recording data.   (Blagg, 1989, p. 11)

The imposition of the National Curriculum coinciding with a more powerful, parental lobby will create the need in schools for a more explicit attempt to teach thinking skills. So how should this be achieved? Glaser's (1984) ideals of teaching thinking skills within each curriculum area is a highly desirable aim and yet the everyday realities of school timetables, subject specialisms, differing teacher styles and expectations, and poor communications within and between departments constantly erode the possibility of achieving these ideals. Although there has been a general trend toward interactive problem-solving approaches across a range of curriculum areas, we are probably still a long way from realizing Glaser's (1984) aims.

Even the planning and development of the UK National Curriculum reflects some of the compartmentalism and problems in schools. The Department of Education and Science brought together specialists in different subject areas to decide on the essential process and content issues within each core and foundation subject. Yet there appears to be no coherent plan relating the deliberations of the various working parties to a comprehensive framework linked to cognitive development.

Thus, the orders for each subject contain a series of ambiguous, loose statements about selected areas of procedural and declarative knowledge deemed essential by committee concencus. These areas of knowledge have been somewhat arbitrarily grouped into attainment targets and arranged into various levels of attainment that pupils are expected to achieve as they progress through the school system. The attainment targets have been clarified by examples of programs of study. Although there are shortcomings in the National Curriculum, the testing and reporting arrangements should at least mean that parents will be better informed about their childrens' progress.

Successful progress through the various levels of attainment will depend crucially on adequate, cognitive development. Thus, teachers will be under increasing pressure to intervene cognitively with those pupils who become "stuck" at particular achievement levels. We have begun to map the relationship between the cognitive processes required by the various levels of attainment within and across the core and foundation subjects, but progress is difficult because of the many ways in which the orders can be interpreted (Blagg & Ballinger, 1990).

Nevertheless, it is possible to identify a number of cognitive skills and procedures that are common to many subjects while noting that some disciplines lend themselves to the development of a wider range of cognitive skills than others. For instance, even allowing for effective mediation, learning a foreign language may not be as cognitively inclusive as the study of science or the humanities. Although an infusion approach to enhancing cognitive development would be ideal, the present curriculum climate suggests that subject compartmentalism would make it difficult for this to be achieved in any coordinated way.

In these circumstances, there is probably a need (at least in the short term) for a comprehensive thinking skills course that can be taught as a separate program yet at the same time provide a model and basis for moving toward an infusion approach. If such a course could be organized in modular themes that could be taught as a sequenced, cross-curricular program or, alternatively, selectively integrated with different curricular areas, this might well provide the flexibility to assist progress toward Glaser's infusion approach.

Teaching for Transfer

A course that lends itself to an infusion approach would not necessarily tackle the key issue of transfer and generalization. There is still the problem of context-specific learning. In a recent report on training for transfer in the adult world, Annett (1989) draws a useful distinction between *transferable skills* and *transfer skills,* which is roughly analogous to the distinction many authors make between lower and higher order cognitive processes.

Annett argues that transferable skills are commonly occurring skills and routines required by many different job contexts. Possession of these transferable skills is assessed by observing trainee performance on a variety of tasks. Trainees are not required to explain how and why they are selecting particular skills and routines to carry out the job in hand but merely demonstrate that they can use the transferable skills. The selection and organization processes involved in using transferable skills are under the control of transfer skills (i.e., transfer skills refer to higher level (executive) metacognitive processes). It is one thing to demonstrate the acquisition of transferable skills in particular contexts but quite another to have the transfer skills to know when to select and use these lower order processes in novel situations. In other words, transferable skills are about the "what" of performance and transfer skills, the "how."

There have been many suggestions on how to teach transferable skills so that they do, in fact, transfer. Annett and Sparrow (1985) and Brown and Campione (1986) have summarized much of this advice. Recurring recommendations include the need to:

1. use discovery learning methods to promote pupil involvement and meaningful learning;
2. raise awareness of the possibilities for transfer and provide explicit examples;
3. use many and varied examples and training contexts.

Annett (1989) suggests that maybe the key to transfer lies in teaching the higher level executive processes rather than the lower order component skills. Nevertheless, the higher level processes need to be taught within the context of a structured program (knowledge lean or knowledge rich). In these circumstances, it makes sense to address both lower and higher order components at the same time. The content of the cognitive skills course will determine which lower order components are addressed, whereas the extent to which higher order processes are elaborated and exercised will be largely determined by the manner in which the tasks are presented and mediated.

Considering these issues in relation to the application of FIE to mainstream adolescents, a number of problems emerge. Pupils and teachers complained about too much repetition—a lack of novelty and stimulus. It was interesting that although task pages in the earlier parts of instruments were relatively easy, their reliance on implicit rather than explicit instructions often prompted considerable debate about the nature of the problem. However, once pupils had ironed out ambiguities in the earlier task pages and became used to the implicit conventions, later task pages needed relatively little problem definition. In some cases this created boredom but more fundamentally it meant there was little need to think out loud or analyze and debate what was required in each task.

In this respect, the metacognitive component of the program was greatly diminished. In addition, as the tasks were often relatively straight forward with only one set of correct answers, it was sometimes difficult to encourage pupils to reflect on their approaches and procedures. All too often, what remained was the practice of particular procedures (such as systematic search, counting, labeling, and eliminating) tied to artificial exercises remote from everyday experience. Thus, the FIE program was often reduced to training in transferable skills, rather than training for transfer. In fairness, the teacher's manual did include many practical examples of transfer or bridging applications but, once again, insufficient challenge, too much repetition, and artificiality in the tasks meant that pupils and teachers did not always take bridging seriously. For example, after working through 10 pages of Organization of Dots, there was a tendency to give up on bridging because pupils were being prompted to reflect on similar types of questions in relation to very similar tasks. Not surprisingly, both pupils and teachers ran out of fresh ideas and novel connections.

A recent study by Alison Wolf (1989) explored the relationship between transfer and course structure/content in the vocational training field. Her findings confirmed that transfer could be enhanced by using many and varied training contexts, but also by teaching sub-skills and processes within the context of whole, complex tasks (that may even go beyond the trainees' competence to complete). This contrasts with the more traditional vocational training approaches in which basic skills or routines are taught using artificial, simple, uncluttered tasks. In Wolf's study, the training materials involved tasks simulating real-life problems that students were likely to meet.

In some ways, her approach is more in tune with Glaser's (1984) ideas. Moreover, Wolf's findings support Perkins and Salomon's (1988) suggestions on "hugging" as a way of promoting transfer. They argue that learning tasks need to be contextualized so that they "hug" (more closely resemble) the potential transfer contexts. For example, an English teacher wanting pupils to relate literature to everyday life might choose an example that is particularly clear for the students to see, for example, *Catcher in the Rye* by Salinger. Of course, integrating more relevant content into cognitive skills courses does not negate Feuerstein's main vehicle for transfer (i.e., bridging). Indeed, it may enhance it. Perkins and Salomon (1988) cite both hugging and bridging as the essential components in what they call a "simple recipe for teaching for transfer" (p. 24). Like Feuerstein, they suggest that at the end of each lesson students might be provoked to think about how they would tackle analogous problems well beyond the original learning context.

Summary

In summary, the kind of cognitive skills program likely to impact most on schools in the present climate needs to take into account the following issues:

- The purpose and function of the program needs to be transparent to both pupils and teachers, with teaching guidelines being sufficiently explicit that teachers can implement the course with minimal training.

- There needs to be a more explicit focus on transfer and generalization with clear links within the program between the cognitive skills it intends to foster and applications to interpersonal and curriculum areas.

- The course needs to take on a modular format so that it can be used selectively and flexibly and adapted to support different curriculum areas, meeting various pupil and teacher needs.

- In keeping with Alison Wolf's (1989) findings on the teaching of transferable skills, complex tasks need to be used from many and varied contexts.

- The program needs to be easily accessible to all teachers and freely photocopiable within schools.

Although the rather clinical FIE program does not meet these needs, Feuerstein's theoretical models do provide a range of starting points and broad perspectives (rather than explicit directives) from which to begin to build a more effective classroom program. If the practical issues just referred to can be overcome, then the "Chinese whispers" effect experienced by any educational innovation should be reduced and progress made toward an approach that integrates the teaching of cognitive skills within and across the curriculum. It was in these circumstances that a curriculum group was established in 1985 to design, pilot, and produce our own locally contextualized thinking skills course. The group brought together individuals intimately involved in teaching and/or researching Feuerstein's ideas but with very different backgrounds (psychological, teaching, and artistic).

The FIE evaluation has already suggested that Feuerstein's program had a greater impact on teachers than it did on pupils. It is probably also true to say that the impact on teachers was greatest among those who were involved with the design issues of our own thinking skills course. While most teachers accepted Feuerstein's ideas about cognitive modifiability and became more conscious of their crucial role in bringing about pupil change, relatively few had the opportunity for further training in Israel or the time to emerse themselves in the wider literature on the teaching of thinking skills. Those involved with the design of the Somerset Thinking Skills Course (STSC) did have this opportunity and have benefited from it.

In a sense, STSC represents a kind of distanced and figural transfer effect of 7 years intensive involvement with Feuerstein's theoretical framework and FIE program. Although we began with Feuerstein's models, the final style, organization, and content of STSC has been influenced by information processing analyses of intelligence, problem-solving approaches, and ideas from a number of recent curriculum projects that have emphasized the importance of small groupwork and the social aspects of learning. The final section of this chapter considers the organization and structure of STSC in relation to the issues raised so far.

SOMERSET THINKING SKILLS COURSE

Introduction

STSC comprises a comprehensive modular course targeted at the full ability range of mainstream 10- to 16-year-olds. As Fig. 7.1 shows, the course involves seven modules organized as a linear sequence together with an additional module (organizing and memorizing) to be used flexibly at any stage in the program. To date, the handbook and the first six modules have been published. Two further modules are in preparation. Each module consists of photocopiable pupil activities

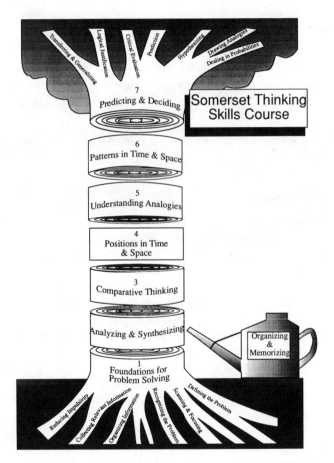

FIG. 7.1.   The Modular Structure of the Somerset Thinking Skills Course (from the forthcoming revised edition of the STSC Handbook, Blagg, Ballinger, & Gardner (in preparation c)).

accompanied by detailed guidelines on the intentions and classroom applications of each task.

Aims and Objectives

The overriding aim of STSC is to enhance pupil ability to learn. This is achieved via a number of specific aims:

1. To enhance self-esteem.
2. To promote positive attitudes and beliefs about being able to learn to learn.
3. To heighten awareness of learning styles and the need to adjust them according to differing demands.
4. To enhance ability to communicate ideas accurately and clearly.
5. To teach basic cognitive resources underpinning problem-solving processes.
6. To develop awareness and control over the use of problem-solving processes.
7. To transform passive recipients of information into active searchers and generators of ideas.
8. To facilitate the ability to transfer and generalize ideas across many different contexts.   (Blagg, Ballinger, & Gardner, 1988, p. 33)

Broad Design Issues

These aims illustrate that we have not confined ourselves to purely cognitive matters. We have also been concerned with interrelating motivational, social, and communication issues that have fundamentally affected the design of the course. There are a number of reasons for this.

Firstly, there is overwhelming evidence to suggest that the extent to which children are active, optimistic, and purposeful in their approach to learning will depend on their previous learning experiences. Pupils who have experienced repeated failure in school work and have been constantly criticized even for their best efforts are likely to have developed poor self-esteem. Many of these children will see little point in putting forward their ideas or making any effort in school tasks. Some will be only too willing to adopt the role of a less able pupil in preference to risking failure. Those who have seen no relationship between effort and achievement will begin to regard successful learning as being governed by factors beyond their control. Thus, any program that might be used with low achievers must address these attitudinal and motivational issues.

Secondly, research evidence points to the importance of the social aspects of learning, which implies the need to shape activities for paired, small group, and class work rather than solely independent work. This is also of practical importance to schools at the moment because of their concern to promote ways of helping pupils to work as members of groups by sharing ideas, acknowledging different viewpoints, and negotiating roles and task interpretations.

Thirdly, the mediational significance of language has also been highlighted in the literature and again at a practical level there is universal concern in schools to develop pupils' communication skills. Written communication has always been recognized as important but more recently a national project has been established in the UK (the National Oracy Project) which seeks to encourage ways of developing oral communication skills within and across the curriculum.

Fourthly, within any group of pupils there will be a wide spread of skills and competencies. As the FIE evaluation showed, this not only applies to mixed ability classes but also to groups of lower achieving pupils. Many pupils with reading and writing difficulties are fluent orally, provided they are given a chance to demonstrate their abilities. Some pupils show sophisticated reasoning skills when tasks are presented in their preferred mode (e.g., pictorial, numerical, diagrammatic). It is important, therefore, to produce a course that has a broad appeal and creates multiple opportunities for pupils of differing abilities to benefit from the tasks.

With these points in mind, STSC tasks have been specifically designed for small group work and class discussion. All of the tasks involve a wide range of visual and verbal demands. Moreover, we have consciously designed activities that enable *differentiation by outcome*. Virtually all of the tasks can be interpreted at different levels of sophistication. This applies especially to the various kinds of open-ended tasks, for example, stimulus tasks open to both literal and figural interpretations, naturalistic tasks with many possible solutions, and artificial tasks which provide opportunities for pupils to design their own activities.

STSC tasks have also been designed to promote children's confidence and self-esteem in a number of ways:

- The use of a wide range of novel discussion/problem-solving tasks that are relatively free from previous failure experience.
- The inclusion of open-ended tasks where there are many alternative, justifiable interpretations communicating to the pupils that the teacher is not necessarily looking for one correct answer.
- The provision of interesting visuals (pictures, cartoons, charts, etc.) to stimulate and extend pupil ideas and provide a learning environment that presents tasks in multiple modes.
- The careful sequencing of pupil activities to enable pupils to reinforce and build on basic skills, resources, and strategies.
- The emphasis on small group work enabling pupils to help one another, comparing, sharing, and reflecting on the skills, procedures, and solutions.

Teacher guidelines have been designed as easily accessible lesson plans that provide "springboards" and starting points rather than "straight jackets." However, there is a consistent emphasis on the need to establish a safe, democratic environment in which:

- pupils' ideas are carefully considered and valued, both by other pupils and the teacher;
- misunderstandings and errors are handled sensitively and constructively;
- pupils are encouraged to challenge ideas rather than personalities;
- it is safe and acceptable to hold a different view from the majority, provided it can be justified;
- it is good to ask questions, both of oneself and of others.

Learning Styles

In relation to attitudes, beliefs, and motivational issues, children often exhibit all-pervasive learning styles irrespective of the problems or contexts that confront them. For example, many children with learning problems are impulsive (Kagan, Rosman, Day, Albert, & Phillips, 1964), tending to rush into tasks before gathering appropriate information, often working in a trial-and-error manner and frequently recording ideas without sufficient attention to planning, accuracy, or detail. Feuerstein et al. (1980) addresses this issue in his deficient functions list and the FIE program is geared especially toward reducing impulsivity. However, at the other end of the impulsivity–reflectivity continuum, there are pupils who are over-reflective, constantly checking and rechecking information and plans so that they take an inordinate amount of time over tasks and often fail to finish.

Baron (1985) emphasizes that no one particular learning style is right or wrong, but rather pupils need to adapt their style to suit the needs of the particular task. There are situations when it is entirely appropriate to scan rapidly and gain a holistic, although perhaps incomplete, appraisal of the detail in a situation. On the other hand, there are times when it is essential to take more time and be far more systematic, serialistic, and attentive to detail. In this regard, the range of activities within STSC enable teachers to prompt pupils to become aware of the need to adapt their learning styles to suit the needs of the situation. Some STSC tasks demand very systematic, accurate, and carefully planned responses, whereas others are more about brainstorming, risk taking, and the generation of many different possibilities.

Cognitive Strategies and Resources

In tune with the wider literature, we seek to promote the acquisition, application, and generalization of both higher and lower order cognitive skills, referred to in STSC as:

- *cognitive resources* (specific, lower order skills and techniques) and
- *cognitive strategies* (coordinated sequences of skills and procedures selected for a particular purpose).

Our primary emphasis has been the teaching of transfer skills (i.e., cognitive strategies and the self-questioning and control procedures that govern their selection and implementation). In order to prepare pupils to manage unfamiliar and real-life problems, we have made intentional use of complexity and ambiguity alongside teacher guidance on facilitation and mediation (as opposed to instruction and direction).

Thus, every activity demands that the pupils register that a problem exists, recognize and define it for themselves, generate their own plan, and so on. Teachers mediate as little as possible but as much as necessary. During the summary phase of each lesson, pupils reflect on their own and each others' procedures and plans and examine the merits of different approaches.

At various stages in the course, design frameworks are introduced within which pupils create their own tasks for others to solve. Naturally, the design of problem-solving tasks provides an opportunity to consider the kinds of options and constraints that operate with different task types. This leads on to a consideration of such issues as:

What makes some problems more difficult than others?

How do you know whether your design plans will work?

What makes a good plan?

Moreover, in common with Sternberg and Feuerstein's programs, we make use of complex mastery tasks at critical stages to enable teachers to assess pupils' growing confidence.

At the strategic level, we have focused on the following domains:

- *Recognizing* (a problem exists)
- *Defining* (the problem)
- *Generating* (alternative approaches)
- *Planning* (selecting the most viable approach)
- *Checking* (self-monitoring)
- *Evaluating* (solutions and approaches)
- *Communicating* (the outcomes to self and others)
- *Transfering and Generalizing* (actively reflecting on the application of skills and procedures learnt in one context to many others, and where possible

deducing general principles or rules that can help with future learning or problem solving).

Within each of these domains, there are numerous issues to consider (Blagg, Ballinger, & Gardner, 1988). For instance, the most basic level of all (i.e., recognizing a problem exists) depends on a state of vigilance and an interrogative, questioning orientation to one's environment in comparison to a passive and non-critical outlook. This kind of orientation involves a reflective rather than impulsive cognitive style in which important fine details and inconsistencies in situations are noted.

Having registered that a problem exists, there are many processes involved in defining it, especially if the problem is unfamiliar, complex, and/or abstract. It is almost as though pupils need to draw down an infinite cognitive "roller blind" as they embark on a whole range of self-questioning processes (see Fig. 7.2).Each question involves many other questions. For instance, deciding what is relevant depends on the problem, but identifying the problem may depend on eliminating irrelevance—so where does the problem solver start? Perhaps on the basis of scanning and focusing the information available, the problem solver creates a series of hypotheses about what the problem might be, eliminating different irrelevancies for each problem definition, and then comparing the various definitions for their comprehensiveness. Finally, the thinker selects the most likely and inclusive problem definition in the time available.

Similar sorts of implicit or explicit questioning processes are implied by each of the main problem-solving domains. It seems likely that some of these questioning processes are more important than others but as yet, there is no clear way forward on taxonomy. Nevertheless, as Fig. 7.3 illustrates, efficient use of strategies depends not only on particular knowledge and experience but also on a wide repertoire of essential cognitive resources (transferable skills).

These cognitive resources are mainly concerned with:

- organizing and processing skills;
- knowledge and experience of codes and conventions;
- linguistic skills.

We have viewed these organizing and processing skills as overlapping, related, and often complementary processes. They underpin all of the main stages of problem solving, enabling the individual to understand, organize, re-organize, memorize, and retrieve information. Examples of organizing and processes skills include: scanning and focusing; analyzing and synthesizing; hypothesizing and testing; including and eliminating; recollecting and anticipating; labeling and coding; describing and comparing; grouping and classifying; imagining and brain-

Recognizing
& Defining

Examples

• Asking questions to clarify the problem

What is clear?
What is ambiguous?
What is relevant?
What is fact/opinion?
What is familiar/
   unfamiliar?
What can I ignore?
What do I notice?
What is important
   information?

• Translating the problem
  into a task with clear goals.

• Selecting the most likely
  task definition that fits
  the available evidence?

FIG. 7.2.   Some of the cognitive issues involved in recognizing and defining problems.

storming; ordering and prioritizing; collating and recording; drafting and redrafting; interpreting and summating; memorizing and recalling.

Some of these organizing and processing skills like analyzing and synthesizing, hypothesizing and testing, involve multiple skills in themselves which are unraveled in the STSC modules. Beyond these important skills, effective learning depends on knowledge and experience of numerous codes and conventions. In particular, pupils need a comprehensive understanding of the way in which we visually represent our world in many different forms. This includes an understanding of abbreviations, codes, symbols, conventions, and reference systems used in cartoons, pictures, charts, tables, graphs, maps, and so on. It also involves an appreciation of concepts and conventions in time and space, to enable reflection, anticipation, sequencing, ordering, and prioritizing. FIE teachers who became

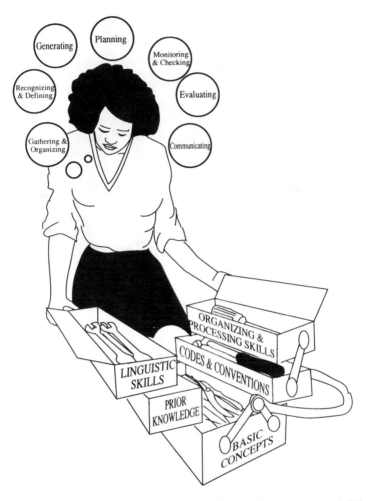

FIG. 7.3. The thinker's need for a range of cognitive resources to build purposeful strategies.

very sensitive to pupil deficiencies noted recurring problems in these basic areas. In view of this, we systematically integrated into the modules activities that prompt pupil understanding of numerous codes, conventions, and reference systems.

The significance of linguistic skills has already been mentioned in the previous section. We recognize the limited communication skills of many low-achieving adolescents and realize that their problem-solving abilities are fundamentally hampered by simply not having the language to cope with many tasks. At a very simple level, some pupils are unable to distinguish between objects and events because they do not have the precise words to describe and label them. Other pupils find enormous difficulties in coping with the language involved in giving precise instructions. In our experience, most adolescents find difficulty in listening to other people's points of view and engaging in a genuine discussion. In view of these considerations, we have throughout the modules demanded high-level oracy skills and the need to acquire and use precise and, if necessary, technical vocabulary. In addition, we have given specific practice in understanding and using language in many forms, functions, and varieties. Thus, STSC provides opportunities to address oral areas specified by the English curriculum committee:

> . . . to persuade; to explain, to instruct; to entertain; to narrate; to speculate; to argue a case; to report; to describe; to find out; to clarify or explore an issue; to solve a problem; to interpret; to summarize; to evaluate; to reflect; to announce; to criticise and respond to criticism.
>
> English for Ages 5–16, DES (1989) paragraph 15.17

Structure and Organization of STSC

STSC involves a series of visually based tasks organized into modular themes and arranged as a spiraling linear model graded in difficulty. Each module revisits and builds on ideas, principles, and strategies established earlier and continually checks for pupil knowledge and use of important cognitive resources and strategies.

The course contains both open-ended tasks that do not have one correct set of answers and more focused, closed tasks that do have particular solutions. Whether the tasks are open or closed, we have deliberately made much use of ambiguity to create disequilibrium and the need to resolve the uncertainties and come to an agreed definition of the problem. Many of the tasks do not have written instruc-

TABLE 7.1
The Main Cognitive Resource Categories Used in STSC Together
With Examples of Each and Their Strategic Application.

Domains	Examples	Purpose
1. Organizing and processing skills	Scanning and focusing analysis and synthesis	To process, organize, memorize, and retrieve information
2. Knowledge and Experience	Of codes and symbols, conventions and rules	To interpret and represent information in many different modes.
3. Linguistic Skills	Vocabulary and terminology, language registers. . . .	To understand and apply language in its many different forms, functions and varieties.

tions and even those that do require careful attention to additional implicit information. There are a number of reasons for this:

1. We wish to break down the familiar pupil expectation that they will be told exactly what to do. From the early stages of the work, pupils are required to think for themselves in defining the task.
2. Use of ambiguity allows for many justifiable interpretations, prompting much debate and discussion among the pupils.
3. The range of viable interpretations provokes close attention to detail and encourages comparative behavior in evaluating the most adequate and logically consistent task definitions.
4. It reduces impulsivity by communicating to the pupils that the tasks are rarely straight forward and have to be thought through.
5. It gradually encourages many more reticent pupils to risk a contribution in group or class discussion work, in the knowledge that teacher is not looking for set answers to the task.
6. It sharpens pupil awareness of the need for precision and accuracy in many everyday communications to avoid unintended ambiguity. . . .
7. It encourages pupils to "read between the lines" when faced with any kind of problem, i.e., it establishes a routine wherein the child searches for implicit clues and information. . . .

(Blagg, Ballinger, & Gardner, 1988, pp. 34 & 35)

As Fig. 7.4 illustrates, the modules contain three different task types:

- artificial
- naturalistic
- stimulus

Artificial tasks focus on the need for particular skills and strategies. These tasks are many and varied and require careful analysis and interpretation. Many of these tasks are closed (i.e., with one set of correct solutions) but open in the sense that the pathways to the solutions are numerous. Some of the tasks are abstract and contextually bare (as in FIE), whereas others are contextualized to a degree. An example from the third module (Comparative Thinking) is given in Fig. 7.5. This abstract artificial task occurs toward the end of the module. It is one of a series of activities that initially develop pupil understanding of the nature of comparison before going on to show how this understanding can help in classification. Classification principles are then developed and practiced in a range of contexts in order to demonstrate how these principles act as important recording and organizational factors across the curriculum and everyday life.

Naturalistic tasks "hug," in Perkins and Salomon's (1986) terms, interpersonal

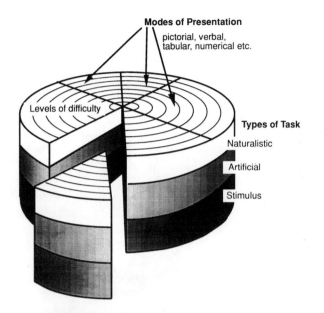

FIG. 7.4. The organization and structure of activities within each STSC module.

and academic areas. In common with the artificial tasks, these types of activities are many and varied and presented in a wide range of modes and formats. These tasks enable the teacher to check for pupil ability to transfer ideas acquired in the artificial situation to more realistic problems. An example of a naturalistic task is given in Fig. 7.6.

This is an example of an open-ended activity related to an everyday situation. The main picture shows a woman whose body language implies she has a problem. Pupils may deduce she is holding a keyring without a key and that she is locked in or locked out. The woman is surrounded by "thought bubbles," which can be identified in terms of cartoon convention and the contents of the bubbles suggest that the woman is indeed locked out. Pupils are implicitly required to consider alternative options and decide the most appropriate actions to take according to the four situations depicted in the bottom frame. The activity lends itself to small group work, enabling comparison of different solutions generated to deal with the various scenarios. Generalization issues include the need to consider consequences before selecting actions appropriate to circumstances and as such offers links with many other subjects by establishing the importance of anticipation and flexibility in planning.

In common with Wolf's (1989) research, some of the naturalistic tasks (particularly the mastery tasks) are whole and complex. For instance, in the activity

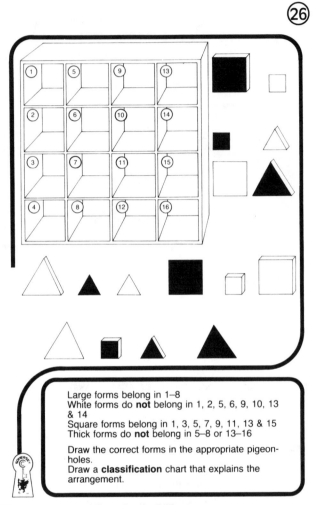

FIG. 7.5. An artificial task from the third STSC module (Comparative Thinking).

Choosing a Holiday (Comparative Thinking) the information pages simulate a holiday brochure containing a complex array of information (in words, pictures, charts, and graphs) and providing details on different resorts (temperature, amenities, accommodation options, costs, and flight details). Pupils are required to select the three most appropriate holiday options to suit a particular set of client needs. Although the task requires comparing information from a bewildering range of different sources, it establishes the principle that complex choices can

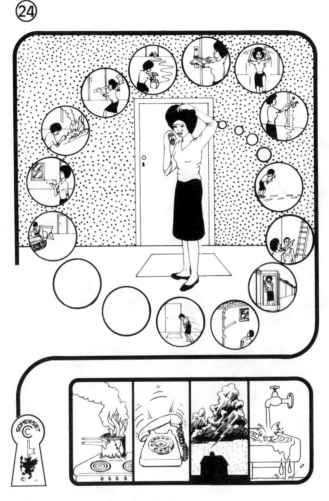

© Basil Blackwell Ltd in association with Somerset County Council, 1988

FIG. 7.6. An example of a naturalistic task taken from the first STSC module (Foundations for Problem Solving).

be simplified if we make our needs explicit and distinguish the relevant from irrelevant parameters, thereby helping to eliminate unnecessary information before analyzing the task into manageable parts.

We include these types of tasks for reasons other than Wolf (1989) expresses. For us, it is not so much that such tasks expose pupils to a contextualized range of transferable skills (although this is obviously useful) but rather that they pose a genuine challenge for pupils and create the opportunity for them to become aware of the questioning processes necessary to manage complexity and ambiguity, provided the teacher facilitates appropriately and does not analyze the problems for the pupils.

Stimulus tasks are discussion tasks that establish a meaningful context and theme for each module. In tune with Perkins' and Salomon's (1986) ideas on "hugging," they include numerous references to all sorts of transfer possibilities, prompting "connectedness" between many different ideas. They are kinds of "application tasks" requiring particular styles of strategic thinking. In comparison to the naturalistic and artificial tasks, the problems are more open-ended, prompting competing, justifiable interpretations. Figure 7.7 illustrates a stimulus task from the first module (Foundations for Problem Solving).

This stimulus page shows a picture of a living room with many people involved in various activities. There are no explicit instructions but the bottom frame is a cartoon serving as a key to the roles of the senses in data gathering. The usual five senses are indicated in the foreground. Two further figures are meant to represent the "sixth" sense and what has been referred to as the "seventh" sense (in common usage, thinking, imagining; in the psychological world, metacognition).

There are many ways in which this activity can be used. For instance, pupils can be helped to scan the main picture and the keyframe before being put into groups to consider questions like:

- What is the main picture all about?
- What does the key frame represent?
- What is the relationship between the two?

The activity is open-ended and full of intentionally ambiguous detail to encourage pupils to share ideas and recognize the diversity of justifiable interpretations. The figures in the key frame are obviously symbolic but there is no entirely secure way of knowing exactly what they symbolize.

At a content level, the task motivates pupils to explore ways in which we obtain information from one or more of our senses and offers the opportunity to consider a wide range of related issues (e.g., the use of technology to heighten sensory information; communication (or lack of it) in the picture; the effects of losing one or more of our senses). As such, there are many links with other curriculum areas including science, English, and humanities.

As Fig.7.1 illustrates, the course involves eight modules. Each contains approximately 25 photocopiable pupil activities with accompanying teacher guidelines. The guidelines for each task involve:

- *a description* of the task (its main features, ambiguities, and intentions) together with examples of key strategies, resources, and vocabulary associated with the activity;

© Basil Blackwell Ltd in association with Somerset County Council, 1988

FIG. 7.7.   A stimulus task from the first STSC module (Foundations for Problem Solving).

- *a lesson plan* divided into three phases (introduction, development, and summary);
- *examples of transfer applications and generalizations.*

The contents of each module can be very briefly summarized as follows:

1. *Foundations for Problem Solving.* Blagg, Ballinger, Gardner, Petty, and Williams (1988a) represents the course in miniature in that it includes activities

that touch upon many of the cognitive resource and strategic issues elaborated in later modules. It also sets the scene for all subsequent modules by establishing the aims, format, and conventions of the course. The module concentrates on a range of procedures and skills essential to gathering and organizing relevant information and recognizing and defining problems. For instance, pupils learn to scan and focus; distinguish between explicit and implicit information; use systematic search strategies; and describe and label essential features. At a content level, many of the tasks integrate successfully with mathematics, humanities, English, and personal and social development courses.

2. *Analyzing and Synthesizing.* Blagg, Ballinger, Petty, and Williams (1988b) develops important vocabulary, concepts, skills, and strategies introduced in the Foundations module but focuses more specifically on the nature of analysis and synthesis in everyday life. Pupil activities consider part–whole relationships in both structures and operations and link understanding in this area to different forms of instructions, error analysis, and design issues. The final stages of the module lead on to an appreciation of the interrelationships between structure, function, and aesthetics, finishing on a complex mastery task in which pupils apply their numerous analytic skills to an evaluative exercise related to the humanities.

3. *Comparative Thinking.* Blagg, Ballinger, Gardner, and Petty (1988a) focuses on the distinction between describing and comparing before developing the nature, meaning, and purpose of comparison utilizing a wide variety of contexts and problem-solving situations from both academic and interpersonal areas. It explores the contribution spontaneous comparative behavior makes to all kinds of decision making (e.g., selecting the most economic buys in a supermarket, choosing a holiday within various constraints, etc.). The later stages of the module demonstrate how comparison forms the basis of classification. The nature and purpose of classification is explored and related in a variety of ways to both subject matter and social organizations.

4. *Positions in Time and Space.* Blagg, Ballinger, Gardner, and Petty (1988b) heightens pupil awareness of the way in which temporal and spatial considerations lie at the heart of planning and anticipating. The module exposes and integrates key concepts and vocabulary relating to reference points in time and space. Analytic behavior is now enhanced with specific spatial labeling systems and given a past–present future dimension. The later stages of the module broaden the activities beyond physical issues into "mental" issues. In particular, the module considers how different people come to adopt very different mental positions or viewpoints. This involves exploring the nature of empathy and prejudice. The content elements in the course provide numerous links with science, mathematics, English, humanities, and personal and social development courses.

5. *Understanding Analogies.* Blagg, Ballinger, and Gardner (1989) explores

the nature of symbolism and analogy in everyday life. The module considers comparative principles involved in understanding a wide range of transformations and relationships (pictorial, figural, and cartoon). It goes on to show how transformations can form the basis of understanding different kinds of analogies and how analogy, metaphor, and simile are related. The activities in this module link with English, mathematics, the sciences, and humanities as well as personal and social development courses.

6. *Patterns in Time and Space*. Blagg, Ballinger, and Gardner (1990) builds on the previous module, extending pupil understanding of spatial and temporal reference systems. It explores the kinds of predictions one can make from understanding patterns and sequences in time and space, and goes on to consider relationships between time, distance, and speed. Once again, the activities provide multiple links across a range of curriculum and interpersonal areas.

7. *Predicting and Deciding*. Blagg, Ballinger, and Gardner (in preparation a) integrates and summarizes aspects from previous modules in the context of a wide range of social, domestic, and academic decision-making activities. It highlights the fact that most decision making is based on probabilities rather than certainties. It encourages pupils to consider how different kinds of evidence and information contribute to probabilistic thinking.

8. *Organizing and Memorizing*. Blagg, Ballinger, and Gardner (in preparation b) revisits many of the ideas and resources emphasized throughout the course, with an explicit focus on techniques and strategies to facilitate recalling, organizing, and memorizing different types of information. The module (supplementary to the rest of STSC) emphasizes flexible strategic thinking through tasks that prompt pupils to consider which types of organizing and memorizing techniques and resources should be used for different purposes.

Transfer and Generalization

The structure and organization of the course addresses the key issues of transfer and generalization in a number of important ways:

- both transferable and transfer skills are emphasized throughout.
- the activities are intentionally ambiguous as a means of promoting discussion, debate, and metacognition.
- the tasks are very different in their style, format and content, level of complexity, and presentation modes. This rich variety of examples and contexts enables teachers to assess spontaneous literal and/or figural transfer in pupils and if necessary heighten awareness of transfer possibilities through sensitive prompts and questions.

- at strategic points, whole, complex mastery activities are included that extend the range and level of transfer demands.

- the increasing use of abstraction and the need to use basic cognitive resources for more sophisticated operations as the course progresses, allows the teacher to check for the transfer of ideas, principles, skills, and strategies both within and between the modules.

In addition to these broad points, transfer possibilities have been integrated into each activity and lesson plan.

The teacher guidelines emphasize that each STSC task should be contextualized by an introductory activity. This enables the teacher to establish pupil attention while preparing the pupil, either literally or figuratively, for the actual task. The teacher guidelines provide examples of suitable introductions, but the choice of introduction will depend on pupil ability and experience. The extent to which pupils can then define the task page provides an immediate opportunity for the teacher to check for transfer of ideas from the introduction to the STSC exercise. Pupils who readily make the connections between a close transfer introduction and the task page can be presented with increasingly distanced transfer introductions in subsequent activities.

In the development phase of each lesson, pupils work on the STSC task in pairs or groups, and then in class discussion are prompted to relate the use of skills and strategies involved to other contexts through inductive and deductive questioning (e.g., Where have you met this or a similar problem before? Where else might you use these skills?).

Each lesson ends with a summative review in which the teacher provides examples of transfer (near and/or far, literal and/or figural, depending on pupil ability and the nature of the task). Naturally, pupils are given the opportunity to offer their own examples of transfer and indeed, spontaneous transfer is expected as the course progresses. Wherever possible, examples of figural transfer are formalized into generalizations (i.e., rules and principles that have wide applicability).

Transfer and generalization does not rest simply with the program design. It also depends heavily on the ability of individual teachers to mediate effectively for transfer. Hopefully, the reader will already appreciate that the kind of teaching style advocated by the course is very much in tune with the models promoted by both Feuerstein et al. (1979) and Glaser (1984).

The STSC teacher guidelines do emphasize the importance of eliciting, facilitating, and cautiously prompting with open-ended questions as opposed to directing, instructing, and using closed questions. The advice moves very sensitively toward more directive prompts and questions in the event of pupil difficulty but moves away from this directive role as soon as possible to enable the child to take on responsibility for their own learning. The STSC Handbook (Blagg,

Ballinger, & Gardner, 1988) elaborates on the role of the teacher as an effective mediator and classroom manager. The issues referred to in the handbook are developed in depth in Blagg and Ballinger (1990).

Finally, transfer and generalization is also an outcome of organizational issues in schools. If thinking skills lessons are seen as a "mysterious activity," with no apparent connection to other areas of the curriculum, benefits to pupils are likely to be limited. Even if pupils acquire new strategies and resources and are prompted to question, maximum transfer and generalization is likely only if all teachers have the same optimistic expectations and sensitive teaching styles. In an ideal world, a whole school approach is required in which everyone is totally committed to enhancing pupils' cognitive development. Progress toward this is possible only with a committed senior management creating opportunities for inservice training, regular discussion groups, and fostering genuine communication within and between subject departments.

Piloting, Evaluation, and Dissemination

STSC is theoretically based and, like FIE, it is eclectically linked to some of the latest developments in the psychological world. The design and development of the course has involved national field trials and observations with many adolescents and their teachers in both inner city and rural schools. The pilot modules received highly enthusiastic user testimonials. Nevertheless, in the light of feedback from early trials, we substantially modified the course so that the final content, presentation, and style of STSC owes much to the suggestions we have received from our pilot schools. In the light of this advice, we contextualized the program rather more to enhance its meaning and relevance and also included more tasks with multiple outcomes that aided differentiation by outcome so that both lower- and higher-achieving pupils could benefit from the course.

In view of the direct involvement of many practicing teachers, the final shape and form of STSC does have a face validity in a number of respects. Undoubtedly, the materials are highly practical in the classroom. They certainly attract and motivate the users and provoke intense discussion among both pupils and teachers. In addition, our decision to include more content-loaded tasks related to academic and interpersonal areas has given the course a credibility in the context of the National Curriculum. In fact, a number of different curriculum specialists have argued that they can use the STSC as a means of delivering certain declarative and procedural aspects of their subjects as illustrated in Blagg and Ballinger (1990). In this respect, we feel we have avoided the dangers of iatrogenic educational programs.

Perhaps these points account in part for the enthusiastic take up of the course and the speed with which teachers begin to feel comfortable and confident with it. We are already quite convinced that the kinds of attitudinal teaching style and even personality changes noted among FIE teachers are now being replicated with STSC teachers. It would seem that, teaching thinking teaches teachers as a few comments from STSC users imply:

> STSC is for us primarily a diagnostic tool that has highlighted problems that we should have been aware of ten years ago.
>
> The course (STSC) has helped to move staff away from their chalk and talk approach. The pupils like the materials and saw much that the teachers missed. Questioning techniques show improvement.
>
> First year pupils took to the work very quickly and the quality of the discussion frankly took me by surprise. Pupils with quite severe deficits in basic skills revelled in the discussions. These children were also being taught in a mixed ability setting for some other subjects and by Christmas some members of staff were noticing their unusual forwardness in discussion work, even by comparison with the brightest pupils.
>
> I never realized how important it was to ask the right questions. Sometimes I kick myself because I know I've lost the pupils for about ten minutes by asking the wrong kind of question. . . .

Interestingly, STSC is being delivered in a variety of ways, ranging from a bolt-on approach, in which the modules are taught to particular groups as a separate subject, through to an infused approach in which different subject areas are taking on responsibility for different modules.

Nevertheless, positive user testimonials and wide dissemination and use does not amount to hard evidence that STSC can produce in pupils the kinds of attitudinal, behavioral, and cognitive changes that it seeks to develop. There is a need for many carefully controlled small-scale studies to consider aspects of the course and/or particular kinds of outcomes. There is also a need for large-scale, independent, and comprehensive evaluations of the kind reported in the present IE study.

We know of many small-scale studies now underway but to date, we have only received the results of one investigation carried out by Lake (1987, 1988). He compared the effects of using Lipman's Philosophy for Children Program with the first STSC module, given under two conditions. In one group, the materials were used for group work with an emphasis on pupils becoming more aware of their own thoughts and problem-solving approaches. A second group used the materials primarily as independent problem-solving tasks, with relatively little mediation, discussion, and reflection.

The pupils (mixed ability, 10- to 12-year-olds) from one class, were randomly assigned to the three groups and independently assessed at the beginning of the study and 3 months later on the GHOST Scale, listed in Appendix 31. Put very simply, the Lipman group improved significantly on Factor A, relating to pupil competence with routine classroom tasks, whereas the discussion-oriented STSC group showed a highly significant improvement on Factor B, referring to pupil ability to manage their own learning and deal with complex tasks. The second STSC group, who received no mediation and worked independently, showed no significant changes in either Factor A or B.

CONCLUDING COMMENTS

The evaluation of IE, set against the context of recent developments in the wider psychological literature, has brought the possibility of teaching cognitive skills within sight. Theory and research have highlighted many issues that have important implications for the design of cognitive skills courses. As far as possible, STSC has taken these ideas into account. STSC was initially inspired by the promise of IE and represents a kind of distanced transfer of our involvement with the program.

We regard STSC as a promising way forward rather than an end product. It is at least prompting teachers to think about their role in fostering pupils' cognitive development and offers vantage points, novel materials, and teaching strategies to enhance that role. Teaching thinking is both a humbling yet illuminating experience that transcends subject dogma. Teachers that seriously embark on this quest find themselves discussing all manner of curriculum issues with colleagues of very different interests, persuasions, and specialisms. Frequently they find that:

> . . . a close look at conventional disciplinary boundaries discloses not a well-defined geography with borders naturally marked by rivers and mountain ranges but, instead, enormous overlap and interrelation. If knowledge and skill are local, the boundaries surely are not the cleavages of the conventional curriculum. Yet because those cleavages are there as part of the organization of schooling, tactics . . . are needed to take the numerous opportunities for fertile transfer across the conventional subject matters. (Perkins & Salomon, 1988, p. 30)

Appendices

INSTRUMENTAL ENRICHMENT
SEMI-STRUCTURED PUPIL INTERVIEW
SCHEDULE

1. Tell me about your typical week—the courses you take day by day and how you feel about them?

2. How do you feel about school this year?

3. What has been different about school this year compared to other years? What have been the important changes for you and why?

4. Which of the subjects are you really enjoying most this year? What do you like about these most?

5. What do you feel about being a pupil at this particular school?

6. How do you feel about the way the groups are organized? I mean, in some schools all of the children are mixed up, so that in the same class you have children who find their school work very difficult alongside other children who find it very easy and are doing very well. Whereas, in other schools the children are grouped into bands and sets according to how well they are doing in the school. How does it work at your school and how do you feel about it?

7. What sort of system would you prefer in your school? What would you like to see and why?

8. What residential experiences have you been involved in this year?

9. Have you been involved with any work experience projects this year? If so, could you tell me a little bit about these.

10. I would like to ask you a little bit about FIE now. First of all, was it an option that you chose to do or was it something that you had to do?

    Option/Compulsory

11. How do you feel about that? Do you think it should be an option or do you think it should be something that all pupils should do? Why?

12. Is it very different to the other subjects you take?

    Yes/No

13. In what way is it different?

14. Is there more discussion work in FIE?

    Yes/No

15. Do you join in the discussions?

    Rarely/Sometimes/Always

16. How do you feel about talking in front of the class?

17. Have your feelings about this changed over the year?

18. Have your parents attended an open evening or talked to your teacher about FIE?

    Yes/No

19. Have they asked you about FIE?

    Yes/No

20. What do they think about it?

21. What can you tell me about the four instruments you have studied this year and what did you think about them?

    Organization of dots:

    Analytic perception:

    Orientation in Space:

    Comparisons:

22. What did you like in particular about FIE?

22. What did you particularly dislike about FIE?

24. In what ways do you think that FIE has helped you in any of your other school subjects?

25. In what way has FIE helped you outside school?

26. In what ways do you think that FIE will help you when you leave school?

27. They do say that FIE makes you very accurate and careful in your work. Have you noticed this in your FIE lessons?

    Yes/No

28. Do you think FIE has helped you to be more careful in your other subjects?

29. Can you think of any other changes that may have happened to you that are to do with studying FIE?

30. FIE involves learning lots of new words and ideas. How has this helped you in other subjects?

    Yes/No

31. Other comments.

NIGEL BLAGG, PhD
Senior Educational Psychologist
and FIE Evaluator for Somerset

APPENDIX 2

INSTRUMENTAL ENRICHMENT— SUMMATIVE DIARY RECORD

FIE TEACHER —————
SCHOOL —————
TERM BEGINNING ———

A TIMETABLE ARRANGEMENTS

1 Number of timetabled FIE lessons —————————

2 Number of FIE lessons taught —————————————

3 Reasons for differences between 1 and 2—

—————————————————————————————

4 Number of timetabled lessons for bridging —————————

5 Number of bridging lessons taught —————————————

—————————————————————————————

NB: 4 and 5 refer to School D only

B VISITORS TO LESSONS

NAME	POSITION	NUMBER OF VISITS

NB: This refers to the number of lessons *taught by the FIE teacher*. FIE lessons *covered* by other members of staff should *not* be included.

C ATTENDANCE RECORD FOR EACH PUPIL FOR FIE LESSONS AS IN A(2):

Pupil's Name	FIE Lessons attended	
	Present	Absent

D THE FIE MATERIAL
1 Units and pages covered.

2 Teacher responses to the material—
(a) Positive
Comments:

(b) Negative
Comments:

3 Student response to the lessons.

(a) Positive
Comments:

(b) Negative
Comments:

E THE NATURE AND EXTENT OF BRIDGING WITHIN FIE LESSONS
(Please tick as appropriate).

1 Teacher gives examples of bridging—always/sometimes/never.

2 Pupils spontaneously bridge—always/sometimes/never.

3 Please indicate main areas where bridging occurs.
Teacher's own subject discipline.
Object subject areas.
Pupil's everyday experiences at home and school.
Careers.
Other.

4 Difficulties and problems with bridging.

F STAFF ROOM RESPONSE

Please list names and subject disciplines of teachers who have shown a particular interest in FIE and FIE Pupils this term. Alongside each name please tick appropriately those teachers who have been involved in attending FIE lessons; bridging activities in their own lessons; spontaneously noting improvement in FIE pupils as compared to their non-FIE peers.

NAME	SUBJECT	BRIDGING	FIE LESSONS ATTENDED	POSITIVE COMMENTS ON FIE PUPILS

G Please comment on developing links with non-FIE staff with respect to bridging.

H Please attach photocopies of positive comments from non-FIE teachers about FIE pupils.

I Please comment on any general developments with respect to pupils as a result of FIE Practice this term.

J Do you feel that your FIE work this term has brought about any differences in the approach to your main subject discipline in terms of preparation, presentation, teaching style, etc. If so please comment in detail.

K Any other comments including: overall highs or lows for the term; suggestions for improvements in the co-ordination of the FIE program; ways of improving time-tabling arrangements, etc.

Signed _____

Date _____

APPENDIX 3

M.L.E. SUMMARY RATING

NAME   SCHOOL

SUBJECT   F.I.E.   PERIOD 1984–86

INTENTIONALITY/RECIPROCITY   Total =

A. Classroom Organization

   1. Preparation and planning   (a) (b) (c) (d)

   2. Lesson beginnings   (b) (c)

   3. Transitions   (c)

B. General Teaching Style   (a) (b) (c) (d) (f) (g) (h) (i) (j) (k)

C. Lesson Content

   1. Introduction   (a) (b) (c) (f) (g) (h) (i) (j) (k) (l)

   2. Independent work   (a) (c) (d)

   3. Discussion   (a) (b) (d) (e) (f) (h) (i) (k) (l)

   4. Summary   (a) (b) (c) (d) (e)

MEANING   Total =

A. Classroom Organization

   1. Preparation and planning   (a) (d)

   2. Lesson beginnings   (b) (c)

   4. Lesson endings   (c)

B. General Teaching Style   (b) (c) (d) (e) (f) (g) (k)

C. Lesson Content

   1. Introduction   (c) (d) (e) (f) (g) (h) (i) (j) (k) (l)

   2. Independent work   (b) (c) (d)

   3. Discussion   (a) (b) (c) (d) (e) (f) (g) (h) (l)

   4. Summary   (a) (b) (d) (e)

TRANSCENDENCE   Total =

C. Lesson Content

   1. Introduction   (d) (e) (f) (g) (h) (j) (k) (l)

   2. Independent work   (b)

   3. Discussion   (a) (c) (d) (e) (f) (g) (h) (j) (l)

   4. Summary   (b)

COMPETENCE   Total =

A. Classroom Organization

   1. Preparation and planning   (a)

B. General Teaching Style   (c) (d) (f) (g) (i)

C. Lesson Content

   2. Independent work   (c) (d) (e)

   3. Discussion   (b) (k)

   4. Summary   (a) (d) (e)

REGULATION AND CONTROL OF BEHAVIOR   Total =

A. Classroom Organization

   1. Preparation and planning   (a) (b) (c)

   2. Lesson beginnings   (a)

   3. Transitions   (a) (b) (d)

   4. Lesson endings   (a) (b) (c) (d)

B. General Teaching Style   (b) (e) (h)

C. Lesson Content

   1. Introduction   (h) (l)

   2. Independent work   (a) (c) (d) (e)

   3. Discussion   (b) (c) (d) (e) (i) (k)

   4. Summary   (c) (d) (e)

SHARING BEHAVIOR   Total =

A. Classroom Organization

   1. Preparation and planning   (a) (b)

   4. Lesson endings   (c)

B. General Teaching Style   (a) (b) (c) (d) (f) (g) (i) (j)

C. Lesson Content

   1. Introduction   (f) (g)

   2. Independent work   (c) (d)

   3. Discussion   (a) (b) (c) (d) (e) (f) (g) (h) (i) (k)
                                   (l)

   4. Summary   (c) (d) (e)

INDIVIDUATION AND PSYCHOLOGICAL DIFFERENTIATION

   4. Lesson beginnings   (c)

B. General Teaching Style   (b) (c) (d) (f) (g) (i)

C. Lesson Content

   1. Introduction   (f) (g)

   2. Independent work   (c) (d) (e)

   3. Discussion   (c) (d) (e) (h) (j) (k) (l)

GOAL SEEKING, GOAL SETTING, PLANNING,
AND GOAL ACHIEVING BEHAVIOR Total =

A. Classroom Organization

    1. Preparation and planning   (c)

    2. Lesson beginnings   (c)

    3. Transitions   (c)

    4. Lesson endings   (c)

B. General Teaching Style   (e)   (g)

C. Lesson Content

    1. Introduction   (c)   (f)   (g)   (h)   (i)   (j)

    2. Independent work   (a)   (b)   (c)   (d)   (e)

    3. Discussion   (b)   (c)   (d)

    4. Summary   (a)   (d)   (e)

CHALLENGE, SEARCH FOR NOVELTY, AND COMPLEXITY   Total =

A. Classroom Organization

    2. Lesson beginnings   (b)

B. General Teaching Style   (d)   (f)   (g)

C. Lesson Content

    1. Introduction   (f)   (g)   (i)   (j)   (k)

    3. Discussion   (b)   (c)   (d)   (e)   (h)   (j)   (l)

APPENDIX 4

(a) The Mean Scores of Control, Low-MLE, and High-MLE Groups at the Beginning of the Study on a Range of Psychometric Measures and (b) Differences Between the Characteristics of Each Group Based on an Analysis of Variance

Variable	Control Mean	N	Low-MLE Mean	N	High-MLE Mean	N	F Ratio	P
ERT quotient	85.88	40	82.63	79	81.96	47	4.18	<0.05
RW1 quotient	87.80	44	84.67	81	86.45	44	1.39	NS
RW2 quotient	84.09	44	83.79	81	83.25	44	0.08	NS
RW3 quotient	84.02	44	81.60	81	80.05	44	1.94	NS
RM1 quotient	85.34	44	82.59	79	88.33	48	0.09	NS
RM2 quotient	87.52	44	88.18	79	88.33	48	0.09	NS
BAS IQ	91.59	46	91.20	71	92.98	53	0.31	NS
BAS WD 'T' scores	42.59	46	41.03	71	42.68	53	1.64	NS
BAS RD 'T' scores	48.22	46	48.63	71	49.45	53	0.20	NS
BAS SIM 'T' scores	45.24	46	43.34	71	45.55	53	1.76	NS
BAS BDP 'T' scores	51.11	46	50.56	71	49.75	53	0.31	NS
BAS MAT 'T' scores	44.37	46	46.27	71	44.91	53	0.99	NS
BAS BD 'T' scores	44.93	46	45.01	71	47.58	53	1.40	NS
CSMS	6.32	46	6.00	75	6.30	42	2.92	NS

MLE = Mediated Learning Experience Rating
N = Number of Subjects
F RATIO = From ANOVA Tables
P = Probability Levles

APPENDIX 5

(a) The Mean Scores of Each Teaching Group at the Beginning of the Study on a Range of Psychometric Tests and (b) Differences Between the Teaching Groups Emerging From an Analysis of Variance

Variables	4	5	6	7	8	9	10	11	12	13	15	16	17	18	F Ratio	P
ERT quotient	84.20	83.75	84.91	83.00	81.82	88.00	82.31	82.15	82.15	81.93	82.00	82.67	84.29	81.42	0.95	NS
RW1 quotient	87.00	91.00	84.06	88.40	87.40	89.00	87.55	89.20	89.20	83.85	82.40	80.81	84.40	85.43	1.22	NS
RW2 quotient	80.92	80.15	80.38	84.70	83.40	91.47	83.00	86.93	86.93	85.15	80.53	86.56	79.13	83.43	1.94	<0.05
RW3 quotient	85.25	85.38	81.81	84.00	80.50	85.20	74.27	79.60	79.60	80.69	78.27	86.19	79.67	80.29	1.76	NS
RM1 quotient	80.46	80.38	85.00	84.60	85.50	90.00	86.15	87.23	87.23	90.54	79.53	81.81	79.40	82.71	2.14	<0.05
RM2 quotient	84.92	83.69	87.44	88.60	90.90	90.93	87.77	89.15	89.15	89.79	88.60	89.69	83.73	89.64	0.91	NS
BAS IQ	91.23	90.15	89.94	92.69	92.38	94.24	94.67	96.21	96.21	94.24	86.71	90.06	89.93	78.00	0.72	NS
BAS WD 'T' scores	39.77	42.31	41.63	41.31	42.85	43.71	42.50	41.86	41.86	44.82	39.88	39.65	42.57	44.00	1.14	NS
BAS RD 'T' scores	49.62	49.85	45.94	49.69	51.62	49.12	46.50	53.79	53.79	50.47	44.47	49.65	45.21	42.00	1.10	NS
BAS SIM 'T' scores	44.62	42.62	46.00	44.46	44.85	46.53	46.92	45.43	45.43	46.12	40.35	42.76	44.29	36.00	1.12	NS
BAS BDP 'T' scores	51.08	49.54	50.25	50.46	47.77	53.12	50.50	52.07	52.07	49.71	49.82	49.47	50.43	45.00	0.36	NS
BAS MAT 'T' scores	42.31	42.08	44.50	47.38	44.77	46.00	48.08	46.57	46.57	45.29	44.29	47.24	44.93	40.00	0.81	NS
BAS BD 'T' scores	47.69	45.15	44.56	46.08	46.31	45.12	50.17	47.36	47.36	47.00	43.41	42.94	45.07	32.00	0.74	NS
CSMS	6.22	6.12	6.29	6.37	6.31	6.47	6.18	5.87	5.87	6.44	5.99	5.95	5.65	6.21	1.15	NS

P = Probability levels.
F RATIO = From ANOVA tables.

APPENDIX 6

Analysis of Variance of the Edinburgh Reading Test Change Scores Exploring Treatment, Sex, and School Factors

Part (a)

Source	S of Squares	Degrees of Freedom	Mean sq.	F (ratio)	P (variance)
Treatment	0.846	1	0.846	.039	.845
Sex	5.712	1	5.712	.260	.611
School	37.339	3	12.446	.567	.638
Explained	45.079	5	9.016	.411	.840
Residual	1689.572	77	21.942		

Part (b)

Treat	School A Sex		School B Sex		School C Sex		School D Sex	
	Boy	Girl	Boy	Girl	Boy	Girl	Boy	Girl
Exp.	1.00	0.36	−1.67	−2.67	1.38	3.67	1.50	1.60
	(16)	(14)	(3)	(3)	(13)	(9)	(6)	(5)
Cont.	—	—	−1.67	2.00	—	—	3.20	−3.67
			(3)	(3)			(5)	(3)

Exp. = IE pupils   Cont. = Control pupils   Treat = Treatment

APPENDIX 7

Analysis of Variance of the Richmond Work Study RW2 Change Scores Exploring Treatment, Sex, and School Factors

Part (a):

Source	S of Squares	Degrees of Freedom	Mean sq.	F (ratio)	P (variance)
Treatment	230.967	1	230.967	1.912	.171
Sex	.886	1	.886	.007	.932
School	59.780	3	19.927	.165	.920
Explained	251.075	5	50.215	.416	.836
Residual	9301.021	77	120.792		

Part (b): Group means

Treat	School A Sex		School B Sex		School C Sex		School D Sex	
	Boy	Girl	Boy	Girl	Boy	Girl	Boy	Girl
Exp.	0.00	4.00	7.33	−7.67	1.15	3.56	−2.17	3.40
	(16)	(14)	(3)	(3)	(13)	(9)	(6)	(5)
Cont.	—	—	7.67	0.33	—	—	12.40	−2.67
			(3)	(3)			(5)	(3)

Exp. = IE pupils   Cont. = Control pupils   Treat = Treatment

APPENDIX 8

Analysis of Variance of the Richmond Work Study RW3 Change Scores Exploring Treatment, Sex, and School Factors

Part (a):

Source	S of Squares	Degrees of Freedom	Mean sq.	F (ratio)	P (variance)
Treatment	4.608	1	4.608	.032	.859
Sex	1.309	1	1.309	.009	.925
School	630.128	3	210.043	1.439	.238
Explained	898.802	5	179.760	1.231	.303
Residual	11241.439	77	145.993		

Part (b): Group means

Treat	School A Sex		School B Sex		School C Sex		School D Sex	
	Boy	Girl	Boy	Girl	Boy	Girl	Boy	Girl
Exp.	2.19	3.21	−1.33	−6.33	6.69	7.22	−2.33	5.60
	(16)	(14)	(3)	(3)	(13)	(9)	(6)	(5)
Cont.	—	—	5.00	−9.67	—	—	−1.40	−0.33
			(3)	(3)			(5)	(3)

Exp. = IE pupils   Cont. = Control pupils   Treat = Treatment

APPENDIX 9

Analysis of Variance of the Richmond Mathematics Test RM2 Change Scores Exploring Treatment, Sex, and School Factors.

Part (a):

Source	S of Squares	Degrees of Freedom	Mean sq.	F (ratio)	P (variance)
Treatment	329.433	1	329.433	1.937	.169
Sex	46.684	1	46.684	.274	.602
School	381.949	3	127.316	.748	.528
Explained	571.034	5	114.207	.671	.647
Residual	9695.950	57	170.104		

Part (b): Group means

Treat	School A Sex		School B Sex		School C Sex		School D Sex	
	Boy	Girl	Boy	Girl	Boy	Girl	Boy	Girl
Exp.	−6.29	5.62	−2.00	−2.50	−0.27	−2.80	−8.25	−3.33
	(7)	(13)	(1)	(2)	(11)	(5)	(8)	(3)
Cont.	—	—	3.67	−7.00	—	—	6.60	−4.67
			(3)	(2)			(5)	(3)

Exp. = IE pupils   Cont. = Control pupils   Treat = Treatment

APPENDIX 10

Analysis of Variance of the Science Reasoning Test CSMSS Change Scores Exploring Treatment, Sex, and School Factors

Part (a): Source	S of Squares	Degrees of Freedom	Mean sq.	F (ratio)	P (variance)
Treatment	.221	1	.221	.401	.529
Sex	.000	1	.000	.000	.996
School	2.375	3	.792	1.433	.242
Explained	2.423	5	.485	.878	.502
Residual	31.474	57	.552		

Part (b): Group means

Treat	School A Sex		School B Sex		School C Sex		School D Sex	
	Boy	Girl	Boy	Girl	Boy	Girl	Boy	Girl
Exp.	0.27	0.18	−0.40	−1.00	−0.14	−0.34	0.10	0.10
	(7)	(13)	(1)	(2)	(11)	(5)	(8)	(3)
Cont.	—	—	−0.30	−0.05	—	—	0.28	−0.20
			(3)	(2)			(5)	(3)

Exp. = IE pupils   Cont. = Control pupils   Treat = Treatment

APPENDIX 11

Analysis of Variance of the British Ability Scales BAS IQ Change Scores Exploring Treatment, Sex, and School Factors.

Part (a): Source	S of Squares	Degrees of Freedom	Mean sq.	F (ratio)	P (variance)
Treatment	1.691	1	1.691	.030	.864
Sex	69.069	1	69.069	1.213	.275
School	230.384	3	76.795	1.349	.268
Explained	250.208	5	50.042	.879	.501
Residual	3245.443	57	56.938		

Part (b): Group means

Treat	School A Sex		School B Sex		School C Sex		School D Sex	
	Boy	Girl	Boy	Girl	Boy	Girl	Boy	Girl
Exp.	2.14	1.85	−7.00	8.50	4.91	9.00	5.38	6.67
	(7)	(13)	(1)	(2)	(11)	(5)	(8)	(3)
Cont.	—	—	9.00	1.00	—	—	0.60	9.67
			(3)	(2)			(5)	(3)

Exp. = IE pupils   Cont. = Control pupils   Treat = Treatment

APPENDIX 12

Analysis of Variance of the BAS Word Definitions Scale Change Scores Exploring Treatment, Sex, and School Factors

Part (a):

Source	S of Squares	Degrees of Freedom	Mean sq.	F (ratio)	P (variance)
Treatment	4.281	1	4.281	.295	.589
Sex	9.113	1	9.113	.627	.432
School	22.066	3	7.355	.506	.679
Explained	44.569	5	8.914	.614	.690
Residual	828.035	57	14.527		

Part (b): Group means

Treat	School A Sex		School B Sex		School C Sex		School D Sex	
	Boy	Girl	Boy	Girl	Boy	Girl	Boy	Girl
Exp.	−2.00	−0.54	−2.00	2.50	−0.36	1.00	0.00	−0.33
	(7)	(13)	(1)	(2)	(11)	(5)	(8)	(3)
Cont.	—	—	1.33	0.00	—	—	1.40	0.67
			(3)	(2)			(5)	(3)

Exp. = IE pupils   Cont. = Control pupils   Treat = Treatment

APPENDIX 13

Analysis of Variance of the BAS RECALL of Designs Scale Change Scores Exploring Treatment, Sex, and School Factors

Part (a):

Source	S of Squares	Degrees of Freedom	Mean sq.	F (ratio)	P (variance)
Treatment	.121	1	.121	.002	.963
Sex	2.589	1	2.589	.046	.830
School	131.044	3	43.948	.788	.506
Explained	163.527	5	32.705	.586	.710
Residual	3179.330	57	55.778		

Part (b): Group means

Treat	School A Sex		School B Sex		School C Sex		School D Sex	
	Boy	Girl	Boy	Girl	Boy	Girl	Boy	Girl
Exp.	1.60	5.20	1.75	1.75	−1.43	4.00	−4.25	1.40
	(5)	(10)	(4)	(4)	(7)	(5)	(4)	(5)
Cont.	—	—	0.75	−5.75	—	—	5.00	−2.00
			(4)	(4)			(7)	(4)

Exp. = IE pupils   Cont. = Control pupils   Treat = Treatment

APPENDIX 14

Analysis of Variance of the BAS Similarities Scale Change Scores Exploring Treatment, Sex, and School Factors

Part (a): Source	S of Squares	Degrees of Freedom	Mean sq.	F (ratio)	P (variance)
Treatment	1121.502	1	1121.502	1.217	.275
Sex	372.889	1	372.889	.405	.527
School	1216.481	3	405.494	.440	.725
Explained	3477.041	5	695.408	.775	.586
Residual	52533.277	57	921.636		

Part (b): Group means

Treat	School A Sex		School B Sex		School C Sex		School D Sex	
	Boy	Girl	Boy	Girl	Boy	Girl	Boy	Girl
Exp.	−15.00	3.80	−10.50	−8.75	−4.00	−28.80	−5.75	−16.40
	(5)	(10)	(4)	(4)	(7)	(5)	(4)	(5)
Cont.	—	—	−17.00	−29.75	—	—	−17.43	−24.25
			(4)	(4)			(7)	(4)

Exp. = IE pupils   Cont. = Control pupils   Treat = Treatment

APPENDIX 15

Analysis of Variance of the BAS Block Design (level) Change Scores Exploring Treatment, Sex, and School Factors.

Part (a): Source	S of Squares	Degrees of Freedom	Mean sq.	F (ratio)	P (variance)
Treatment	3507.253	1	3507.253	4.818	.032
Sex	43.508	1	43.508	.060	.808
School	4809.581	3	1603.194	2.202	.098
Explained	5519.694	5	1103.939	1.516	.199
Residual	41495.734	57	727.995		

Part (b): Group means

Treat	School A Sex		School B Sex		School C Sex		School D Sex	
	Boy	Girl	Boy	Girl	Boy	Girl	Boy	Girl
Exp.	4.60	−3.40	37.75	11.25	−5.29	−2.00	14.00	13.20
	(5)	(10)	(4)	(4)	(7)	(5)	(4)	(5)
Cont.	—	—	−2.75	−.75	—	—	−7.57	11.00
			(4)	(4)			(7)	(4)

Exp. = IE pupils   Cont. = Control pupils   Treat = Treatment

APPENDIX 16

Analysis of Variance of the BAS Matrices Change Scores Exploring Treatment, Sex, and School Factors.

Part (a): Source	S of Squares	Degrees of Freedom	Mean sq.	F (ratio)	P (variance)
Treatment	81.460	1	81.460	.107	.745
Sex	783.011	1	783.011	1.028	.315
School	1139.144	3	379.715	.499	.685
Explained	2278.063	5	455.613	.598	.701
Residual	43396.255	57	761.338		

Part (b): Group means

Treat	School A Sex		School B Sex		School C Sex		School D Sex	
	Boy	Girl	Boy	Girl	Boy	Girl	Boy	Girl
Exp.	−15.60	−12.70	6.50	0.25	−3.14	−18.40	−8.50	−5.20
	(5)	(10)	(4)	(4)	(7)	(5)	(4)	(5)
Cont.	—	—	−12.25	−15.50	—	—	10.43	−9.50
			(4)	(4)			(7)	(4)

Exp. = IE pupils   Cont. = Control pupils   Treat = Treatment

APPENDIX 17

Analysis of Covariance of Edinburgh Reading Test, Change Scores Exploring the Differential Effects of Attendance and MLEU on Treatment Outcome

Part (a): Source	S of Squares	Degrees of Freedom	Mean sq.	F (ratio)	P (variance)
Attendance	70.015	1	70.015	3.363	.072
MLEU	47.263	1	47.263	2.270	.137
Sex	1.058	1	1.058	.051	.822
School Sex	31.667	3	10.556	.507	.679
School	66.636	3	22.212	1.067	.370
Explained	205.051	9	22.782	1.094	.381
Residual	1207.478	58	20.819		

Part (b): Adjusted Means

	1	2		
Sex	1.037	1.287		
	(37)	(31)		

	A	B	C	D
School	−1.003	1.297	.827	1.717
	(6)	(30)	(11)	(21)

APPENDIX 18

Analysis of Covariance of Richmond Work Study, RW1, Change Scores, Exploring the Differential Effects of Attendance and MLEU on Treatment Outcome.

Part (a): Source	S of Squares	Degrees of Freedom	Mean sq.	F (ratio)	P (variance)
Attendance	51.311	1	51.311	.504	.480
MLEU	202.407	1	202.407	1.990	.164
Sex	.150	1	.150	.001	.969
School	375.814	3	125.271	1.232	.306
Sex					
School	271.644	3	90.548	.890	.452
Explained	926.486	9	102.943	1.012	.441
Residual	5899.205	58	101.710		

Part (b): Adjusted Means

	1	2		
Sex	2.681	2.791		
	(37)	(31)		

	A	B	C	D
School	−4.669	3.781	.811	4.321
	(6)	(30)	(11)	(21)

APPENDIX 19

Analysis of Covariance of Richmond Work Study, RW2, Change Scores Exploring the Differential Effects of Attendance and MLEU on Treatment Outcome.

Part (a): Source	S of Squares	Degrees of Freedom	Mean sq.	F (ratio)	P (variance)
Attendance	132.727	1	132.727	1.497	.226
MLEU	20.293	1	20.293	.229	.634
Sex	95.492	1	95.492	1.077	.304
School	51.425	3	17.142	.193	.901
Sex					
School	601.031	3	200.344	2.260	.091
Explained	886.317	9	98.480	1.111	.370
Residual	5141.492	58	88.646		

Part (b): Adjusted Means

	1	2		
Sex	0.278	2.668		
	(37)	(31)		

	A	B	C	D
School	−1.872	1.948	1.248	1.518
	(6)	(30)	(11)	(21)

APPENDIX 20

Analysis of Covariance of Richmond Work Study, RW3, Change Scores Exploring the Differential Effects of Attendance and MLEU on Treatment Outcome.

Part (a): Source	S of Squares	Degrees of Freedom	Mean sq.	F (ratio)	P (variance)
Attendance	.262	1	.262	.002	.964
MLEU	11.095	1	11.095	.087	.769
Sex	69.548	1	69.548	.548	.462
School	582.061	3	194.020	1.527	.217
Sex					
School	195.116	3	65.039	.512	.676
Explained	841.638	9	93.514	.736	.674
Residual	7367.429	58	127.025		

Part (b): Adjusted Means

Sex	1	2		
	1.952	3.992		
	(37)	(31)		

School	A	B	C	D
	−6.078	3.512	1.192	5.422
	(6)	(30)	(11)	(21)

APPENDIX 21

Analysis of Covariance of Richmond Maths Test, RM1, Change Scores Exploring the Differential Effects of Attendance and MLEU on Treatment Outcome.

Part (a): Source	S of Squares	Degrees of Freedom	Mean sq.	F (ratio)	P (variance)
Attendance	10.871	1	10.871	.140	.710
MLEU	257.770	1	257.770	3.316	.074
Sex	61.200	1	61.200	.787	.379
School	919.878	3	306.656	3.945	.013
Sex					
School	112.918	3	37.639	.484	.695
Explained	1371.914	9	152.435	1.961	.061
Residual	4508.557	58	77.734		

Part (b): Adjusted Means

Sex	1	2		
	.542	2.452		
	(37)	(31)		

School	A	B	C	D
	−8.878	6.132	0.732	−2.038
	(6)	(30)	(11)	(21)

APPENDIX 22

Analysis of Covariance of Richmond Maths Test, RM2, Change Scores Exploring the Differential Effects of Attendance and MLEU on Treatment Outcome.

Part (a): Source	S of Squares	Degrees of Freedom	Mean sq.	F (ratio)	P (variance)
Attendance	278.983	1	278.983	1.865	.180
MLEU	7.874	1	7.874	.053	.820
Sex	318.714	1	318.714	2.131	.152
School	694.310	3	231.437	1.547	.218
Sex					
School	387.661	3	129.220	.864	.468
Explained	1771.324	9	196.814	1.316	.260
Residual	5834.064	39	149.591		

Part (b): Adjusted Means

	1	2		
Sex	−4.037 (27)	1.913 (22)		

	A	B	C	D
School	−12.087 (3)	4.483 (19)	−4.887 (11)	−3.887 (16)

APPENDIX 23

Analysis of Covariance of Science Reasoning Test Change Scores Exploring the Differential Effects of Attendance and MLEU on Treatment Outcome.

Part (a): Source	S of Squares	Degrees of Freedom	Mean sq.	F (ratio)	P (variance)
Attendance	.234	1	.234	.381	.541
MLEU	1.234	1	1.234	2.007	.164
Sex	.013	1	.013	.022	.883
School	1.321	3	.440	.717	.548
Sex					
School	.720	3	.240	.391	.760
Explained	4.105	9	.456	.742	.669
Residual	23.975	39	.615		

Part (b): Adjusted Means

	1	2		
Sex	.051 (27)	.091 (22)		

	A	B	C	D
School	−0.669 (3)	.121 (19)	.101 (11)	.131 (16)

APPENDIX 24

**Analysis of Covariance of BASIQ Change Scores Exploring the
Differential Effects of Attendance and MLEU on Treatment Outcome.**

Part (a): Source	S of Squares	Degrees of Freedom	Mean sq.	F (ratio)	P (variance)
Attendance	58.084	1	58.084	1.206	.279
MLEU	151.566	1	151.566	3.147	.084
Sex	127.207	1	127.207	2.641	.112
School Sex	95.432	3	31.811	.661	.581
School	185.801	3	61.934	1.286	.293
Explained	550.878	9	61.209	1.271	.283
Residual	1878.183	39	48.159		

Part (b): Adjusted Means

	1	2		
Sex	2.555 (27)	6.315 (22)		

	A	B	C	D
School	4.075 (3)	2.065 (19)	5.845 (11)	5.765 (16)

APPENDIX 25

**Analysis of Covariance of BASIQ Subtest WORT Change Scores Exploring the
Differential Effects of Attendance and MLEU on Treatment Outcome.**

Part (a): Source	S of Squares	Degrees of Freedom	Mean sq.	F (ratio)	P (variance)
Attendance	.218	1	.218	.016	.901
MLEU	1.346	1	1.346	.098	.756
Sex	12.825	1	12.825	.932	.340
School Sex	40.870	3	13.623	.990	.408
School	13.718	3	4.573	.332	.802
Explained	67.290	9	7.477	.543	.834
Residual	536.710	39	13.762		

Part (b): Adjusted Means

	1	2		
Sex	−0.969 (27)	0.231 (22)		

	A	B	C	D
School	2.251 (3)	−1.999 (19)	−0.099 (11)	0.701 (16)

APPENDIX 26

Analysis of Covariance of BASIQ Subtest RECALLT Change Scores Exploring the Differential Effects of Attendance and MLEU on Treatment Outcome.

Part (a): Source	S of Squares	Degrees of Freedom	Mean sq.	F (ratio)	P (variance)
Attendance	.272	1	.272	.005	.946
MLEU	24.104	1	24.104	.416	.523
Sex	167.163	1	167.163	2.885	.099
School	108.698	3	36.233	.625	.604
Sex School	44.626	3	14.875	.257	.856
Explained	373.183	9	41.465	.716	.691
Residual	1930.363	34	57.952		

Part (b): Adjusted Means

	1	2
Sex	−0.598 (20)	3.582 (24)

	A	B	C	D
School	2.102 (8)	3.402 (15)	−1.128 (9)	1.352 (12)

APPENDIX 27

Analysis of Covariance of BASIQ subtest SIMT Change Scores Exploring the Differential Effects of Attendance and MLEU on Treatment Outcome.

Part (a): Source	S of Squares	Degrees of Freedom	Mean sq.	F (ratio)	P (variance)
Attendance	1157.188	1	1157.188	1.109	.300
MLEU	.001	1	.001	.000	.999
Sex	246.219	1	246.219	.236	.630
School	3267.889	3	1089.296	1.044	.386
Sex School	1682.131	3	560.710	.537	.660
Explained	6516.392	9	724.044	.694	.710
Residual	35486.040	34	1043.707		

Part (b): Adjusted Means

	1	2
Sex	−6.116 (20)	11.196 (24)

	A	B	C	D
School	−21.076 (8)	6.354 (15)	−12.506 (9)	−17.096 (12)

APPENDIX 28

Analysis of Covariance of BASIQ Subtest BLOCKT Change Scores Exploring the Differential Effects of Attendance and MLEU on Treatment Outcome.

Part (a): Source	S of Squares	Degrees of Freedom	Mean sq.	F (ratio)	P (variance)
Attendance	79.061	1	79.061	.076	.784
MLEU	11.261	1	11.261	.011	.918
Sex	2505.110	1	2505.110	2.418	.129
School	1093.117	3	364.372	.352	.788
Sex					
School	1348.868	3	449.623	.434	.730
Explained	5433.314	9	603.702	.583	.802
Residual	35229.664	34	1036.167		

Part (b): Adjusted Means

	$\overline{1}$	$\overline{2}$		
Sex	7.797 (20)	−8.375 (24)		

	$\overline{A}$	$\overline{B}$	$\overline{C}$	$\overline{D}$
School	8.597 (8)	−9.283 (15)	−1.353 (9)	3.137 (12)

APPENDIX 29

Analysis of Covariance of BASIQ Subtest POWERT Change Scores Exploring the Differential Effects of Attendance and MLEU on Treatment Outcome.

Part (a): Source	S of Squares	Degrees of Freedom	Mean sq.	F (ratio)	P (variance)
Attendance	686.934	1	686.934	.891	.352
MLEU	1248.016	1	1248.016	1.618	.212
Sex	206.435	1	206.435	.268	.608
School	5040.365	3	1680.122	2.178	.109
Sex					
School	1103.533	3	367.844	.477	.700
Explained	7645.974	9	849.553	1.101	.3 88
Residual	26225.662	34	771.343		

Part (b): Adjusted Means

	$\overline{1}$	$\overline{2}$		
Sex	8.439 (20)	3.799 (24)		

	$\overline{A}$	$\overline{B}$	$\overline{C}$	$\overline{D}$
School	27.679 (8)	−2.491 (15)	13.939 (9)	−4.131 (12)

APPENDIX 30

Analysis of Covariance of BASIQ Subtest MATT Change Scores Exploring the Differential Effects of Attendance and MLEU on Treatment Outcome.

Part (a): Source	S of Squares	Degrees of Freedom	Mean sq.	F (ratio)	P (variance)
Attendance	699.119	1	699.119	.836	.367
MLEU	42.724	1	42.724	.051	.823
Sex	388.506	1	388.506	.464	.500
School	905.754	3	301.918	.361	.782
Sex School	771.088	3	257.029	.307	.820
Explained	3231.052	9	359.006	.429	.910
Residual	28440.948	34			

Part (b): Adjusted Means

	1	2		
Sex	−4.530 (20)	−10.900 (24)		

	A	B	C	D
School	3.070 (8)	−13.140 (15)	−6.720 (9)	−9.910 (12)

APPENDIX 31

THE GATEHOUSE OBSERVATION SCHEDULE FOR TEACHERS (Lake 1987)
(Developed from the Somerset Observation Schedule (Blagg 1983))

School _____ Child's Name _____
Teacher _____

The following pairs of statements describe aspects of a child's current learning characteristics in the classroom. They are divided into seven categories. Please make your judgments from your own knowledge and observations of each child, by ticking in the appropriate column, according to the following guide:

Column 1. The Left Hand statement is true all or nearly all of the time
2. The Left Hand statement is much more often true.
3. The Left Hand statement is more often true.
4. The child currently falls between the two—sometimes one way, sometimes the other.
5. The Right Hand statement is more often true.
6. The Right Hand statement is much more often true.
7. The Right Hand statement is true all or nearly all of the time.

	1	2	3	4	5	6	7	
1. Settles down to work quickly.	—	—	—	—	—	—	—	Takes a long time to settle down to work.
2. Has appropriate equipment ready.	—	—	—	—	—	—	—	Seldom has appropriate equipment ready.
3. Listens to other pupils' comments during discussions.	—	—	—	—	—	—	—	Seldom listens to other pupils' comments during discussions.
4. Concentrates right up to the end of a period of work.	—	—	—	—	—	—	—	Tends to become unsettled before the end of a period of work.
5. Spontaneously reads and follows instructions carefully before starting on a task.	—	—	—	—	—	—	—	Ignores or fails to consider all the instructions carefully beforehand.
6. Is self-motivated toward work.	—	—	—	—	—	—	—	Is unmotivated toward work.
7. Is self-disciplined in class.	—	—	—	—	—	—	—	Needs constant reminders to stay on task.
8. Produces neat, careful written and number work.	—	—	—	—	—	—	—	Produces untidy, slapdash written and number work.
9. Tends to think a problem through, before embarking on it.	—	—	—	—	—	—	—	Approaches problems using trial and error.
10. Is highly responsive to direct questioning.	—	—	—	—	—	—	—	Is unresponsive to direct questioning.

11. Spontaneously makes links — — — — — — — Has difficulty in making
    across different curricular   links across different
    areas.   curricular areas.

12. Can describe a number of — — — — — — — Is unable to describe
    different strategies for   more than one way of
    solving.   solving a problem.

13. Approaches new tasks with — — — — — — — Apprehensive about
    confidence.   unfamiliar tasks.

14. Will defend own opinions — — — — — — — Tends not to defend own
    that feels are right.   opinions.

15. Shows evidence of being — — — — — — — Seems able to use only
    able to handle two or more   one source of information
    sources of information at   at a time when tackling a
    one time when solving   problem.
    problems.

16. Contributes to class — — — — — — — Rarely contributes to class
    discussions.   discussions.

17. Readily gives advice to — — — — — — — Rarely gives advice to
    other children.   other children.

18. Spontaneously volunteers — — — — — — — Seldom volunteers
    relevant information   relevant information.

Scoring and Interpretation

1. Can be scored as a Total of 18 items and as two separate sections: A: 1–9; B: 10–18.

2. Norms for the final version are based—so far—on 224 middle schools children (3rd and 4th years, ages 10–12), from six Milton Keynes schools.

   The Mean for each section is approximately 32. Actual figures are:

	A	B	Total
Mean	31.71	32.27	63.93
SD	13.87	12.55	23.56

3. Difference scores between the two sections are normally distributed. A difference of 11 or 12 points falls within normal limits.

4. Item analyses: In each section, tetrachoric correlation is above .9 for all items, except one in each case (above 8).

5. Reliability: test-retest, 2–3 weeks; 6 teachers, in 2 schools, each retesting 10 children; Pearson r.

Section A:	+ .96
Section B:	+ .96
Total:	+ .97

   No individual teacher's r, for any section, was less than + .96, despite widespread protestations of not being able to remember how they had rated first time, etc.

6. Validity: difficult, obviously, but: using "the Child at School" observation schedule (CAS) of the Inner London Education Authority, which provides a Total Score of adjustment to school and 3 subscales, for Anxiety, Aggression and Learning Problems, the following r's were found for one class (n=32):

GHOST Total and CAS Total:	+ .85
GHOST Total and Learning:	+ .84
Section A and CAS Learning:	+ .87*
Section B and CAS Learning:	+ .57*

*further confirmation that the 2 sections do measure different aspects of school learning.

References

Annett, J., & Sparrow, J. (1985). Transfer of training: a review of research and practical implications. *Journal of Progressive Learning and Educational Technology, 22.* 116–124. (Manpower Services Commission, Review and Development, No. 23, London, England.)

Annett, J (1989). *Training in transferable skills.* Sheffield, England: The Training Agency.

Arbitman-Smith, R. (1982, March). *Can we improve the learning ability of slow-learners? A preliminary study of cognitive modifiability.* Paper delivered at the meeting of the American Education Research Association, New York.

Arbitman-Smith, R., & Haywood, H. C. (1980). Cognitive education for learning-disabled adolescents. *Journal of Abnormal Child Psychology, 8,* 51.

Arbitman-Smith, R., Haywood, H. C., & Bransford, J. D. (1985). Assessing cognitive change. In C. M. McCauley, R. Sperber, & P. Brooks. (Eds), *Learning and cognition in the mentally retarded.* Baltimore, MD: University Park Press.

Baron, J. (1985). *Rationality and intelligence.* New York: Cambridge University Press.

Barrows, H. S., & Tamblyn, R. M. (1980). *Problem-based learning: An approach to medical education.* New York: Springer.

Beasley, P. F. (1984). *An evaluation of Feuerstein's model for the remediation of adolescents' cognitive deficits.* Unpublished doctoral dissertation, University of London.

Belmont, J. M., & Butterfield, E. C. (1977) The instructional approval to developmental cognitive research. In R. Kail & J. Hagen (Eds.), *Perspectives on the development of memory and cognition.* Hillsdale, NJ: Lawrence Erlbaum Associates.

Belmont, J.M., Butterfield, E. C., & Ferretti, R. P. (1982). To secure transfer of training, instruct self-management skills. In D. K. Detterman & R. J. Sternberg, (Eds.), *How and how much can intelligence be increased?* (pp. 147–154). Norwood, NJ: Ablex.

Blagg, N. R. (1983). *Instrumental Enrichment Lesson Observation Form.* Unpublished article. Somerset County Council, Somerset, England.

Blagg, N. R. (1987). *School phobia and its treatment* (2nd ed.). London: Routledge.

Blagg, N. R. (1989). Thinking as a skill. *Education, 174,* 11–12.

Blagg, N. R., & Ballinger, M. P. (1990). *Thinking to learn, learning to think.* London: Routledge.

Blagg, N. R., Ballinger, M. P., & Gardner, R. J. (1988). *The Somerset Thinking Skills Course: Teacher's manual.* Oxford, England: Blackwell.

Blagg, N. R., Ballinger, M. P., & Gardner, R. J. (1989). *The Somerset Thinking Skills Course: 5. Understanding analogies.* Oxford, England: Blackwell.

Blagg, N. R., Ballinger, M. P., & Gardner, R. J. (1990). *The Somerset Thinking Skills Course: 6: Patterns in time and space.* Oxford, England: Blackwell.

Blagg, N. R., Ballinger, M. P., & Gardner, R. J. (in preparation -a). *The Somerset Thinking Skills Course: 7: Predicting and deciding.* Oxford, England: Blackwell.

Blagg, N. R., Ballinger, M. P., & Gardner, R. J. (in preparation-b). *The Somerset Thinking Skills Course: 8: Organizing and memorizing.* Oxford, England: Blackwell.

Blagg, N. R., Ballinger, M. P., & Gardner, R. J. (in preparation-c). *The Somerset Thinking Skills Course: Handbook.* (Revised Edition) Oxford, England: Blackwell.

Blagg, N. R., Ballinger, M. P., Gardner, R. J., & Petty, M. (1988a). *The Somerset Thinking Skills Course: 3. Comparative thinking.* Oxford, England: Blackwell.

Blagg, N. R., Ballinger, M. P., Gardner, & R. J., Petty, M. (1988b). *The Somerset Thinking Skills Course: 4. Positions in time and space.* Oxford, England: Blackwell.

Blagg, N. R., Ballinger, M. P., Gardner, R. J., Petty, M., & Williams, G. (1988a). *The Somerset Thinking Skills Course: 1. Foundations for problem solving.* Oxford, England: Blackwell.

Blagg, N. R., Ballinger, M. P., Gardner, R. J., Petty, M., & Williams, G. (1988b). *The Somerset Thinking Skills Course: 2. Analyzing and Synthesizing.* Oxford, England: Blackwell.

Blagg, N. R., & Tincknell, B. (1984). *Instrumental Enrichment Project—Piagetian tasks.* Unpublished article. Somerset County Council, Somerset, England.

Bradley, T. B. (1983). Remediation of cognitive deficits: A critical appraisal of the Feuerstein model, in: *Journal of Mental Deficiency Research, 27,* 79–92.

Bransford, J. D., Arbitman-Smith, R., Stein, B. S., & Vye, N. J. (1985). Improving thinking and learning skills: An analysis of three approaches. In J. W. Segal, S. F. Chipman, & R. Glaser (Eds.), *Thinking and learning skills: Vol. 1. Relating instruction to basic research* (pp. 133–206). Hillsdale, NJ: Lawrence Erlbaum Associates.

Brown, A. L., & Campione, J. C. (1986). Training for transfer: Guidelines for promoting flexible use of trained skills. In M. Wade (Ed.), *Motor skill acquisition of the mentally handicapped.* North Holland: Elsevier.

Brown, A. L., & Ferrara, R. A. (1985). Diagnosing zones of proximal development. In J. V. Wertsch (Ed.), *Culture, communication and cognition: Vygotskian perspectives* (pp. 273–305). New York: Cambridge University Press.

Budoff, M., & Friedman, M. (1964). "Learning Potential" as an assessment approach to the adolescent mentally retarded. *Journal of Consulting Psychology, 28,* 434–439.

Burden, R. L. (1987). Feuerstein's Instrumental Enrichment program: Important issues in research and evaluation. *European Journal of Psychology of Education, 2,* 3–16.

Campione, J. C., Brown, A. L., & Ferrara, R. A. (1982). Mental retardation and intelligence. In R. J. Sternberg (Ed.), *Handbook of human intelligence.* Cambridge, England: Cambridge University Press.

Cattell, R. B. (1956). Validation and intensification of the Sixteen Personality Factor Questionnaire. *Journal of Clinical Psychology, 12,* 205–214 (c).

Chipman, S. F. Segal, J. W., & Glaser, R. (Eds.). (1985b). *Thinking and learning skills: vol. 2. Research and open questions.* Hillsdale, NJ: Lawrence Erlbaum Associates.

Chisholm, B., Kearney, D., Knight, G., Little, H., Morris, S., & Tweddle, D. (1986). *Preventative approaches to disruption.* London: Macmillan Education.

Clarke, A. D. B., & Clarke, A. M. (1976). *Early experience: Myth and evidence.* New York: Free Press

de Bono, E. (1969). *The mechanism of mind.* Jonathon Cape, Harmondsworth, England: Penguin.

de Bono, E. (1976). *Teaching thinking.* London: Temple Smith.

de Bono, E. (1979). *Future postitive: A book for the energetic eighties.* London: Temple Smith.

de Bono, E. (1981). *CoRT thinking lessons.* Oxford: Pergamon Press.

Department of Education and Science. (1989). *National Curriculum Document: English for ages 5 to 16 (June 1989)*. London: Department of Education and Science, Her Majesties Stationary Office.

Feuerstein, R. (1987). *Mediated learning theory*. Presented at the International Workshop in Theoretical and Applied Aspects of Structural Cognitive Modifiability, Jersalem.

Feuerstein, R., Rand, Y., & Hoffman, M. (1979). *The dynamic assessment of retarded performers*. Baltimore, MD: University Park Press.

Feuerstein, R., Rand, Y., Hoffman, M., & Miller, R. (1979a). Cognitive modifiability in retarded adolescents: Effects of instrumental enrichment. *American Journal of Mental Deficiency, 83,* 539–550.

Feuerstein, R., Rand, Y., Hoffman, M., & Miller, R. (1980). *Instrumental enrichment*. Baltimore, MD: University Park Press.

Feuerstein, R., Rand, Y., Jensen, M. R., Kaniel, S., & Tzuriel, D. (1987). Prerequisite for assessment of learning potential: The LPAD model. In C. S. Lidz (Ed.), *Dynamic assessment: An interactional approach to evaluating learning potential* (pp. 35–51). New York: Guilford Press.

Flavell, J. H. (1977). *Cognitive development*. Englewood Cliffs, NJ: Prentice-Hall.

Galton, F. (1869). *Hereditary genius: An enquiry into its laws and consequences* (Reprinted 1907, New York: Dutton)

Gardner, H. (1983). *Frame of mind: The theory of multiple intelligences*. London: Paladin.

Glaser, R. (1984). Education and thinking: The role of knowledge. *American Psychologist, 39,* 93–104.

Hammill, D. D., & Larsen, S. C. (1974). The effectiveness of psycholinguistic training. *Exceptional Children, 41,* 5–14.

Hamilton, D. (1976). *Curriculum evaluation*. London: Open Books

Haywood, H. C., & Arbitman-Smith, R. (1981). Modification of cognitive functions in slow-learning adolescents. In P. Mittler (Ed.), *Frontiers of knowledge in mental retardation* (Vol. 1). Baltimore, MD: University Park Press.

Hunter-Grundin, E. (1985). *Teaching thinking: An evaluation of Edward de Bono's classroom materials:* London: Schools Councils Publications.

Kagan, J., Rosman, B. B., Day, D., Albert, J., & Phillips, W. (1964). Information processing in the child: Significance of analytic and reflective attitudes. *Psychological Monographs, 78* (Whole No, 578).

Kirby, J. R. (1984). *Cognitive strategies and educational performance*. London and New York: Academic Press.

Kirk, S., McCarthey, J., & Kirk, W. (1968). *Illinois test of psycholinguistic abilities*. Urbana: University of Illinois Press.

Lake, M. (1987). *Thinking skills in the middle school*. Unpublished MPhil Thesis. Cranfield Institute of Technology. Cranfield, England

Lake, M. (1988). Group participation compared with individual problem solving. *Thinking Skills Network Newsletter*. Number 5 Issue, Milton Keynes, London.

Lawrence, D. (1988). *Enhancing self esteem in the classroom*. London: Paul Chapman.

Link, F. (1983, June). Introductory talk given at IE Training Course, Level 1, Oxford, England.

Lipman, M. (1974). *Harry Stottlemeier's discovery*. Upper Montclair, NJ: IAPC.

Lipman, M., Sharp, A. N., & Oscanyon, F. S. (1980). *Philosophy in the classroom*. Philadelphia: Temple University Press.

Lidz, C. S. (Ed.) (1987). *Dynamic assessment. An interractional approach to evaluating learning potential*. New York: Guilford Press.

Luria, A. (1959). The directive function of speech in development. *Word, 15,* 341–352.

Luria, A. (1961). *The role of speech in the regulation of normal and abnormal behaviours*. New York: Liveright.

Mays, W. (1985). *Thinking skills programmes: An analysis*. Unpublished proceedings from the

Manchester Intellectual Skills Project one day conference on the Teaching of Thinking Skills at Manchester Polytechnic.

Meeker, M. (1969). *The structure of intellect: Its interpretation and uses.* Columbus, OH: Merrill.

Mehl, M. C. (1985). *The cognitive difficulties of first-year physics students at the University of the Western Cape and various compensatory programmes.* Unpublished PhD thesis, University of Cape Town.

Meichenbaum, D. (1977). Cognitive behaviour modification: An integrative approach. Teaching children self-control. In B. Lahey & A. Kazdin (Eds.), *Advances in child clinical psychology* (Vol. 2). New York: Plenum Press.

Meichenbaum, D. H. (1985). A cognitive-behavioural perspective. In S. F. Chipman, J. W. Segal, & R. Glaser (Eds.), *Thinking and learning skills: vol. 2. Research and open questions.* Hillsdale, NJ: Lawrence Erlbaum Associates.

Meichenbaum, D. H., & Goodman, J. (1971). Training impulsive children to talk to themselves. A means of developing self-control. *Journal of Abnormal Psychology, 77,* 115–126

Newcomer, P., Larsen, S., & Hammill, D. (1975). A response. *Exceptional Children, 42,* 144–148.

Newland, T. E. (1980). Psychological assessment of exceptional children and youth. In W. Cruickshank, (Ed.), *Psychology of exceptional children and youth* (4th ed.). Englewood Cliffs, NJ: Prentice-Hall.

Nisbet, J., & Shucksmith, J. (1986). *Learning strategies.* London: Routledge and Kegan Paul.

Perkins, D. N., & Salomon, G. (1988, September). Teaching for transfer. *Educational Leadership, 46*(1), 22–32.

Resnick, L., & Beck, I. L. (1976). Designing instruction in reading: Interaction of theory and practice. In J. T. Guthrie (Ed.), *Aspects of reading acquisition.* Baltimore, MD: Johns Hopkins University Press.

Rousseau, J. J. (1762). *Emile.* London: Everyman Edition.

Salomon, G., & Perkins, D. N. (1987). Transfer of cognitive skills from programming: When and how? *Journal of Educational Computing Research, 3* 149–69

Segal, J. W., Chipman, S. F., & Glaser, R. (Eds.). (1985). *Thinking and learning skills: Vol. 1. Relating instruction to research.* Hillsdale, NJ: Lawrence Erlbaum Associates.

Sharron, H. (1987). *Changing children's minds,* London: Souvenir Press.

Shayer, M., & Beasley, F. (1987). Does instrumental enrichment work? *British Educational Research Journal, 13,* 101–119.

Sternberg, R. J. (1977). *Intelligence, information processing, and analogical reasoning: The componential analysis of human abilities.* Hillsdale, NJ: Lawrence Erlbaum Associates.

Sternberg, R. J. (1985). Approaches to intelligence. In S. F. Chipman, J. W. Segal, & R. Glaser (Eds.), *Thinking and learning skills: Research and open questions* (Vol. 2). Hillsdale, NJ: Lawrence Erlbaum Associates.

Sternberg, R. J., & Bhana, K. (1986, October). Synthesis of research on the effectiveness of intellectual skills programs: Snake-oil remedies or miracle cures? *Educational Leadership, 44*(2), 60–67.

Stufflebeam, D. L. (1971). *Educational evaluation and decision making.* Itasca, IL: F. E. Peacock.

Thurstone, L. L. (1938). *Primary mental abilities.* Chicago: University of Chicago Press.

Turberfield, A. F. (1984, May). Unpublished paper. Conference of the lower attaining pupils' program.

Vernon, P. E. (1971). *The structure of human abilities.* London: Methuen.

Vygotsky, L. S. (1962). *Thought and language* (E. Hanfmann & F. Vakar, Eds. & Trans.). Cambridge, MA: MIT Press.

Vygotsky, L. S. (1978a). Interaction between learning and development. In L. S. Vygotsky, *Mind in society: The development of higher psychological processes* (M. Cole, V. John Steiner, S. Scribner, & E. Souberman, Eds. & Trans.; pp. 79–91). Cambridge, MA: Harvard University Press. (Original work published 1935)

Vygotsky, L. S. (1978b). *Mind in society*. Cambridge, MA: Harvard University Press.

Weller, K., & Craft, A. (1983). *Making up our minds: An exploratory study of instrumental enrichment*. London: Schools Council.

Whimbey, A., & Lochhead, J. (1979). *Problem solving and comprehension: A short course in analytic reasoning*. Philadelphia: Franklin Institute Press.

Wolf, A. (1989). *What should 'teaching for transfer' mean?* Paper delivered to an invitational seminar on transfer, Warwick University, Warwick, England.

Ysseldyke, J. E., & Salvia, J. (1974). Diagnostic-prescriptive teaching: Two models. *Exceptional Children, 41*, 181.

Author Index

Subject Index